MCQ in IoT

For Intermediate Level Volume:- 2 of 3

Prepare for success with IoT multiple choice questions

Dr. Dheeraj Mehrotra
Dr. Brijesh Bakariya

www.bpbonline.com

First Edition 2026

ISBN: 978-93-65894-103

LIMITS OF LIABILITY AND DISCLAIMER OF WARRANTY

To View Complete
BPB Publications Catalogue
Scan the QR Code:

www.bpbonline.com

Dedicated to

Our family members who have supported us in all respects of life and career. Our journey proved to be a boon by following their words and experiences.

About the Authors

- **Dr. Dheeraj Mehrotra**, with an MS, MPhil, and Ph.D. (education management), is also an H.C., a white and yellow belt in Six Sigma, and a certified NLP business diploma holder. He is an educational innovator and author with expertise in Six Sigma in education, academic audits, **neuro-linguistic programming (NLP)**, and total quality management.

Dr. Mehrotra is also an experiential educator and a CBSE resource for school assessment (SQAA), CCE, JIT, Five S, and Kaizen. He has authored over 100 books on topics including computer science, AI, digital body language, NLP, quality circles, school management, classroom effectiveness, and safety and security in schools.

He is a former principal at De Indian Public School, New Delhi (India), NPS International School, Guwahati, and education officer at GEMS, Gurgaon, with over two decades of teaching experience. He is a certified trainer for quality circles/TQM in education and QCI standards for school accreditation/school audits and management.

He was honored with the president of India's National Teacher Award in 2006, the Best Science Teacher State Award from the Ministry of Science and Technology, Uttar Pradesh, and the Innovation in Education Award for his inception of Six Sigma in Education by Education Watch, New Delhi. He also received the Education World-Best Teacher Award, the BOLT Learner Teacher Award by Air India, and the Innovation in Education Award 2016 by Higher Education Forum (HEF), Gujarat Chapter, among others. He developed over 150 free educational mobile apps for the Google Play Store exclusively for teachers, students, and parents. This work has been recognized by the Limca Book of Records and India Book of Records as the only Indian to achieve that feat. Dr. Mehrotra currently serves as the principal at Kunwars Global School, Lucknow, in India. He has conducted over 1000 workshops globally on excellence in education, integrating total quality management and six sigma, **technology integration in education (TIE)**, and developing Rockstar Teachers. His workshops cover topics such as cyberspace, cyber security, classroom management, school leadership and management, and innovative teaching within classrooms via Mind Maps, NLP, and experiential learning in academics. He is also an active TEDx speaker, with talks available on the YouTube TEDx channel.

As a premium Udemy instructor, he has developed over 450 courses, serving over 8 Lakh students from 180 countries.

- **Dr. Brijesh Bakariya**, MCA, Ph.D. (computer applications), is an academician, researcher, and author with extensive expertise in data science, artificial intelligence, machine learning, IoT, and programming languages. He is currently serving as an assistant professor in the department of computer science and engineering at I.K. Gujral Punjab Technical University, Hoshiarpur Campus (Punjab, India). With over 15 years of teaching experience, he has contributed significantly to higher education, research supervision, and academic leadership.

He earned his Ph.D. in computer applications from Maulana Azad **National Institute of Technology (NIT)**, Bhopal, 2016, and completed his MCA from DAVV University, Indore, 2009. Over the years, he has supervised and awarded three Ph.D. scholars and is currently guiding several more in cutting-edge areas such as machine learning for healthcare, deep learning-based human activity recognition, and predictive modeling.

His research contributions are remarkable, with more than 40 publications in SCI and Scopus-indexed journals, etc (including Springer, Elsevier, CRC Press, and Bentham Science). His work spans across AI-driven medical diagnosis, sentiment analysis, human activity recognition, weblog analysis, and IoT-based intelligent systems. He has also presented papers at prestigious international and national conferences. He is the author and co-author of multiple books with reputed publishers such as BPB Publications and Springer. He has also contributed book chapters in advanced domains like smart schools, lung cancer detection, and sentiment analysis techniques. A prolific innovator, He has filed and published multiple patents in the domains of data science, clustering, COVID-19 detection via mobile applications, and big data efficiency.

He is an active member of professional bodies such as IRED, IAENG, and SDIWC. Dedicated to continuous learning, He has attended numerous **faculty development programs (FDPs)**, **short-term training programs (STTPs)**, and workshops conducted by IITs, NITs, NITTTR, and AICTE across domains like Python, machine learning, deep learning, data science, cloud computing, and cryptography. His professional journey reflects his passion for quality education, research excellence, and innovation in technology integration. His commitment to advancing computer science education and guiding the next generation of researchers continues to inspire students, peers, and the academic community at large.

About the Reviewers

❖ **Rakesh Kumar Pal** is a highly experienced technology leader with over two decades of progressive experience in pre-sales, customer success, project management, AI/ML, cloud computing design/architecture, implementation, and cloud and DevSecOps solutions. Rakesh brings a high-energy, people-centric approach, combining creative thinking with a collaborative management style. He is renowned for delivering error-free, efficient services and applications that consistently pass rigorous testing, on-time, and within budget, offering a unique blend of technical skills and diverse industry experience.

He is currently working in Amazon and part of the cloud solution team.

❖ **Banani Mohapatra** is an AI/ML data science leader at Walmart, operating at the intersection of product development and applied AI. She shapes strategy from inception to launch through machine learning, causal inference, and experimental design. With over 13 years of experience spanning e-commerce (Walmart), payments (Visa), and real estate (Realtor.com), she currently leads a global team of more than 25 data scientists and data engineers at Walmart. She has led cutting-edge research to accelerate the adoption of Walmart Labs' subscription products by applying AI across the customer journey - including advanced item recommendation systems, IoT-powered personalized content generation for user engagement, and creative optimization for marketing campaigns. These initiatives have resulted in more relevant experiences for millions of customers and contributed directly to subscription growth and operational efficiency.

❖ **Abhishek Arya** is a seasoned solutions architect and technology leader with over two decades of experience delivering innovative IoT, cloud, data, and AI solutions across industries including retail, finance, telecom, and supply chain. He specializes in designing scalable, secure, and high-performance IoT architectures using leading cloud platforms such as AWS, Azure, Google Cloud Platform, and Microsoft Fabric. His expertise spans the complete IoT ecosystem, from edge device integration and data ingestion to real-time analytics and cloud-based insights, empowering organizations to accelerate digital transformation through connected technologies. A notable achievement includes developing an NHVR (Australia)-compliant driver fatigue management algorithm, leveraging advanced sensor data, AI models, and regulatory logic to enhance transport safety and compliance.

Abhishek is proficient in modern architecture paradigms, including microservices, serverless computing, containerization, DevSecOps, CI/CD automation, and infrastructure as code. With deep expertise in data lake architecture, streaming pipelines, and AI/ML frameworks like GPT-4, Hugging Face, and LangChain, he consistently delivers intelligent, data-driven insights from complex IoT ecosystems while optimizing cloud spend and leading global teams. He is a member of a non-profit organisation contributing to the innovation and growth of AI and IoT solutions in India and has published various articles on IoT, blockchain, and AI across both digital and print media, establishing himself as a thought leader who aligns technology strategies with business objectives for measurable impact.

❖ **Shreya Solanke** is a passionate IoT engineer and leader with extensive professional experience in the domain of IoT, IoT devices, IoT communication stacks, wireless short range radio protocols, IIoT, building controller and EMS ecosystems. Shreya specializes in IoT devices integration to the cloud through multiple patterns and multiple diverse range of devices. She has an extensive with IoT platforms like Microsoft Azure, ThingWorx, AWS, Thingsboard etc. She is an active contributor in two of the IEEE standards P2994 and P1931.1

Acknowledgements

This book culminates a few years of intense learning and research experience. We have been fortunate to interact with many people who have influenced us greatly. One of the pleasures of finally finishing is this opportunity to thank them. We would like to place on record and acknowledge the works of all those great authors whose work we have referred to in preparing this book.

We want to thank a few people for the continued and ongoing support they have given us while writing this book. First and foremost, we would like to thank our family members for continuously encouraging us to write the book; we could never have completed this book without their support.

We are also grateful to BPB Publications for their guidance and expertise in bringing this book to fruition. Revising this book was a long journey, with the valuable participation and collaboration of reviewers, technical experts, and editors.

We would also like to acknowledge the valuable contributions of our colleagues and co-workers during many years working in academia, who have taught us so much and provided valuable feedback on this work.

Finally, we would like to thank all the readers who have taken an interest in our book and for their support in making it a reality. Your encouragement has been invaluable.

Preface

This book emphasizes mastering the key concepts, technologies, and applications in the **Internet of Things (IoT)** through targeted multiple-choice questions.

This book explores the introduction, multiple protocols, Python logical design system, challenges, and future scope of IoT, online simulation software of IoT, offline simulation software of IoT, IoT ecosystem, IoT platforms, and interview questions. This book contains more than 2100 MCQ questions and their answer keys. These questions and answers serve as an effective means to assess your proficiency in IoT. If you possess prior knowledge of IoT concepts, you can utilize this book to determine how many questions you can attempt independently without external assistance. Before facing academic examinations, competitive tests, or job interviews, it would be highly advisable to review these MCQs. For teachers or trainers instructing IoT, these multiple-choice questions serve as a valuable assessment tool to evaluate the extent to which learners have grasped the material taught. An answer key for self-assessment accompanies each question.

The book is divided into **nine chapters**, covering MCQs from all aspects of IoT problem-solving, with special emphasis on multiple protocols, logical design, challenges, and future scope, online and offline simulation software, IoT ecosystem, IoT platforms, and IoT interview questions at an intermediate level.

Chapter 1: Introduction to IoT- This chapter presents MCQs related to intermediate-level concepts of the **Internet of Things (IoT)**. It goes beyond the basics, covering layered architectures, interoperability issues, IoT standards, and security considerations. Learners will strengthen their understanding of how IoT systems function in real-world environments, enabling smarter analysis and design of IoT solutions.

Chapter 2: Multiple Protocols in IoT- This chapter contains MCQs focused on the communication protocols essential for IoT systems, including **Message Queuing Telemetry Transport (MQTT), Constrained Application Protocol (CoAP), Advanced Message Queuing Protocol (AMQP), Zigbee, Bluetooth Low Energy (BLE), Long Range Wide Area Network (LoRaWAN),** and **IPv6 over Low-Power Wireless Personal Area Networks (6LoWPAN).** These questions help learners understand the role of protocols in ensuring connectivity, reliability, and efficiency across diverse IoT networks.

Chapter 3: Python Logical Design of an IoT System- This chapter presents MCQs related to the logical design of IoT systems using Python. It covers concepts such as data flow, sensor integration, control logic, **application programming interfaces (APIs)**, and basic Python libraries used for IoT development. Learners will gain insights into how Python facilitates device-to-cloud communication and data-driven decision-making.

Chapter 4: Challenges and Future Scope of IoT- This chapter provides MCQs on the current challenges and future opportunities of IoT. It addresses issues such as scalability, security, privacy, interoperability, energy efficiency, and data management. It also highlights the emerging trends and future scope of IoT in shaping the Fourth Industrial Revolution (Industry 4.0), smart cities, and digital transformation.

Chapter 5: Online Simulation Software of IoT- This chapter contains MCQs on various online simulation tools used to design and test IoT applications virtually. It introduces tools like Cisco Packet Tracer, Tinkercad, and IoT-specific cloud simulators. Learners will understand how online platforms support prototyping and experimentation without physical hardware.

Chapter 6: Offline Simulation Software of IoT- This chapter presents MCQs focused on offline simulation tools such as **Matrix Laboratory (MATLAB)**, **Network Simulator 2 (NS-2)**, **Network Simulator 3 (NS-3)**, and Proteus. These tools are vital for in-depth IoT system modeling, network simulation, and testing at a professional level. Questions help learners compare and evaluate the effectiveness of different offline environments for IoT research and practice.

Chapter 7: IoT Ecosystem- This chapter provides MCQs on the IoT ecosystem, including devices, gateways, connectivity, cloud services, applications, and end-users. Learners will explore how these components interact to create functional IoT solutions and understand the business and technological aspects that drive the IoT ecosystem.

Chapter 8: IoT Platforms- This chapter contains MCQs on IoT platforms such as **Amazon Web Services (AWS)** IoT, Google Cloud IoT, Microsoft Azure IoT, and IBM Watson IoT. It emphasizes how platforms provide infrastructure, data management, and analytics capabilities, enabling developers and businesses to deploy scalable IoT applications.

Chapter 9: Interview Questions- This chapter presents interview-focused MCQs designed for learners with an intermediate understanding of IoT. It includes scenario-based, technical, and problem-solving questions, helping students and professionals prepare for interviews by testing their applied knowledge and conceptual clarity.

Errata

We take immense pride in our work at BPB Publications and follow best practices to ensure the accuracy of our content to provide with an indulging reading experience to our subscribers. Our readers are our mirrors, and we use their inputs to reflect and improve upon human errors, if any, that may have occurred during the publishing processes involved. To let us maintain the quality and help us reach out to any readers who might be having difficulties due to any unforeseen errors, please write to us at :

errata@bpbonline.com

Your support, suggestions and feedbacks are highly appreciated by the BPB Publications' Family.

At www.bpbonline.com, you can also read a collection of free technical articles, sign up for a range of free newsletters, and receive exclusive discounts and offers on BPB books and eBooks. You can check our social media handles below:

Instagram   Facebook   Linkedin   YouTube

Get in touch with us at: business@bpbonline.com for more details.

Piracy

If you come across any illegal copies of our works in any form on the internet, we would be grateful if you would provide us with the location address or website name. Please contact us at business@bpbonline.com with a link to the material.

If you are interested in becoming an author

If there is a topic that you have expertise in, and you are interested in either writing or contributing to a book, please visit www.bpbonline.com. We have worked with thousands of developers and tech professionals, just like you, to help them share their insights with the global tech community. You can make a general application, apply for a specific hot topic that we are recruiting an author for, or submit your own idea.

Reviews

Please leave a review. Once you have read and used this book, why not leave a review on the site that you purchased it from? Potential readers can then see and use your unbiased opinion to make purchase decisions. We at BPB can understand what you think about our products, and our authors can see your feedback on their book. Thank you!

For more information about BPB, please visit www.bpbonline.com.

Join our Discord space

Join our Discord workspace for latest updates, offers, tech happenings around the world, new releases, and sessions with the authors:

https://discord.bpbonline.com

Table of Contents

CHAPTER 1
Introduction to IoT

Introduction

The **Internet of Things (IoT)** is one of the most important new technologies of the 21st century. It is a network of devices, machines, sensors, actuators, and software systems that are all connected to each other and may send and receive data over the internet or other communication networks. IoT makes it possible to create smart environments where machines and people can work together to make life better, more productive, and more efficient by seamlessly connecting the physical and digital worlds. The IoT connects *things*, from small wearable devices to big industrial machines, and makes them part of a system that can perceive, analyze, and respond to changes in the environment. These *things* have sensors built in to collect data, actuators to carry out tasks, and communication modules to send information. IoT systems not only store and analyze huge volumes of data, but they also give you real-time insights that you can act on. They do this through cloud computing, edge computing, and AI. IoT is a key part of next-generation technologies like smart homes, smart cities, precision agriculture, connected healthcare, industrial automation, and intelligent transportation systems.

We have built a good base for comprehending the IoT at the novice level by looking at its basic ideas, important parts, and real-world uses. In the previous volume, we started our discussion with *Introduction to IoT*, where we learnt that IoT is a network of linked devices that can sense, share, and act on data. We also learnt how IoT is becoming more important in altering industries like healthcare, agriculture, transportation, and smart cities. In the *Building Blocks of IoT* chapter, we explored the main parts that make up functional IoT systems, which are sensors, actuators, communication technologies, cloud infrastructure, and applications. The *Domain-distinct IoT* chapter discussed how IoT solutions are different in different fields. It shows how they may be used in precision farming, remote healthcare, industrial automation, and traffic management, each of which is made to fulfil distinct needs. Further, we looked at sensors and actuators, which are the important hardware parts that make up the IoT. Sensors collect data and send it to actuators, which make decisions like turning on devices or controlling machinery. Lastly, the chapter on *IoT Applications* discussed a wide range of real-world examples, such as smart homes, wearable gadgets, linked cars, and industrial systems. These examples show how IoT can make life easier, more efficient, and less expensive. These chapters gave us the basic knowledge we needed to comprehend the more sophisticated topics that will be explored in this volume, like IoT protocols, system design, simulation tools, ecosystems, and platforms. We have explored the basic parts of the IoT, its areas, the roles of sensors and actuators, and some of the places where it can be used. These chapters will help to comprehend the basics of how the IoT works and why it is crucial in today's environment. However, to really understand IoT, you need to learn more than just the basics. You need to know about the advanced parts that make these systems work well, grow, and last.

We are focusing on these more advanced parts of IoT:

- Communication protocols, which provide rules for how devices talk to each other and make sure they can work together even if they are different types of systems.

- Using Python to construct logical systems, which lets you think about and test IoT operations in real-world situations.

- The problems and future potential of the IoT, which show both the problems it has right now and the new chances for innovation that are coming up.

- Simulation environments, both online and offline, that give learners and developers cheap and flexible places to try things out.

- The IoT ecosystem brings together different people, technologies, and services into one system.

- IoT systems, which act as middleware for managing devices, analyzing data, and making apps.

Studying these things gives students and professionals the theoretical and practical expertise they need to create, test, and implement IoT systems successfully.

IoT is not only a new technology; it is also a force that changes society and the economy. Companies are utilizing IoT to make their operations more efficient, governments are using it to improve public services and smart governance, and people are using it for health, safety, and convenience. IoT also brings up crucial issues of security, privacy, interoperability, and sustainability at the same time. So, to understand IoT, we need to look at both its pros and cons in a fair way. This broader focus makes the following chapters very important for the overall study of IoT. They not only expand on what was learnt in previous topics, but they also get ready for research and real-world use. Each topic adds to our understanding of IoT, whether it is how protocols like MQTT or CoAP let devices talk to each other, how simulation tools like Packet Tracer or MATLAB create testing environments, or how platforms like AWS IoT Core and Azure IoT Hub provide integration and scalability.

This introduction makes it clear that IoT is a technology with many sides. It will only work if all its hardware, software, communication technologies, simulation environments, platforms, and ecosystems work together. Readers will not only be able to comprehend IoT on a conceptual level by studying these advanced topics, but they will also be able to build, simulate, and manage IoT solutions that are safe, dependable, and ready for the future.

Understanding how IoT systems function requires an exploration of several key areas. First, it is essential to comprehend the multiple protocols in IoT that facilitate efficient communication. These include protocols for short and long-distance communication as well as those at the application layer, such as Bluetooth, Zigbee, LoRaWAN, MQTT, and CoAP. A Python logical design of an IoT system involves investigating how these systems are logically built on various levels: perception, network, and application. This also includes using Python programming to create models, run simulations, and build IoT prototypes.

The challenges and future scope of IoT are also significant. Challenges include problems with privacy, cybersecurity, interoperability, scalability, and energy use. Future scope involves new potential such as AI integration, IoT with blockchain, and IoT with 6G. To test these systems, both online simulation software for IoT and offline simulation software for IoT can be used. Online tools like Cisco Packet Tracer and Tinkercad allow students and developers to test systems without real hardware, while offline tools like MATLAB, NS-3, and IoT-Lab are used for advanced, research-focused analysis, customization, and large-scale performance testing.

Finally, a deep understanding of the IoT ecosystem is crucial. This involves analyzing the interactions among devices, networks, platforms, analytics, and stakeholders, and understanding how cloud services, big data, and AI contribute to it. A look at various IoT platforms such as AWS IoT, Azure IoT Hub, Google Cloud IoT, and ThingsBoard (both paid and free) reveals how these platforms simplify device management, data integration, and application development.

Applications

The applications are as follows:

- **Multiple protocols in IoT:**
    - **Bluetooth-enabled**: The wearables keep an eye on patients' vital signs in healthcare.
    - **Smart homes**: Zigbee and Z-Wave give power to smart lights and appliances.
    - **Industrial IoT (IIoT)**: LoRaWAN and NB-IoT make it possible for factories to talk to each other across vast distances.

- o **Transportation**: 5G helps manage traffic and connects cars.
- **Python logical design of an IoT system:**
  - o **Smart irrigation**: Python scripts use sensor data to automatically distribute water.
  - o **Monitoring the environment**: Python-based data pipelines gather and process information about air quality or temperature.
  - o **Machine learning in IoT**: Python adds AI models to IoT devices so they can do predictive analytics.
  - o **Rapid prototyping**: Developers use Python frameworks like Flask or Django to make IoT prototypes that can connect to the cloud.
- **Challenges and future scope of IoT:**
  - o **Problems**: Keeping IoT devices safe from hackers, making sure that different protocols can work together, handling huge amounts of data, and using less energy.
  - o **Future scope**: AI-powered IoT for making decisions in real time, blockchain-based IoT for safe transactions, and 6G IoT for super-fast, reliable connections.
- **Online simulation software of IoT:**
  - o **Cisco Packet Tracer**: A tool for simulating IoT networks for learning and training.
  - o **Tinkercad**: Making simple IoT circuits and Arduino-based systems online.
  - o **Cloud labs**: places where students can work together to design IoT solutions from afar.
- **Offline simulation software for IoT:**
  - o **MATLAB/Simulink**: Making models of IoT systems that use less energy and looking at how well they work.
  - o **NS-3**: Study of IoT network protocols and how they can grow.
  - o **IoT lab**: Testing out big IoT deployments for research in schools and businesses.
- **IoT ecosystem:**
  - o **Smart cities**: Using devices, clouds, and data analytics to control traffic and energy.
  - o **Healthcare**: The healthcare ecosystem is made up of wearables, cloud services, and hospital systems that all work together.
  - o **Agriculture**: An IoT ecosystem featuring sensors, cloud platforms, and mobile apps for farmers.

- **IoT platforms:**
  - **AWS IoT Core**: Connect devices, collect data, and analyze it.
  - **Azure IoT Hub**: Safe communication and connection to Microsoft services.
  - **Google Cloud IoT**: Analytics in real time for devices that are connected.
  - **ThingsBoard (open-source)**: An IoT platform that is flexible and good for entrepreneurs and researchers.

The study of several intermediate-level IoT subjects has given us a complete picture of how this technology works, changes, and adapts to future needs. The examination of multiple protocols in IoT underscored the necessity of uninterrupted communication across diverse devices, hence guaranteeing interoperability, dependability, and efficiency in practical systems. The chapter on *Python Logical Design of an IoT System* showed how programming may help organize IoT systems by showing how logical flow and modular design can make it easier to handle data, operate devices, and build apps. The chapter on *Challenges and Future Scope of IoT* provided important information about the problems that need to be solved, such as scalability, security, privacy, and standardization. It also stressed how IoT could change sectors in the next few years.

The addition of *Online Simulation Software of IoT* and *Offline Simulation Software of IoT* also showed how simulation tools are important for testing, prototyping, and validating IoT systems before they are used on a wide scale. This saves money, time, and resources. The talk about the *IoT Ecosystem* gave a complete picture of how devices, networks, platforms, and applications interact to create a dynamic and collaborative ecosystem. Finally, the study of *IoT Platforms* shows how cloud-based and on-premises solutions may help with device administration, data processing, analytics, and application integration, which makes IoT deployments more stable and scalable.

In general, these subjects together fill up the gaps between theory and practice. They not only help us comprehend the current state of the IoT better, but they also help us get ready to create, analyze, and use IoT solutions that are smarter, safer, and more environmentally friendly in the future.

Join our Discord space

Join our Discord workspace for latest updates, offers, tech happenings around the world, new releases, and sessions with the authors:

https://discord.bpbonline.com

CHAPTER 2
Multiple Protocols in IoT

Introduction

The capacity of devices to interact without a hitch is fundamentally relevant in the wide terrain of the IoT. No single communication protocol can meet the needs of the wide variety of Internet of Things applications, from smart homes to industrial automation. As a result, several different IoT protocols have emerged, each optimized for a different set of requirements, such as data rate, range, battery consumption, and so on. Anyone wanting to dabble in the IoT must be familiar with these protocols.

Message Queuing Telemetry Transport

Message Queuing Telemetry Transport (MQTT) is a low-overhead protocol that was originally designed for use in the oil and gas sector, making it perfect for low-powered devices. It is well-suited for use with distant sensors and mobile devices since it runs via TCP/IP and uses a publish-subscribe mechanism. Due to its modest data transfer needs, it excels in situations when network bandwidth is scarce. You may rely on the web transfer protocol known as the **Constrained Application Protocol (CoAP)** for limited resources. CoAP is a UDP-based protocol that was intended to readily transfer to HTTP for seamless online integration while still catering to the needs of limited-resource gadgets and networks.

Hypertext Transfer Protocol

The foundation of the World Wide Web is also heavily used in IoT. Since developers already know and are comfortable with **Hypertext Transfer Protocol** (**HTTP**), it is typically the protocol of choice for IoT applications, particularly when the data will be shown in web browsers.

- **Zigbee**: Zigbee is a wireless protocol developed for low-data-rate, low-power applications based on the IEEE 802.15.4 standard. Zigbee's mesh networking capabilities make it a great choice for use in smart energy and home automation systems.

- **BLE**: Traditional Bluetooth is well-known for short-range connections, but its power-optimized form, **Bluetooth Low Energy** (**BLE**), is excellent for the IoT. Due to its low power requirements and short communication intervals, BLE is well-suited for devices that run on batteries.

- **Z-Wave**: Z-Wave is a wireless technology that works in the sub-1GHz range; it is mostly used for home automation. There is little interference and a decent trade-off between range and data transfer speed. With its capacity to accommodate over 230 items per network, Z-Wave is well-suited for the development of comprehensive, distributed smart home infrastructures.

- **Long Range (LoRa)**: LoRa is a communication protocol developed specifically for use over extended distances. This low-power, spread-spectrum technology is widely used in contexts where devices may be geographically dispersed, such as in agriculture and smart cities.

- **Narrowband IoT (NB-IoT):** NB-IoT is a cellular technology that provides extensive coverage and was created for gadgets that only need to send little data on an as-needed basis. Because of its powerful penetrating abilities, it may be used successfully in subterranean or very deep interior settings.

Multiple choice questions

1. **Which communication protocol is known for its low power consumption and is commonly used in wireless sensor networks for IoT applications?**

    a. HTTP

    b. MQTT

    c. CoAP

    d. OPC UA

2. **Which protocol is used for efficient and reliable communication between IoT devices and cloud services, making use of lightweight publish-subscribe messaging?**

    a. HTTP

    b. MQTT

    c. CoAP

    d. AMQP

3. Which protocol is designed for real-time communication between IoT devices and is commonly used in industrial automation and control systems?

    a. HTTP

    b. MQTT

    c. OPCUA

    d. CoAP

4. Which protocol is widely used for transferring data between IoT devices and web services, often over the internet?

    a. HTTP

    b. MQTT

    c. CoAP

    d. AMQP

5. Which protocol provides a standard way to interface IoT devices with the cloud, enabling secure and scalable communication?

    a. HTTP

    b. MQTT

    c. CoAP

    d. MQTT-SN

6. Which protocol is specifically designed for constrained devices with low bandwidth, allowing them to communicate with IoT gateways and cloud platforms?

    a. HTTP

    b. MQTT-SN

    c. CoAP

    d. AMQP

7. Which protocol is commonly used for device discovery, configuration, and control in IoT networks and is often implemented on top of UDP?

    a. HTTP

    b. MQTT

    c. CoAP

    d. SSDP

8. Which protocol is used for secure authentication and authorization of IoT devices in enterprise environments, often integrating with existing directory services?

    a. OAuth

    b. JWT

    c. LDAP

    d. SAML

9. Which protocol is used for communication between IoT devices and gateways over short distances, commonly employed in home automation and personal area networks?

    a. Wi-Fi

    b. Bluetooth

    c. Zigbee

    d. LoRa

10. Which protocol is a lightweight alternative to HTTP, designed for constrained devices and low-power networks, using a request-response model?

    a. MQTT

    b. CoAP

    c. OPCUA

    d. AMQP

11. Which protocol is commonly used to communicate between IoT devices and cloud services, using structured messages with headers and payloads?

    a. HTTP

    b. MQTT

    c. CoAP

    d. AMQP

12. Which protocol is specifically designed for industrial IoT applications, ensuring device interoperability from different manufacturers?

    a. HTTP

    b. MQTT

    c. OPCUA

    d. CoAP

13. Which protocol is used for secure token-based authentication and authorization in IoT applications, often integrated with OAuth?

    a. JWT

    b. LDAP

    c. SAML

    d. RADIUS

14. Which protocol is used for communication between IoT devices and cloud services, based on RESTful principles and commonly used in home automation?

    a. HTTP

    b. MQTT

    c. CoAP

    d. AMQP

15. Which protocol is commonly used for communication between IoT devices and cloud services, ensuring secure and reliable data transmission?

    a. HTTP

    b. MQTT

    c. CoAP

    d. AMQP

16. Which protocol is commonly used for communication between IoT devices and cloud services, ensuring secure and efficient data transmission with low overhead?

    a. HTTP

    b. MQTT

    c. CoAP

    d. AMQP

17. Which protocol is commonly used for communication between IoT devices and cloud services, providing lightweight publish-subscribe messaging?

    a. HTTP

    b. MQTT

    c. CoAP

    d. AMQP

18. **Which protocol is commonly used for communication between IoT devices and cloud services, using structured data packets and reliable messaging?**

    a. HTTP

    b. MQTT

    c. CoAP

    d. AMQP

19. **Which protocol is designed for communication between IoT devices and cloud services, based on a RESTful architecture and using lightweight data formats?**

    a. HTTP

    b. MQTT

    c. CoAP

    d. AMQP

20. **In IoT systems, which layer of the OSI model does the CoAP primarily operate in, and what transport layer protocol does it typically use?**

    a. Transport layer, TCP

    b. Application layer, UDP

    c. Data link layer, TCP

    d. Network layer, UDP

21. **Which protocol is designed for communication between IoT devices and cloud services, using a publish-subscribe messaging pattern?**

    a. HTTP

    b. MQTT

    c. CoAP

    d. AMQP

22. **Which protocol is designed for communication between IoT devices and cloud services, using lightweight, stateless interactions?**

    a. HTTP

    b. MQTT

    c. CoAP

    d. AMQP

23. Which protocol is designed for communication between IoT devices and cloud services, ensuring reliable data transmission with low latency?

    a. HTTP

    b. MQTT

    c. CoAP

    d. AMQP

24. Which protocol uses a publish-subscribe model to enable efficient data transmission in IoT networks and allows clients to receive messages only on topics they are interested in?

    a. HTTP

    b. CoAP

    c. MQTT

    d. SNMP

25. Which protocol is used for secure communication between IoT devices and cloud services, often using token-based authentication?

    a. OAuth

    b. JWT

    c. LDAP

    d. SAML

26. Which protocol is commonly used for communication between IoT devices and cloud services based on a client-server architecture?

    a. HTTP

    b. MQTT

    c. CoAP

    d. AMQP

27. Which protocol is used for communication between IoT devices and cloud services, ensuring secure and authenticated data transmission?

    a. HTTP

    b. MQTT

    c. CoAP

    d. AMQP

28. Which protocol is commonly used for communication between IoT devices and cloud services, ensuring secure and reliable messaging?

    a. HTTP

    b. MQTT

    c. CoAP

    d. AMQP

29. Which protocol is commonly used for communication between IoT devices and cloud services, ensuring efficient and lightweight data transmission?

    a. HTTP

    b. MQTT

    c. CoAP

    d. AMQP

30. Which protocol is used for communication between IoT devices and cloud services, providing bidirectional communication with low latency?

    a. HTTP

    b. MQTT

    c. CoAP

    d. AMQP

31. Which protocol is used for communication between IoT devices and cloud services, providing a standardized way to describe and discover IoT resources?

    a. HTTP

    b. MQTT

    c. CoAP

    d. OCF

32. Which protocol is designed for communication between IoT devices and cloud services, using a simple request-response pattern and XML-based messages?

    a. HTTP

    b. MQTT

    c. CoAP

    d. SOAP

33. Which protocol is used for communication between IoT devices and cloud services, providing a secure and lightweight method for device authentication and authorization?

    a. OAuth

    b. JWT

    c. OAuth2

    d. SAML

34. Which protocol is designed for communication between IoT devices and cloud services, providing a way to transfer and manage large binary objects?

    a. HTTP

    b. MQTT

    c. CoAP

    d. HTTP/2

35. Which protocol is used for communication between IoT devices and cloud services, allowing devices to be discovered and controlled over the internet?

    a. MQTT

    b. HTTP

    c. UPnP

    d. CoAP

36. Which protocol is designed for communication between IoT devices and cloud services, enabling efficient and reliable data transmission using message brokers?

    a. HTTP

    b. MQTT

    c. CoAP

    d. Extensible Messaging and Presence Protocol (XMPP)

37. Which protocol is used for communication between IoT devices and cloud services, enabling real-time communication through a publish-subscribe model?

    a. HTTP

    b. MQTT

    c. CoAP

    d. XMPP

38. Which protocol is designed for communication between IoT devices and cloud services, providing a secure way to exchange data using JSON format?

    a. HTTP

    b. MQTT

    c. CoAP

    d. HTTPS

39. Which protocol is used for communication between IoT devices and cloud services, providing a way to manage and control devices remotely over the internet?

    a. MQTT

    b. CoAP

    c. HTTP

    d. XMPP

40. Which protocol is designed for communication between IoT devices and cloud services, providing a way to control and monitor devices using HTTP remotely?

    a. MQTT

    b. CoAP

    c. HTTP

    d. XMPP

41. Which protocol is used for communication between IoT devices and cloud services, allowing devices to publish and subscribe to data streams?

    a. MQTT

    b. CoAP

    c. HTTP

    d. XMPP

42. Which protocol is designed for communication between IoT devices and cloud services, providing a way to monitor and manage devices using XML remotely?

    a. MQTT

    b. CoAP

    c. HTTP

    d. XMPP

43. Which protocol is used for communication between IoT devices and cloud services, providing a way to manage and control constrained devices using RESTful principles?

    a. MQTT

    b. CoAP

    c. HTTP

    d. XMPP

44. Which protocol is designed for communication between IoT devices and cloud services, allowing devices to be discovered and configured dynamically?

    a. MQTT

    b. CoAP

    c. HTTP

    d. XMPP

45. Which protocol is used for communication between IoT devices and cloud services, providing a lightweight and efficient method for device registration and authentication?

    a. MQTT

    b. CoAP

    c. HTTP

    d. DTLS

46. Which protocol is designed for communication between IoT devices and cloud services, providing a secure and standardized way to manage device metadata and capabilities?

    a. MQTT

    b. CoAP

    c. HTTP

    d. OMA LwM2M

47. Which protocol is used for communication between IoT devices and cloud services, providing a way to manage and control devices using a lightweight binary protocol?

    a. MQTT

    b. CoAP

    c. HTTP/2

    d. OMA LwM2M

48. Which protocol is designed for communication between IoT devices and cloud services, providing a way to exchange messages in a resource-constrained environment?

    a. MQTT

    b. CoAP

    c. AMQP

    d. DDS

49. Which protocol is used for communication between IoT devices and cloud services, providing a standardized way to control and manage devices remotely?

    a. MQTT

    b. CoAP

    c. AMQP

    d. OMA LwM2M

50. In IoT edge computing, what advantage does the data distribution service (DDS) protocol provide over MQTT in terms of communication model?

    a. DDS supports point-to-point connections, while MQTT only supports broadcast

    b. DDS enables real-time, data-centric communication and provides QoS controls

    c. DDS operates exclusively on the application layer, unlike MQTT

    d. DDS provides stronger encryption than MQTT

51. Which protocol is used for communication between IoT devices and cloud services, providing a standardized way to exchange messages in real-time?

    a. MQTT

    b. CoAP

    c. AMQP

    d. DDS

52. Which protocol is designed for communication between IoT devices and cloud services, providing a way to discover and manage devices using a web-based API?

    a. MQTT

    b. CoAP

    c. AMQP

    d. HTTP

53. Which protocol is used for communication between IoT devices and cloud services, providing a way to transfer data and events between devices using a publish-subscribe model?

    a. MQTT

    b. CoAP

    c. AMQP

    d. DDS

54. Which protocol is designed for communication between IoT devices and cloud services, providing a way to discover, control, and manage devices using RESTful principles?

    a. MQTT

    b. CoAP

    c. AMQP

    d. HTTP

55. Which protocol is used for communication between IoT devices and cloud services, providing a way to exchange messages in a decentralized and peer-to-peer manner?

    a. MQTT

    b. CoAP

    c. AMQP

    d. DDS

56. Which protocol is commonly used for communication between IoT devices and cloud services, allowing devices to publish and receive messages using a lightweight messaging protocol?

    a. MQTT

    b. CoAP

    c. AMQP

    d. DDS

57. Which protocol is designed for communication between IoT devices and cloud services, providing a way to manage and control devices using binary encoding efficiently?

    a. MQTT

    b. CoAP

    c. AMQP

    d. MQTT-SN

58. Which protocol is used for communication between IoT devices and cloud services, enabling secure and efficient data transmission over unreliable networks?

    a. MQTT

    b. CoAP

    c. AMQP

    d. MQTT-SN

59. Which protocol is commonly used for communication between IoT devices and cloud services, ensuring secure and reliable data transmission using message brokers and queues?

    a. MQTT

    b. CoAP

    c. AMQP

    d. MQTT-SN

60. Which protocol is designed for communication between IoT devices and cloud services, providing a way to exchange data using token-based authentication securely?

    a. OAuth

    b. JWT

    c. CoAP

    d. DTLS

61. Which protocol is used for communication between IoT devices and cloud services, providing a way to manage and control devices using a simple request-response pattern?

    a. MQTT

    b. CoAP

    c. HTTP

    d. DDS

62. Which protocol is designed for communication between IoT devices and cloud services, providing a way to control and manage devices using lightweight binary messages?

    a. MQTT

    b. CoAP

    c. HTTP

    d. DDS

63. Which protocol is used for communication between IoT devices and cloud services, enabling efficient and secure data transmission over constrained networks?

   a. MQTT

   b. CoAP

   c. AMQP

   d. MQTT-SN

64. Which protocol is designed for communication between IoT devices and cloud services, providing a way to securely exchange data using a publish-subscribe model?

   a. MQTT

   b. CoAP

   c. AMQP

   d. XMPP

65. Which protocol is used for communication between IoT devices and cloud services, allowing devices to publish and subscribe to data streams using a publish-subscribe model?

   a. MQTT

   b. CoAP

   c. AMQP

   d. XMPP

66. Which protocol is designed for communication between IoT devices and cloud services, providing a way to efficiently manage and control constrained devices?

   a. MQTT

   b. CoAP

   c. OMA LwM2M

   d. XMPP

67. Which protocol is used for communication between IoT devices and cloud services, allowing devices to discover and exchange information about available services?

   a. MQTT

   b. CoAP

   c. UPnP

   d. XMPP

68. Which protocol is designed for communication between IoT devices and cloud services, providing a way to exchange data using XML-based messages securely?

    a. MQTT

    b. CoAP

    c. AMQP

    d. SOAP

69. Which protocol is used for communication between IoT devices and cloud services, enabling secure and efficient data transmission using a lightweight messaging pattern?

    a. MQTT

    b. CoAP

    c. AMQP

    d. MQTT-SN

70. Which protocol is designed for communication between IoT devices and cloud services, providing a way to exchange data using a request-response pattern securely?

    a. MQTT

    b. CoAP

    c. AMQP

    d. MQTT-SN

71. Which protocol is used for communication between IoT devices and cloud services, allowing devices to discover and exchange data using RESTful principles?

    a. MQTT

    b. CoAP

    c. AMQP

    d. XMPP

72. Which protocol is designed for communication between IoT devices and cloud services, providing a way to exchange data using publish-subscribe messaging securely?

    a. MQTT

    b. CoAP

    c. AMQP

    d. XMPP

73. **Which protocol is used for communication between IoT devices and cloud services, enabling efficient and secure data transmission using a publish-subscribe model?**

    a. MQTT

    b. CoAP

    c. AMQP

    d. XMPP

74. **Which protocol is designed for communication between IoT devices and cloud services, providing a way to monitor and control devices using binary encoding remotely?**

    a. MQTT

    b. CoAP

    c. AMQP

    d. OMA LwM2M

75. **Which security feature is provided by the Datagram Transport Layer Security (DTLS) protocol in an IoT system that uses CoAP over UDP?**

    a. Encryption and integrity of data at the application layer

    b. Secure key exchange and message encryption over unreliable networks

    c. Authentication of data sources at the Data link layer

    d. Protection of broadcast packets in constrained devices

76. **Which protocol is designed for communication between IoT devices and cloud services, providing a way to exchange data using binary messages securely?**

    a. MQTT

    b. CoAP

    c. AMQP

    d. DDS

77. **For IoT applications requiring high scalability and minimal overhead, which protocol is generally preferred over HTTP for lightweight communication between devices?**

    a. AMQP

    b. MQTT

    c. CoAP

    d. FTP

78. Which protocol is designed for communication between IoT devices and cloud services, providing a way to exchange data using publish-subscribe messaging securely?

    a. MQTT

    b. CoAP

    c. AMQP

    d. XMPP

79. Which protocol is used for communication between IoT devices and cloud services, allowing devices to discover and manage devices using a web-based API?

    a. MQTT

    b. CoAP

    c. AMQP

    d. HTTP

80. Which protocol is designed for communication between IoT devices and cloud services, providing a way to efficiently manage and control constrained devices using binary encoding?

    a. MQTT

    b. CoAP

    c. AMQP

    d. MQTT-SN

81. Which protocol is used for communication between IoT devices and cloud services, enabling secure and efficient data transmission over unreliable networks?

    a. MQTT

    b. CoAP

    c. AMQP

    d. MQTT-SN

82. Which protocol is designed for communication between IoT devices and cloud services, providing a way to monitor and control devices using XML remotely?

    a. MQTT

    b. CoAP

    c. AMQP

    d. HTTP

83. Which protocol is used for communication between IoT devices and cloud services, allowing devices to publish and receive messages using a lightweight messaging pattern?

   a. MQTT

   b. CoAP

   c. AMQP

   d. DDS

84. Which protocol is designed for communication between IoT devices and cloud services, providing a way to exchange data using a publish-subscribe model securely?

   a. MQTT

   b. CoAP

   c. AMQP

   d. XMPP

85. In IoT applications where devices need to communicate within a mesh network topology, which of the following protocols is widely adopted?

   a. LoRaWAN

   b. BLE

   c. Zigbee

   d. MQTT

86. Which protocol is designed for communication between IoT devices and cloud services, providing a way to exchange data using JSON format securely?

   a. MQTT

   b. CoAP

   c. AMQP

   d. HTTPS

87. Which protocol is used for communication between IoT devices and cloud services, enabling efficient and reliable data transmission using message brokers?

   a. MQTT

   b. CoAP

   c. AMQP

   d. HTTPS

88. Which protocol is designed for communication between IoT devices and cloud services, providing a way to control and monitor devices using HTTP remotely?

    a. MQTT

    b. CoAP

    c. AMQP

    d. HTTPS

89. Which of the following best describes the role of the IPv6 over Low-Power Wireless Personal Area Networks (6LoWPAN) protocol in IoT?

    a. It enables efficient message queuing and subscription management

    b. It allows for packet fragmentation and IPv6 header compression over low-power networks

    c. It enhances security by encrypting data at the transport layer

    d. It manages high-speed data transmission over large distances

90. Which protocol is designed for communication between IoT devices and cloud services, providing a way to exchange data using a request-response pattern securely?

    a. MQTT

    b. CoAP

    c. AMQP

    d. HTTPS

91. Which protocol is used for communication between IoT devices and cloud services, enabling secure and efficient data transmission over unreliable networks?

    a. MQTT

    b. CoAP

    c. AMQP

    d. HTTPS

92. Which protocol is designed for communication between IoT devices and cloud services, providing a way to exchange data using a publish-subscribe model securely?

    a. MQTT

    b. CoAP

    c. AMQP

    d. HTTPS

93. Which protocol is used for communication between IoT devices and cloud services, allowing devices to discover and exchange information about available services?

    a. MQTT

    b. CoAP

    c. AMQP

    d. HTTPS

94. Which protocol is designed for communication between IoT devices and cloud services, providing a way to exchange data using binary encoding securely?

    a. MQTT

    b. CoAP

    c. AMQP

    d. HTTPS

95. Which protocol is used for communication between IoT devices and cloud services, enabling efficient and secure data transmission over unreliable networks?

    a. MQTT

    b. CoAP

    c. AMQP

    d. HTTPS

96. Which protocol is designed for communication between IoT devices and cloud services, providing a way to monitor and control devices using XML remotely?

    a. MQTT

    b. CoAP

    c. AMQP

    d. HTTPS

97. Which protocol is used for communication between IoT devices and cloud services, allowing devices to publish and receive messages using a lightweight messaging pattern?

    a. MQTT

    b. CoAP

    c. AMQP

    d. HTTPS

98. Which protocol is designed for communication between IoT devices and cloud services, providing a way to exchange data using a publish-subscribe model securely?

    a. MQTT

    b. CoAP

    c. AMQP

    d. HTTPS

99. Which protocol is used for communication between IoT devices and cloud services, enabling real-time communication through a publish-subscribe model?

    a. MQTT

    b. CoAP

    c. AMQP

    d. HTTPS

100. Which protocol is designed for communication between IoT devices and cloud services, providing a way to exchange messages in a resource-constrained environment?

    a. MQTT

    b. CoAP

    c. AMQP

    d. DDS

101. Which protocol is used for communication between IoT devices and cloud services, allowing devices to publish and subscribe to data streams using a publish-subscribe model?

    a. MQTT

    b. CoAP

    c. AMQP

    d. DDS

102. Which protocol is designed for communication between IoT devices and cloud services, providing a way to manage and control devices using binary encoding remotely?

    a. MQTT

    b. CoAP

    c. AMQP

    d. OMA LwM2M

103. Which protocol is used for communication between IoT devices and cloud services, allowing devices to discover and exchange information about available services?

   a. MQTT

   b. CoAP

   c. UPnP

   d. XMPP

104. Which protocol is designed for communication between IoT devices and cloud services, providing a way to exchange data using JSON format securely?

   a. MQTT

   b. CoAP

   c. AMQP

   d. HTTPS

105. Which protocol is used for communication between IoT devices and cloud services, enabling efficient and reliable data transmission using message brokers and queues?

   a. MQTT

   b. CoAP

   c. AMQP

   d. HTTPS

106. Which protocol is designed for communication between IoT devices and cloud services, providing a way to control and monitor devices using HTTP remotely?

   a. MQTT

   b. CoAP

   c. AMQP

   d. HTTPS

107. Which protocol is used for communication between IoT devices and cloud services, allowing devices to publish and subscribe to data streams using a publish-subscribe model?

   a. MQTT

   b. CoAP

   c. AMQP

   d. DDS

108. Which protocol is designed for communication between IoT devices and cloud services, providing a way to exchange data using a request-response pattern securely?

    a. MQTT

    b. CoAP

    c. AMQP

    d. DDS

109. Which protocol is used for communication between IoT devices and cloud services, enabling secure and efficient data transmission over unreliable networks?

    a. MQTT

    b. CoAP

    c. AMQP

    d. DDS

110. Which protocol is designed for communication between IoT devices and cloud services, providing away to securely exchange data using publish-subscribe messaging?

    a. MQTT

    b. CoAP

    c. AMQP

    d. XMPP

111. Which protocol is used for communication between IoT devices and cloud services, allowing devices to discover and manage devices using a web-based API?

    a. MQTT

    b. CoAP

    c. AMQP

    d. HTTP

112. Which protocol is designed for communication between IoT devices and cloud services, providing a way to manage and control constrained devices using binary encoding efficiently?

    a. MQTT

    b. CoAP

    c. AMQP

    d. MQTT-SN

113. Which protocol is used for communication between IoT devices and cloud services, enabling secure and efficient data transmission over unreliable networks?

    a. MQTT

    b. CoAP

    c. AMQP

    d. MQTT-SN

114. Which protocol is designed for communication between IoT devices and cloud services, providing a way to monitor and control devices using XML remotely?

    a. MQTT

    b. CoAP

    c. AMQP

    d. HTTP

115. Which protocol is used for communication between IoT devices and cloud services, allowing devices to publish and receive messages using a lightweight messaging pattern?

    a. MQTT

    b. CoAP

    c. AMQP

    d. DDS

116. Which protocol is designed for communication between IoT devices and cloud services, providing a way to securely exchange data using publish-subscribe messaging?

    a. MQTT

    b. CoAP

    c. AMQP

    d. XMPP

117. Which protocol is used for communication between IoT devices and cloud services, enabling real-time communication through a publish-subscribe model?

    a. MQTT

    b. CoAP

    c. AMQP

    d. XMPP

118. Which protocol is designed for communication between IoT devices and cloud services, providing a way to exchange data using JSON format securely?

    a. MQTT

    b. CoAP

    c. AMQP

    d. HTTPS

119. Which protocol is used for communication between IoT devices and cloud services, enabling efficient and reliable data transmission using message brokers and queues?

    a. MQTT

    b. CoAP

    c. AMQP

    d. HTTPS

120. Which protocol is designed for communication between IoT devices and cloud services, providing a way to control and monitor devices using HTTP remotely?

    a. MQTT

    b. CoAP

    c. AMQP

    d. HTTPS

121. Which protocol is used for communication between IoT devices and cloud services, allowing devices to publish and subscribe to data streams using a publish-subscribe model?

    a. MQTT

    b. CoAP

    c. AMQP

    d. DDS

122. Which protocol is designed for communication between IoT devices and cloud services, providing a way to exchange data using a request-response pattern securely?

    a. MQTT

    b. CoAP

    c. AMQP

    d. DDS

123. Which protocol is used for communication between IoT devices and cloud services, enabling secure and efficient data transmission over unreliable networks?

    a. MQTT

    b. CoAP

    c. AMQP

    d. DDS

124. Which protocol is designed for communication between IoT devices and cloud services, providing a way to exchange data using publish-subscribe messaging securely?

    a. MQTT

    b. CoAP

    c. AMQP

    d. XMPP

125. Which protocol is used for communication between IoT devices and cloud services, allowing devices to publish and receive messages using a lightweight messaging pattern?

    a. MQTT

    b. CoAP

    c. AMQP

    d. DDS

126. Which protocol is designed for communication between IoT devices and cloud services, providing a way to manage and control devices using binary encoding efficiently?

    a. MQTT

    b. CoAP

    c. AMQP

    d. MQTT-SN

127. Which protocol is used for communication between IoT devices and cloud services, enabling secure and efficient data transmission over unreliable networks?

    a. MQTT

    b. CoAP

    c. AMQP

    d. MQTT-SN

128. Which protocol is designed for communication between IoT devices and cloud services, providing a way to manage and control devices using binary encoding remotely?

    a. MQTT

    b. CoAP

    c. AMQP

    d. OMA LwM2M

129. Which protocol is used for communication between IoT devices and cloud services, allowing devices to discover and exchange information about available services?

    a. MQTT

    b. CoAP

    c. AMQP

    d. XMPP

130. Which protocol is designed for communication between IoT devices and cloud services, providing a way to exchange data using JSON format securely?

    a. MQTT

    b. CoAP

    c. cAMQP

    d. HTTPS

131. Which protocol is used for communication between IoT devices and cloud services, enabling efficient and reliable data transmission using message brokers and queues?

    a. MQTT

    b. CoAP

    c. AMQP

    d. HTTPS

132. Which protocol is designed for communication between IoT devices and cloud services, providing a way to control and monitor devices using HTTP remotely?

    a. MQTT

    b. CoAP

    c. AMQP

    d. HTTPS

133. Which protocol is used for communication between IoT devices and cloud services, allowing devices to publish and subscribe to data streams using a publish-subscribe model?

    a. MQTT

    b. CoAP

    c. Advanced Message Queuing Protocol (AMQP)

    d. DDS

134. Which protocol is designed for communication between IoT devices and cloud services, providing a way to exchange data using a request-response pattern securely?

    a. MQTT

    b. CoAP

    c. AMQP

    d. HTTPS

135. Which protocol is used for communication between IoT devices and cloud services, enabling secure and efficient data transmission over unreliable networks?

    a. MQTT

    b. CoAP

    c. AMQP

    d. HTTPS

136. Which protocol is designed for communication between IoT devices and cloud services, providing a way to exchange data using publish-subscribe messaging securely?

    a. MQTT

    b. CoAP

    c. AMQP

    d. XMPP

137. Which protocol is used for communication between IoT devices and cloud services, enabling real-time communication through a publish-subscribe model?

    a. MQTT

    b. CoAP

    c. AMQP

    d. XMPP

138. Which protocol is designed for communication between IoT devices and cloud services, providing a way to manage and control devices using binary encoding remotely?

    a. MQTT

    b. CoAP

    c. AMQP

    d. MQTT-SN

139. Which protocol is used for communication between IoT devices and cloud services, allowing devices to discover and exchange information about available services?

    a. MQTT

    b. CoAP

    c. AMQP

    d. XMPP

140. Which protocol is designed for communication between IoT devices and cloud services, providing a way to exchange data using JSON format securely?

    a. MQTT

    b. CoAP

    c. AMQP

    d. HTTPS

141. Which protocol is used for communication between IoT devices and cloud services, enabling efficient and reliable data transmission using message brokers and queues?

    a. MQTT

    b. CoAP

    c. AMQP

    d. HTTPS

142. Which protocol is designed for communication between IoT devices and cloud services, providing a way to control and monitor devices using HTTP remotely?

    a. MQTT

    b. CoAP

    c. AMQP

    d. HTTPS

143. Which protocol is used for communication between IoT devices and cloud services, allowing devices to publish and subscribe to data streams using a publish-subscribe model?

    a. MQTT

    b. CoAP

    c. AMQP

    d. DDS

144. Which protocol is designed for communication between IoT devices and cloud services, providing a way to exchange data using a request-response pattern securely?

    a. MQTT

    b. CoAP

    c. AMQP

    d. HTTPS

145. Which protocol is used for communication between IoT devices and cloud services, enabling secure and efficient data transmission over unreliable networks?

    a. MQTT

    b. CoAP

    c. AMQP

    d. HTTPS

146. Which protocol is designed for communication between IoT devices and cloud services, providing a way to exchange data using publish-subscribe messaging securely?

    a. MQTT

    b. CoAP

    c. AMQP

    d. XMPP

147. Which protocol is used for communication between IoT devices and cloud services, enabling real-time communication through a publish-subscribe model?

    a. MQTT

    b. CoAP

    c. AMQP

    d. XMPP

148. **Which protocol is designed for communication between IoT devices and cloud services, providing a way to exchange messages in a resource-constrained environment?**

    a. MQTT

    b. CoAP

    c. AMQP

    d. DDS

149. **Which protocol is used for communication between IoT devices and cloud services, allowing devices to publish and receive messages using a lightweight messaging pattern?**

    a. MQTT

    b. CoAP

    c. AMQP

    d. DDS

150. **Which of the following protocols is commonly used for communication in IoT devices?**

    a. HTTP

    b. FTP

    c. MQTT

    d. SMTP

151. **What is the primary purpose of the CoAP protocol in IoT?**

    a. File transfer

    b. Messaging

    c. Remote procedure calls

    d. Device management

152. **Which protocol is designed to be lightweight and optimized for constrained environments in IoT?**

    a. HTTP

    b. CoAP

    c. MQTT

    d. WebSocket

153. Which of the following protocols uses a publish-subscribe model?

   a. HTTP

   b. CoAP

   c. MQTT

   d. FTP

154. In which layer of the OSI model does the HTTP protocol operate?

   a. Application layer

   b. Presentation layer

   c. Session layer

   d. Transport layer

155. Which protocol is often used for low-power, low-bandwidth communication in IoT?

   a. HTTP

   b. MQTT

   c. CoAP

   d. XMPP

156. What type of protocol is XMPP considered to be?

   a. Request/Response

   b. Publish/Subscribe

   c. Query/Response

   d. Peer-to-peer

157. What does the acronym MQTT stand for?

   a. Message Queuing Telemetry Transport

   b. Multi-Queue Transport Technology

   c. Message Query Transfer Technique

   d. Mobile Queueing Telemetry Transport

158. Which protocol is designed for asynchronous communication and often used for instant messaging?

   a. HTTP

   b. XMPP

   c. MQTT

   d. CoAP

159. **Which protocol is best suited for highly constrained devices and low-bandwidth networks?**

    a. MQTT

    b. CoAP

    c. HTTP

    d. WebSocket

160. **What is the main difference between HTTP and MQTT?**

    a. MQTT is more lightweight and efficient for IoT

    b. HTTP supports encryption, while MQTT does not

    c. HTTP uses a publish-subscribe model, while MQTT uses request-response

    d. MQTT is suitable for high-bandwidth environments, unlike HTTP

161. **Which protocol is specifically designed for reliable communication over unreliable networks in IoT?**

    a. MQTT

    b. CoAP

    c. HTTP

    d. XMPP

162. **Which of the following protocols is not commonly used in IoT applications?**

    a. HTTP

    b. SNMP

    c. FTP

    d. CoAP

163. **What is the primary function of the WebSocket protocol in IoT?**

    a. Data encryption

    b. Real-time bidirectional communication

    c. Lightweight messaging

    d. Remote procedure calls

164. **Which protocol uses a GET method to retrieve data from a server?**

    a. CoAP

    b. MQTT

    c. HTTP

    d. XMPP

165. **Which of the following is an advantage of using MQTT over HTTP in IoT systems?**

   a. Lower latency

   b. Higher bandwidth usage

   c. More complex implementation

   d. Less efficient for small payloads

166. **What is the role of the broker in MQTT?**

   a. Manage device connections

   b. Route messages between clients

   c. Encrypt messages

   d. Store messages

167. **Which protocol is used primarily for IoT applications requiring high-frequency updates?**

   a. CoAP

   b. HTTP

   c. MQTT

   d. FTP

168. **Which protocol is designed to facilitate low-power communication between constrained devices?**

   a. HTTP

   b. CoAP

   c. MQTT

   d. SNMP

169. **What is the primary advantage of CoAP compared to HTTP in IoT scenarios?**

   a. Better security features

   b. Lower overhead and more efficient for constrained devices

   c. Higher data transfer rate

   d. Supports more complex request types

170. **Which protocol is known for its use in applications requiring low latency and high reliability?**

   a. HTTP

   b. MQTT

   c. CoAP

   d. SNMP

171. **Which of the following is a key feature of the CoAP protocol?**

    a. Stateful communication

    b. Request-response model

    c. Binary payloads only

    d. High data throughput

172. **Which protocol is designed to handle large volumes of data and is often used for web-based applications?**

    a. MQTT

    b. HTTP

    c. CoAP

    d. WebSocket

173. **In which scenarios is the use of XMPP most advantageous?**

    a. Real-time messaging applications

    b. Low-bandwidth communication

    c. High-throughput data transfer

    d. Constrained device environments

174. **What type of network communication does the WebSocket protocol provide?**

    a. One-way communication

    b. Bi-directional, full-duplex communication

    c. Request-response communication

    d. Publish-subscribe communication

175. **Which protocol is optimized for use in environments with low power and limited processing capacity?**

    a. HTTP

    b. MQTT

    c. CoAP

    d. WebSocket

176. **Which of the following protocols supports the use of message queues for managing communication between devices?**

    a. CoAP

    b. MQTT

    c. HTTP

    d. XMPP

177. Which protocol is based on the Extensible Messaging and Presence Protocol (XMPP)?

    a. MQTT

    b. CoAP

    c. HTTP

    d. XMPP

178. Which IoT protocol is characterized by its use of lightweight UDP for transport?

    a. HTTP

    b. CoAP

    c. MQTT

    d. XMPP

179. Which protocol uses a publish and subscribe model to distribute messages between devices?

    a. HTTP

    b. MQTT

    c. CoAP

    d. SNMP

180. Which protocol is commonly used in conjunction with RESTful web services?

    a. CoAP

    b. HTTP

    c. MQTT

    d. WebSocket

181. What type of communication does the MQTT protocol primarily support?

    a. Asynchronous communication

    b. Synchronous communication

    c. Request-response communication

    d. Peer-to-peer communication

182. **Which protocol is particularly effective for constrained devices with limited resources and intermittent connectivity?**

    a. HTTP

    b. CoAP

    c. MQTT

    d. XMPP

183. **Which protocol is designed to work efficiently over TCP/IP networks and provides support for streaming data?**

    a. MQTT

    b. CoAP

    c. HTTP

    d. WebSocket

184. **Which of the following protocols is used to monitor and manage network devices?**

    a. SNMP

    b. HTTP

    c. MQTT

    d. CoAP

185. **Which protocol allows for easy integration with existing web technologies and supports secure communication via HTTPS?**

    a. HTTP

    b. MQTT

    c. CoAP

    d. XMPP

186. **Which protocol is most appropriate for applications requiring minimal overhead and small message sizes?**

    a. HTTP

    b. CoAP

    c. MQTT

    d. WebSocket

187. **Which protocol is designed to work well in unreliable network conditions with support for message acknowledgment?**

    a. CoAP

    b. MQTT

    c. HTTP

    d. WebSocket

188. **Which protocol is best suited for high-frequency, real-time data updates in IoT systems?**

    a. CoAP

    b. MQTT

    c. HTTP

    d. XMPP

189. **Which protocol is known for its support of both presence and instant messaging features?**

    a. HTTP

    b. XMPP

    c. CoAP

    d. MQTT

190. **Which protocol is commonly used at the network layer for IoT devices?**

    a. HTTP

    b. MQTT

    c. IPv6

    d. CoAP

191. **Which IPv6 feature is particularly useful for IoT devices?**

    a. Broadcast communication

    b. Large address space

    c. Statelessness

    d. Connection-oriented communication

192. **What does the RPL protocol stand for?**

    a. Routing Protocol for Low-power and Lossy Networks

    b. Routing Protocol for Lightweight Networks

    c. Reliable Protocol for Low-power Networks

    d. Redundant Protocol for Link-layer Networks

193. **Which of the following is a key characteristic of CoAP?**

    a. Connection-oriented

    b. Designed for high-latency environments

    c. Uses UDP

    d. Requires a reliable transport layer

194. **What is the main purpose of the 6LoWPAN adaptation layer?**

    a. To enable IPv4 over low-power networks

    b. To provide encryption for data transmission

    c. To compress IPv6 headers for low-power networks

    d. To convert TCP to UDP

195. **Which protocol is designed for constrained environments and small packets?**

    a. TCP

    b. UDP

    c. CoAP

    d. FTP

196. **What is the role of the 6LoWPAN in IoT networks?**

    a. It manages network security

    b. It provides routing information

    c. It enables IPv6 packets to be sent over IEEE 802.15.4 networks

    d. It handles data encryption

197. **What does the term Low-power and Lossy Networks (LLNs) refer to?**

    a. Networks with high bandwidth and reliable connectivity

    b. Networks with low power, intermittent connectivity, and high packet loss

    c. Networks with high power and low latency

    d. Networks with high bandwidth and low latency

198. **Which protocol is used to manage and discover IoT devices in a network?**

    a. DHCP

    b. SNMP

    c. DNS

    d. CoAP

199. **In which layer does the Neighbor Discovery Protocol (NDP) operate?**
    a. Application layer
    b. Transport layer
    c. Network layer
    d. Data link layer

200. **What is the primary goal of the Routing Protocol for Low-power and Lossy Networks (RPL)?**
    a. To ensure secure communication
    b. To optimize energy consumption and reliability in routing
    c. To increase data transfer speed
    d. To enable voice communication

201. **What does the term stateless protocol mean in the context of CoAP?**
    a. The protocol maintains the state of every connection
    b. The protocol does not maintain session state between requests
    c. The protocol is stateful and requires a connection to function
    d. The protocol only works in a stateful network environment

202. **Which protocol is designed to provide a simple and efficient way to communicate with constrained devices?**
    a. HTTP
    b. MQTT
    c. CoAP
    d. SNMP

203. **What is the primary purpose of the lightweight IP (6LoWPAN) protocol?**
    a. To enhance security in IoT communications
    b. To provide high-speed data transfer
    c. To optimize IPv6 communication over low-power wireless networks
    d. To manage device authentication

204. **What kind of address space does IPv6 provide?**
    a. 32-bit address space
    b. 64-bit address space
    c. 128-bit address space
    d. 256-bit address space

205. Which protocol is used for dynamic address allocation in IoT networks?

a. DHCP

b. ARP

c. RARP

d. NDP

206. What type of communication does the RPL protocol support?

a. Point-to-point communication

b. Broadcast communication

c. Multicast communication

d. Peer-to-peer communication

207. Which protocol is commonly used in conjunction with 6LoWPAN for low-power wireless networks?

a. Zigbee

b. Bluetooth

c. Wi-Fi

d. LTE

208. Which layer in the OSI model does the RPL protocol operate?

a. Data link layer

b. Network layer

c. Transport layer

d. Application layer

209. What is the purpose of the border router in a 6LoWPAN network?

a. To provide encryption for data packets

b. To translate between IPv6 and the 6LoWPAN protocol

c. To manage device authentication

d. To handle multicast communication

210. Which protocol provides a mechanism for device discovery and service advertisement in IoT networks?

a. DHCP

b. DNS

c. CoAP

d. Bonjour

211. **In which type of network is the RPL protocol primarily used?**

    a. High-bandwidth networks

    b. Low-power and Lossy Networks

    c. Cellular networks

    d. Fiber-optic networks

212. **What is the primary function of the network layer in IoT?**

    a. To provide end-to-end communication

    b. To handle error correction

    c. To manage the data flow between devices

    d. To provide logical addressing and routing

213. **Which of the following is a key feature of IPv6 in IoT applications?**

    a. Supports large-scale multicast communication

    b. Provides low-latency communication

    c. Offers simple packet structure

    d. Supports only IPv4 addresses

214. **Which protocol is often used for real-time data exchange in IoT networks?**

    a. TCP

    b. UDP

    c. HTTP

    d. MQTT

215. **What does the acronym LLN stand for in the context of RPL?**

    a. Low-power Link Network

    b. Low-level Node Network

    c. Low-latency Network

    d. Low-power and Lossy Network

216. **What type of address is used in 6LoWPAN to identify a device on the network?**

    a. IPv4 address

    b. MAC address

    c. IPv6 address

    d. Port number

217. **Which protocol is used for endpoint communication in a constrained environment?**

    a. CoAP

    b. HTTP

    c. FTP

    d. SMTP

218. **Which of the following is a key characteristic of the IEEE 802.15.4 standard used in IoT?**

    a. High-speed data transmission

    b. Long-range communication

    c. Low-power operation

    d. High-bandwidth support

219. **Which network layer protocol is often used with IoT devices that require low latency and low power consumption?**

    a. IPv4

    b. IPv6

    c. TCP

    d. UDP

220. **What is the primary advantage of using IPv6 over IPv4 in IoT applications?**

    a. Reduced header size

    b. Increased address space

    c. Faster data transfer

    d. Better encryption

221. **Which of the following is a standard used for communication in IoT networks?**

    a. IEEE 802.15.4

    b. IEEE 802.11ac

    c. IEEE 802.3

    d. IEEE 802.16

222. **Which protocol is designed for device-to-device communication in a low-power network?**

    a. Bluetooth

    b. Wi-Fi

    c. Zigbee

    d. LTE

223. What does the term stateless imply about the CoAP protocol?

    a. It keeps track of connection states

    b. It does not maintain the state of requests and responses

    c. It requires a continuous connection

    d. It uses a connection-oriented approach

224. Which of the following protocols is used to manage IP addresses in an IoT network?

    a. DNS

    b. ARP

    c. DHCP

    d. NDP

225. What does the acronym CoAP stand for?

    a. Constrained Application Protocol

    b. Connected Application Protocol

    c. Communication Access Protocol

    d. Constrained Access Protocol

226. In which type of network is the 6LoWPAN protocol commonly used?

    a. High-speed internet networks

    b. Cellular networks

    c. Low-power wireless networks

    d. Satellite networks

227. Which of the following is a feature of RPL?

    a. Real-time data transfer

    b. High throughput

    c. Energy-efficient routing

    d. High-speed communication

228. Which layer in the OSI model is responsible for logical addressing and routing?

    a. Physical layer

    b. Data link layer

    c. Network layer

    d. Transport layer

229. **What type of communication does CoAP support?**

   a. Unicast

   b. Multicast

   c. Broadcast

   d. Peer-to-peer

230. **Which IoT protocol is designed for real-time data exchange and operates over UDP?**

   a. CoAP

   b. HTTP

   c. MQTT

   d. FTP

231. **What is the role of the border router in a 6LoWPAN network?**

   a. To manage encryption

   b. To handle data compression

   c. To provide translation between IPv6 and 6LoWPAN

   d. To manage device discovery

232. **What is a key advantage of using IPv6 in IoT networks?**

   a. Simpler packet structure

   b. Smaller address space

   c. Support for large-scale addressing

   d. Better compression algorithms

233. **Which protocol is used for device discovery and service advertisement in IoT environments?**

   a. CoAP

   b. SNMP

   c. Bonjour

   d. MQTT

234. **What is the primary purpose of the Neighbor Discovery Protocol (NDP) in IPv6?**

   a. To provide encryption

   b. To discover neighboring nodes and manage addresses

   c. To route packets between devices

   d. To handle multicast communication

235. **Which of the following protocols is often used for small data transfers in IoT networks?**

    a. TCP

    b. UDP

    c. FTP

    d. HTTP

236. **What does the acronym RPL stand for in IoT networks?**

    a. Routing Protocol for Low-power and Lossy Networks

    b. Reliable Protocol for Low-power Networks

    c. Routing Protocol for Lightweight Networks

    d. Redundant Protocol for Link-layer Networks

237. **What type of network does 6LoWPAN primarily support?**

    a. High-bandwidth networks

    b. Low-power, low-data-rate networks

    c. Cellular networks

    d. Satellite networks

238. **Which layer of the OSI model does the 6LoWPAN adaptation layer operate?**

    a. Application layer

    b. Network layer

    c. Data link layer

    d. Transport layer

239. **Which protocol is designed to work with the IEEE 802.15.4 standard for IoT communication?**

    a. CoAP

    b. MQTT

    c. RPL

    d. 6LoWPAN

240. **What does the term constrained network refer to?**

    a. Networks with high bandwidth and high power

    b. Networks with limited resources, such as low power and low bandwidth

    c. Networks with high-speed data transfer

    d. Networks with no connectivity issues

241. **Which protocol is used for low-latency communication in IoT networks?**

    a. MQTT

    b. HTTP

    c. CoAP

    d. TCP

242. **What is the primary benefit of using UDP over TCP in IoT networks?**

    a. Better reliability

    b. Lower latency and overhead

    c. Improved error correction

    d. Connection-oriented communication

243. **Which layer of the OSI model is responsible for packet routing in IoT networks?**

    a. Application layer

    b. Data link layer

    c. Network layer

    d. Transport layer

244. **Which IoT protocol is designed for high-throughput and low-power consumption?**

    a. CoAP

    b. MQTT

    c. HTTP

    d. FTP

245. **Which feature of IPv6 is particularly advantageous for IoT devices?**

    a. Smaller header size

    b. Simplified packet structure

    c. Large address space

    d. Improved security

246. **Which protocol is used to optimize header compression in IoT networks?**

    a. IPv6

    b. 6LoWPAN

    c. RPL

    d. CoAP

247. **What type of communication does RPL support in IoT networks?**

    a. Unicast only

    b. Broadcast only

    c. Multicast and anycast

    d. Point-to-point only

248. **Which protocol is best suited for constrained devices with limited computational power?**

    a. HTTP

    b. CoAP

    c. MQTT

    d. FTP

249. **What is the main function of the Neighbor Discovery Protocol (NDP) in IPv6?**

    a. To manage device connections

    b. To discover and configure neighboring devices

    c. To handle data encryption

    d. To route packets efficiently

250. **Which protocol is often used for device and service discovery in IoT?**

    a. CoAP

    b. DNS

    c. Bonjour

    d. SNMP

251. **What is a primary feature of CoAP?**

    a. Connection-oriented communication

    b. Designed for high-bandwidth scenarios

    c. Operates over UDP for low-overhead communication

    d. Supports large data payloads

252. **Which protocol is used for routing in Low-power and Lossy Networks ?**

    a. TCP

    b. RPL

    c. HTTP

    d. CoAP

253. **What type of addressing does IPv6 use?**

    a. 32-bit addresses

    b. 64-bit addresses

    c. 128-bit addresses

    d. 256-bit addresses

254. **What is the main advantage of using 6LoWPAN in IoT networks?**

    a. High-speed data transfer

    b. Compression of IPv6 headers

    c. Large address space

    d. Enhanced security features

255. **Which protocol is specifically designed to work with the IEEE 802.15.4 standard?**

    a. CoAP

    b. MQTT

    c. 6LoWPAN

    d. HTTP

256. **What does the term low-power imply in the context of IoT networks?**

    a. High energy consumption

    b. Low energy consumption

    c. High bandwidth

    d. High processing power

257. **Which of the following is a key feature of MQTT?**

    a. High throughput

    b. Low latency

    c. Connection-oriented communication

    d. Reliable delivery

258. **Which protocol is used for reliable message delivery in IoT?**

    a. HTTP

    b. CoAP

    c. MQTT

    d. UDP

259. What is the main purpose of CoAP in IoT networks?

    a. To provide high-speed communication

    b. To handle large data payloads

    c. To enable efficient communication in constrained environments

    d. To provide end-to-end encryption

260. Which protocol is designed to work with constrained devices and networks?

    a. HTTP

    b. MQTT

    c. CoAP

    d. FTP

261. What is the function of the border router in a 6LoWPAN network?

    a. To translate IPv6 packets to and from 6LoWPAN

    b. To handle network encryption

    c. To manage device authentication

    d. To perform data compression

262. Which protocol is best suited for applications requiring real-time communication?

    a. HTTP

    b. CoAP

    c. MQTT

    d. TCP

263. What does the term constrained environment refer to?

    a. High-speed, high-bandwidth environments

    b. Low-power, low-bandwidth environments

    c. High-power, high-bandwidth environments

    d. Environments with unlimited resources

264. Which layer in the OSI model provides logical addressing and routing?

    a. Application layer

    b. Network layer

    c. Data link layer

    d. Transport layer

265. **What does the acronym CoAP represent?**

    a. Constrained Application Protocol

    b. Communication Access Protocol

    c. Connected Application Protocol

    d. Constrained Access Protocol

266. **Which protocol is designed to manage low-power wireless networks?**

    a. HTTP

    b. MQTT

    c. RPL

    d. CoAP

267. **What is the main feature of the 6LoWPAN adaptation layer?**

    a. Data encryption

    b. Header compression for IPv6

    c. High-speed data transfer

    d. Device authentication

268. **Which protocol provides efficient communication in constrained environments?**

    a. HTTP

    b. CoAP

    c. MQTT

    d. FTP

269. **What does the term low-latency imply for IoT communication protocols?**

    a. High delay in data transmission

    b. Minimal delay in data transmission

    c. High data transfer rate

    d. High computational overhead

270. **Which protocol is used to enable communication between IPv6 and low-power wireless networks?**

    a. HTTP

    b. 6LoWPAN

    c. CoAP

    d. RPL

271. **What is the primary function of the Neighbor Discovery Protocol (NDP)?**
    a. To handle packet routing
    b. To manage network security
    c. To discover and configure neighboring nodes
    d. To compress headers

272. **Which protocol is designed for energy-efficient routing in IoT networks?**
    a. RPL
    b. CoAP
    c. HTTP
    d. MQTT

273. **What is the main advantage of using CoAP in IoT networks?**
    a. High bandwidth
    b. Low energy consumption
    c. High security
    d. Low latency and overhead

274. **Which protocol is optimized for constrained devices with limited resources?**
    a. CoAP
    b. HTTP
    c. FTP
    d. SMTP

275. **Which feature of IPv6 is beneficial for large-scale IoT deployments?**
    a. Reduced packet size
    b. Large address space
    c. Simplified routing
    d. Enhanced security

276. **What does the acronym RPL stand for in IoT networking?**
    a. Routing Protocol for Low-power and Lossy Networks
    b. Reliable Protocol for Low-power Networks
    c. Routing Protocol for Lightweight Networks
    d. Redundant Protocol for Link-layer Networks

277. **Which protocol is commonly used for real-time communication in constrained networks?**

    a. CoAP

    b. HTTP

    c. MQTT

    d. FTP

278. **What is the main role of the border router in a 6LoWPAN network?**

    a. To handle network security

    b. To perform data compression

    c. To manage address translation between IPv6 and 6LoWPAN

    d. To route data packets

279. **Which protocol is designed to handle low-power and low-bandwidth communication?**

    a. HTTP

    b. CoAP

    c. MQTT

    d. FTP

280. **What is the main advantage of using MQTT in IoT networks?**

    a. High bandwidth

    b. Low latency

    c. High security

    d. Large payload support

281. **Which protocol provides header compression for IPv6 in IoT networks?**

    a. CoAP

    b. MQTT

    c. 6LoWPAN

    d. RPL

282. **What does the term constrained device refer to in IoT?**

    a. A device with high processing power

    b. A device with limited computational resources and low power

    c. A device with unlimited connectivity

    d. A device with high bandwidth capabilities

283. **Which protocol is optimized for low-power and low-bandwidth networks?**

   a. HTTP

   b. CoAP

   c. MQTT

   d. FTP

284. **Which feature of RPL is crucial for IoT networks?**

   a. Real-time data transfer

   b. Energy-efficient routing

   c. High-speed communication

   d. Large payload support

285. **What is the main role of CoAP in IoT networks?**

   a. To provide high-speed data transfer

   b. To enable efficient communication in constrained environments

   c. To support large data payloads

   d. To manage device security

286. **Which protocol is used for efficient communication in constrained networks?**

   a. CoAP

   b. HTTP

   c. MQTT

   d. FTP

287. **What does the acronym CoAP stand for?**

   a. Constrained Application Protocol

   b. Communication Access Protocol

   c. Connected Application Protocol

   d. Constrained Access Protocol

288. **Which protocol provides header compression to optimize IPv6 communication in IoT networks?**

   a. CoAP

   b. MQTT

   c. 6LoWPAN

   d. RPL

289. **Which protocol is ideal for handling small data transfers and low-power devices?**

    a. HTTP

    b. CoAP

    c. MQTT

    d. FTP

Join our Discord space

Join our Discord workspace for latest updates, offers, tech happenings around the world, new releases, and sessions with the authors:

https://discord.bpbonline.com

Answers

Q. No.	Answer	Q. No.	Answer	Q. No.	Answer	Q. No.	Answer	Q. No.	Answer
1	c	31	d	61	c	91	b	121	d
2	b	32	d	62	a	92	a	122	c
3	c	33	a	63	d	93	b	123	d
4	a	34	d	64	a	94	c	124	a
5	a	35	c	65	a	95	a	125	a
6	b	36	b	66	c	96	c	126	d
7	d	37	d	67	c	97	b	127	d
8	c	38	d	68	d	98	d	128	d
9	b	39	c	69	a	99	a	129	c
10	b	40	c	70	c	100	b	130	d
11	d	41	a	71	b	101	a	131	c
12	c	42	c	72	a	102	d	132	d
13	a	43	b	73	c	103	c	133	a
14	c	44	b	74	d	104	d	134	c
15	b	45	b	75	d	105	c	135	a
16	d	46	d	76	c	106	d	136	a
17	b	47	d	77	d	107	d	137	d
18	d	48	b	78	c	108	c	138	d
19	c	49	d	79	d	109	d	139	c
20	b	50	a	80	d	110	a	140	d
21	b	51	c	81	d	111	d	141	c
22	c	52	d	82	d	112	d	142	d
23	d	53	d	83	a	113	d	143	d
24	b	54	d	84	a	114	d	144	c
25	a	55	d	85	d	115	a	145	a
26	a	56	a	86	d	116	a	146	a
27	b	57	d	87	c	117	d	147	d
28	d	58	d	88	d	118	d	148	b
29	c	59	c	89	d	119	c	149	a
30	b	60	b	90	d	120	d	150	c

Q. No.	Answer	Q. No.	Answer	Q. No.	Answer	Q. No.	Answer	Q. No.	Answer
151	c	179	b	207	a	235	b	263	b
152	b	180	b	208	b	236	a	264	b
153	c	181	a	209	b	237	b	265	a
154	a	182	b	210	d	238	b	266	c
155	c	183	d	211	b	239	d	267	b
156	d	184	a	212	d	240	b	268	b
157	a	185	a	213	a	241	a	269	b
158	b	186	b	214	b	242	b	270	b
159	b	187	b	215	d	243	c	271	c
160	a	188	b	216	c	244	b	272	a
161	a	189	b	217	a	245	c	273	d
162	c	190	c	218	c	246	b	274	a
163	b	191	b	219	b	247	c	275	b
164	c	192	a	220	b	248	b	276	a
165	a	193	c	221	a	249	b	277	c
166	b	194	c	222	c	250	c	278	c
167	c	195	c	223	b	251	c	279	b
168	b	196	c	224	c	252	b	280	b
169	b	197	b	225	a	253	c	281	c
170	b	198	d	226	c	254	b	282	b
171	b	199	c	227	c	255	c	283	b
172	b	200	b	228	c	256	b	284	b
173	a	201	b	229	b	257	b	285	b
174	b	202	c	230	c	258	c	286	a
175	c	203	c	231	c	259	c	287	a
176	b	204	c	232	c	260	c	288	c
177	d	205	a	233	c	261	a	289	b
178	b	206	c	234	b	262	c		

CHAPTER 3

Python Logical Design of an IoT System

Introduction

In the IoT age, ordinary things are connected to the digital world. These systems look simple to users, but they need careful logical design. Python is a popular language for IoT system design due to its flexibility, durability, and extensive library support. We use Python to create an IoT system's logic. The fundamental components of an IoT system are sensors/actuators, a communication interface, data storage, and a user interface. These parts must communicate, analyze data, and provide meaningful insights.

Python's flexibility enables all aspects of logical flow:

- **RPi.GPIO**: For Raspberry Pi lets Python gather sensor data, for instance, temperature sensor readings.

- **Data transmission**: Python libraries like **paho-mqtt** support IoT protocols like MQTT. Data may be sent and received from a central server or cloud.

- **Data processing and storage**: Python's interoperability with SQLite and AWS offers efficient data storage, retrieval, and processing. This data may be preprocessed using pandas.

- **User interaction**: Python frameworks like Flask or Django may provide web-based dashboards or REST APIs for monitoring, control, and decision-making for IoT data.

- **Modular design**: Python encourages modularity. Modules or scripts may read sensor data, communicate with a server, and interact with users. Modularity facilitates testing, scalability, and troubleshooting.

  Python is ideal for quick prototyping because of its interpretive nature. Development teams can rapidly test logical ideas, make changes, and improve the system. Python's scikit-learn simplifies prototyping predictive maintenance systems using machine learning.

- **Security considerations**: Connected IoT systems are susceptible to assaults. Python has cryptography packages for data encryption and safe communication. MQTT communication may use SSL/TLS for security.

- **Scalability**: Python's architecture supports scaling. Python can evolve when an IoT system adds devices or needs more complex data processing. Dask makes large-scale data processing possible.

- **Integration with advanced technologies**: IoT often integrates with machine learning, AI, and Blockchain. Python, the dominating language in many fields, provides smooth integration. A logical design may use Python's TensorFlow to identify sensor anomalies.

- **Event-driven programming**: Often reactive, IoT systems respond to events. Event-driven programming in Python, particularly with `asyncio`, lets developers run many activities at once, which is essential for real-time IoT systems.

Multiple choice questions

1. **In the context of IoT system design, what does logical design refer to?**
    a. The physical components of the IoT devices.
    b. The software and programming aspects of the IoT system.
    c. The wireless communication protocols used by IoT devices.
    d. The power source requirements for IoT devices.

2. **Which programming language is commonly used for logical design in IoT systems?**
    a. C++
    b. Java
    c. Python
    d. Ruby

3. **What role does Python play in the logical design of an IoT system?**
    a. It facilitates the creation of hardware components.
    b. It handles wireless communication between devices.
    c. It helps in writing code for data processing and control in the IoT system.
    d. It manages the power consumption of IoT devices.

4. **Which of the following Python libraries is commonly used for IoT application development?**
    a. NumPy
    b. Matplotlib
    c. TensorFlow
    d. Flask

5. **What is Flask used for in IoT system design?**
    a. Data visualization
    b. Wireless communication
    c. Web server development
    d. Machine learning

6. **Which Python library is often used for connecting IoT devices to the cloud?**
    a. Requests
    b. Flask
    c. MQTT
    d. Pandas

7. **In IoT systems, what does MQTT stand for?**
    a. Message Queue Telemetry Transport
    b. Message Query Telemetry Transfer
    c. Main Query Telemetry Transport
    d. Message Queue Transfer Telemetry

8. **What is the primary purpose of MQTT in an IoT system?**
    a. Data visualization
    b. Real-time data streaming
    c. Web server development
    d. Data encryption

9. **Which Python library is used for interacting with physical sensors and actuators in an IoT system?**

   a. NumPy

   b. Matplotlib

   c. RPi.GPIO

   d. Requests

10. **What does RPi.GPIO library allows you to do this in an IoT system.**

    a. Develop web servers

    b. Establish wireless communication

    c. Control and read GPIO pins on a Raspberry Pi

    d. Analyze sensor data

11. **Which Python module can generate random numbers in IoT applications?**

    a. Random

    b. Math

    c. NumPy

    d. Randomize

12. **What is the purpose of generating random numbers in an IoT system?**

    a. To improve power efficiency

    b. To simulate real-world scenarios

    c. To establish wireless communication

    d. To reduce latency in data transmission

13. **Which Python library is often used for sending HTTP requests and receiving HTTP responses in an IoT system?**

    a. json

    b. http

    c. requests

    d. urllib

14. **In an IoT system, what is the purpose of sending HTTP requests using the requests library?**

    a. To control actuators

    b. To visualize sensor data

    c. To establish wireless communication

    d. To calculate data statistics

15. **Which Python library is commonly used for working with JSON data in IoT applications?**

    a. jsonify

    b. jsonlib

    c. jsonencode

    d. json

16. **What is the primary use of the json library in IoT systems?**

    a. Wireless communication

    b. Data visualization

    c. Data serialization and deserialization

    d. Web server development

17. **Which Python library is used for creating and manipulating web services in IoT applications?**

    a. webutils

    b. urllib

    c. requests

    d. Flask

18. **What is the role of Flask in an IoT system?**

    a. Real-time data streaming

    b. Handling wireless communication

    c. Creating web services and APIs

    d. Data serialization

19. **Which Python library implements machine learning algorithms in an IoT system?**

    a. TensorFlow

    b. Matplotlib

    c. NumPy

    d. Scikit-learn

20. **What is the main purpose of using TensorFlow in an IoT system?**
    a. Data visualization
    b. Wireless communication
    c. Web server development
    d. Implementing machine learning models

21. **In the context of IoT systems, what is GPIO short for?**
    a. General-purpose input/output
    b. General protocol input/output
    c. Graphical processor input/output
    d. Graphical protocol input/output

22. **Which Python library is used for interacting with GPIO pins in IoT applications?**
    a. gpio
    b. gpiocontrol
    c. RPi.GPIO
    d. gpioaccess

23. **What is the primary purpose of interacting with GPIO pins in an IoT system?**
    a. Real-time data streaming
    b. Handling wireless communication
    c. Controlling sensors and actuators
    d. Developing web services

24. **Which Python library is commonly used for sending and receiving data over a network connection in IoT systems?**
    a. socket
    b. networkutils
    c. networkio
    d. socketio

25. **What is the role of the socket library in an IoT system?**
    a. Data visualization
    b. Wireless communication
    c. Web server development
    d. Establishing network connections and data transfer

26. **Which Python library is commonly used for parsing XML data in IoT applications?**

    a. xmlparser

    b. xmlutils

    c. xmlencode

    d. xml

27. **What is the primary purpose of using the xml library in an IoT system?**

    a. Data visualization

    b. Wireless communication

    c. Data serialization and deserialization

    d. Web server development

28. **Which Python library is often used for time-related calculations and scheduling tasks in IoT systems?**

    a. timer

    b. time

    c. datetime

    d. schedule

29. **In the context of IoT systems, what does the datetime library help you with?**

    a. Data visualization

    b. Handling wireless communication

    c. Managing time-related calculations and scheduling tasks

    d. Developing web services

30. **Which Python library is commonly used for data analysis and manipulation in IoT applications?**

    a. Pandas

    b. NumPy

    c. SciPy

    d. Analysis

31. **What is the primary purpose of using the Pandas library in an IoT system?**

    a. Real-time data streaming

    b. Data visualization

    c. Data analysis and manipulation

    d. Developing machine learning models

32. **Which Python library is used for handling URLs and sending HTTP requests in IoT applications?**

    a. urllib

    b. http

    c. urlrequest

    d. requests

33. **What is the role of the urllib library in an IoT system?**

    a. Real-time data streaming

    b. Data serialization and deserialization

    c. Handling URLs and sending HTTP requests

    d. Developing web services

34. **Which Python library is often used for data visualization in IoT applications?**

    a. Matplotlib

    b. Seaborn

    c. Plotly

    d. Visual

35. **What is the primary purpose of using the matplotlib library in an IoT system?**

    a. Real-time data streaming

    b. Data analysis and manipulation

    c. Data visualization

    d. Developing machine learning models

36. **Which Python library is commonly used for implementing machine learning algorithms in IoT applications?**

    a. TensorFlow

    b. Sklearn

    c. Keras

    d. mlpython

37. **What is the primary purpose of using the TensorFlow library in an IoT system?**

    a. Real-time data streaming

    b. Data analysis and manipulation

    c. Data visualization

    d. Implementing machine learning models

38. **Which Python library is used for working with databases and SQL in IoT applications?**

   a. dbutils

   b. database

   c. sqlalchemy

   d. dbpython

39. **What is the role of the SQLAlchemy library in an IoT system?**

   a. Real-time data streaming

   b. Data analysis and manipulation

   c. Web server development

   d. Interacting with databases and SQL

40. **In an IoT system, which library can be used to encrypt and decrypt data for secure communication?**

   a. cryptolib

   b. ssl

   c. encryption

   d. secureio

41. **What is the primary purpose of using the SSL library in an IoT system?**

   a. Real-time data streaming

   b. Data analysis and manipulation

   c. Establishing secure communication channels

   d. Developing machine learning models

42. **Which Python library is used for creating and interacting with RESTful APIs in IoT applications?**

   a. apiutils

   b. requests

   c. http

   d. flask-restful

43. **What is the role of the flask-restful library in an IoT system?**

   a. Real-time data streaming

   b. Data analysis and manipulation

   c. Handling HTTP requests

   d. Creating and interacting with RESTful APIs

44. **Which Python library is used for working with JSON Web Tokens (JWT) in IoT applications?**

    a. jwt

    b. jsonweb

    c. webtoken

    d. jwtlib

45. **What is the primary purpose of using the jwt library in an IoT system?**

    a. Real-time data streaming

    b. Data analysis and manipulation

    c. Implementing authentication and authorization using JSON Web Tokens

    d. Developing machine learning models

46. **Which Python library is used for working with messaging protocols and brokers in IoT applications?**

    a. messageio

    b. mqtt

    c. messageutils

    d. broker

47. **What is the role of the mqtt library in an IoT system?**

    a. Data visualization

    b. Data analysis and manipulation

    c. Real-time data streaming through messaging protocols

    d. Web server development

48. **In an IoT system, which library can be used to parse and manipulate HTML and XML documents?**

    a. webutils

    b. htmlxml

    c. xmlparse

    d. BeautifulSoup

49. **What is the primary purpose of using the BeautifulSoup library in an IoT system?**

    a. Real-time data streaming

    b. Data analysis and manipulation

    c. Parsing and manipulating HTML and XML documents

    d. Developing web services

50. **Which Python library is often used for handling asynchronous tasks and event-driven programming in IoT systems?**

    a. asyncio

    b. asyncpython

    c. eventutils

    d. asyncioio

51. **Which Python library works with IoT devices and protocols, providing a platform for building IoT applications?**

    a. iotlib

    b. iotutils

    c. iotpy

    d. paho-mqtt

52. **What is the role of the paho-mqtt library in an IoT system?**

    a. Real-time data streaming

    b. Data analysis and manipulation

    c. Handling MQTT communication and protocols

    d. Web server development

53. **In an IoT system, which library can work with databases using an Object-Relational Mapping (ORM) approach?**

    a. dbutils

    b. database

    c. sqlalchemy

    d. orm-python

54. **What is the primary purpose of using the SQLAlchemy library with an ORM approach in an IoT system?**

    a. Real-time data streaming

    b. Data analysis and manipulation

    c. Interacting with databases using an ORM approach

    d. Developing web services

55. **Which Python library is used for creating and managing web sockets in IoT applications?**

    a. websockets

    b. socketio

    c. sockutils

    d. iotsockets

56. **What is the role of the websockets library in an IoT system?**

    a. Real-time data streaming through web sockets

    b. Data analysis and manipulation

    c. Handling HTTP requests

    d. Developing machine learning models

57. **Which Python library is often used for creating interactive and dynamic data visualizations in IoT applications?**

    a. Matplotlib

    b. Seaborn

    c. Plotly

    d. Visual Python

58. **What is the primary purpose of using the Plotly library in an IoT system?**

    a. Real-time data streaming

    b. Data analysis and manipulation

    c. Creating interactive and dynamic data visualizations

    d. Developing machine learning models

59. **Which Python library is commonly used for working with IoT devices and protocols, providing support for CoAP and other protocols?**

    a. iotpy

    b. iotutils

    c. CoAPython

    d. aiocoap

60. **What is the role of the aiocoap library in an IoT system?**

    a. Real-time data streaming

    b. Data analysis and manipulation

    c. Handling CoAP communication and protocols

    d. Developing web services

61. **Which Python library is used for building web-based user interfaces in IoT applications?**

    a. webui

    b. webkit

    c. webutils

    d. dash

62. **What is the primary purpose of using the dash library in an IoT system?**

    a. Real-time data streaming

    b. Data analysis and manipulation

    c. Building interactive web-based user interfaces

    d. Developing machine learning models

63. **Which Python library is often used for real-time data streaming and synchronization in IoT applications?**

    a. syncio

    b. realtime

    c. asyncio

    d. socketio

64. **What is the role of the socketio library in an IoT system?**

    a. Real-time data streaming and synchronization

    b. Data analysis and manipulation

    c. Handling HTTP requests

    d. Developing machine learning models

65. **Which Python library is used for working with RESTful APIs and making HTTP requests in IoT applications?**

    a. requests

    b. restio

    c. http

    d. apiutils

66. **What is the primary purpose of using the requests library in an IoT system?**

   a. Real-time data streaming

   b. Data analysis and manipulation

   c. Making HTTP requests and interacting with RESTful APIs

   d. Developing machine learning models

67. **In an IoT system, which library can handle and manage tasks concurrently, allowing for efficient use of resources?**

   a. async

   b. multitask

   c. concurrency

   d. asyncio

68. **What is the primary purpose of using the asyncio library in an IoT system?**

   a. Real-time data streaming

   b. Data analysis and manipulation

   c. Handling and managing tasks concurrently

   d. Developing machine learning models

69. **Which Python library is often used for data analysis and manipulation in IoT applications, providing support for multi-dimensional arrays?**

   a. Pandas

   b. NumPy

   c. datautils

   d. arraypy

70. **What is the primary purpose of using the NumPy library in an IoT system?**

   a. Real-time data streaming

   b. Data analysis and manipulation with multi-dimensional arrays

   c. Data visualization

   d. Developing machine learning models

71. **Which Python library is used for working with geographic information and mapping in IoT applications?**

   a. geoutils

   b. maplib

    c. geopy

    d. locationpy

72. **What is the primary purpose of using the geopy library in an IoT system?**

    a. Real-time data streaming

    b. Data analysis and manipulation of geographic information

    c. Creating and managing web services

    d. Developing machine learning models

73. **Which Python library is often used for handling time series data and performing analysis on temporal data in IoT applications?**

    a. timeio

    b. datetime

    c. timeseries

    d. Pandas

74. **What is the primary purpose of using the Pandas library for time series data analysis in an IoT system?**

    a. Real-time data streaming

    b. Data analysis and manipulation of temporal data

    c. Data visualization

    d. Developing machine learning models

75. **In an IoT system, which library can handle machine learning tasks, such as classification and regression?**

    a. sklearn

    b. mlutils

    c. tensorlearn

    d. pyml

76. **What is the primary purpose of using the sklearn library in an IoT system?**

    a. Real-time data streaming

    b. Data analysis and manipulation

    c. Developing web-based interfaces

    d. Implementing machine learning models

77. **Which Python library is used for building graphical user interfaces (GUIs) in IoT applications?**

    a. guilib

    b. tkinter

    c. uigui

    d. guiutils

78. **What is the role of the Tkinter library in an IoT system?**

    a. Real-time data streaming

    b. Data analysis and manipulation

    c. Developing web-based interfaces

    d. Building graphical user interfaces (GUIs)

79. **Which Python library is commonly used for working with natural language processing (NLP) in IoT applications?**

    a. nltk

    b. nlpio

    c. languagepy

    d. textutils

80. **What is the primary purpose of using the NLTK library in an IoT system?**

    a. Real-time data streaming

    b. Data analysis and manipulation of natural language data

    c. Developing web-based interfaces

    d. Implementing machine learning models for NLP

81. **In an IoT system, which library can be used to work with audio and sound processing tasks?**

    a. soundio

    b. audio-utils

    c. audiopy

    d. librosa

82. **What is the primary purpose of using the librosa library in an IoT system?**

    a. Real-time data streaming

    b. Data analysis and manipulation of audio data

    c. Developing web-based interfaces

    d. Implementing machine learning models for audio processing

83. Which Python library is often used for performing mathematical calculations and advanced mathematical operations in IoT applications?

    a. mathutils

    b. advancedmath

    c. mathpy

    d. sympy

84. What is the role of the sympy library in an IoT system?

    a. Real-time data streaming

    b. Data analysis and manipulation

    c. Developing web-based interfaces

    d. Performing mathematical calculations and advanced operations

85. Which library can work with images and perform image processing tasks in an IoT system?

    a. imgpy

    b. imageutils

    c. PIL

    d. imager

86. What is the primary purpose of using the PIL library in an IoT system?

    a. Real-time data streaming

    b. Data analysis and manipulation of images

    c. Developing web-based interfaces

    d. Implementing machine learning models for image processing

87. Which Python library is often used for handling and manipulating Excel spreadsheets in IoT applications?

    a. xlslib

    b. xlrd

    c. excelutils

    d. spreadsheetpy

88. **What is the primary purpose of using the xlrd library in an IoT system?**

    a. Real-time data streaming

    b. Data analysis and manipulation of Excel spreadsheets

    c. Developing web-based interfaces

    d. Implementing machine learning models for spreadsheet data

89. **Which library can work with computer vision tasks and object detection in an IoT system?**

    a. visionpy

    b. opencv

    c. computer-vision

    d. imagevision

90. **What is the primary purpose of using the opencv library in an IoT system?**

    a. Real-time data streaming

    b. Data analysis and manipulation of visual data

    c. Developing web-based interfaces

    d. Implementing computer vision tasks and object detection

91. **Which Python library is used for working with 3D graphics and creating interactive 3D applications in IoT applications?**

    a. graphicpy

    b. pygame

    c. graphics3d

    d. pyglet

92. **What is the primary purpose of using the pyglet library in an IoT system?**

    a. Real-time data streaming

    b. Data analysis and manipulation of 3D graphics

    c. Developing web-based interfaces

    d. Creating interactive 3D applications

93. **In an IoT system, which library can be used to work with physical quantities and units of measurement?**

    a. unitpy

    b. quantities

    c. physicalpy

    d. pint

94. **What is the primary purpose of using the pint library in an IoT system?**

    a. Real-time data streaming

    b. Data analysis and manipulation of physical quantities

    c. Developing web-based interfaces

    d. Implementing unit conversions and calculations

95. **Which Python library is often used for working with and manipulating graphs and networks in IoT applications?**

    a. graphio

    b. networkx

    c. graphutils

    d. netpy

96. **What is the primary purpose of using the networkx library in an IoT system?**

    a. Real-time data streaming

    b. Data analysis and manipulation of graphs and networks

    c. Developing web-based interfaces

    d. Implementing machine learning models for graph data

97. **Which library can work with geographic information systems (GIS) and spatial data in an IoT system?**

    a. gispy

    b. geospatial

    c. spatialpy

    d. geopandas

98. **What is the primary purpose of using the geopandas library in an IoT system?**

    a. Real-time data streaming

    b. Data analysis and manipulation of geographic and spatial data

    c. Developing web-based interfaces

    d. Implementing machine learning models for spatial data

99. **Which Python library works with and manipulates structured data in IoT applications, including creating and querying databases?**

    a. datastore

    b. databasepy

    c. dbutils

    d. sqlite3

100. **What is the primary purpose of using the sqlite3 library in an IoT system?**

    a. Real-time data streaming

    b. Data analysis and manipulation of structured data

    c. Developing web-based interfaces

    d. Creating and querying databases

101. **Which Python library is commonly used for creating RESTful APIs in an IoT system?**

    a. NumPy

    b. Flask

    c. Matplotlib

    d. OpenCV

102. **What is the primary purpose of using MQTT in an IoT system?**

    a. Data storage

    b. Secure data transfer

    c. Message brokering

    d. Data visualization

103. **Which Python module is used to interface with GPIO pins on a Raspberry Pi for IoT applications?**

    a. socket

    b. RPi.GPIO

    c. requests

    d. pandas

104. **What function in Python is used to convert a Python object into a JSON string for IoT communication?**

    a. json.dump()

    b. json.loads()

    c. json.dumps()

    d. json.load()

105. **In an IoT system, which of the following is used to securely store sensitive configuration data like API keys?**

    a. Plain text files

    b. Environment variables

    c. JSON files

    d. CSV files

106. **Which Python library can be used for asynchronous programming, which is useful in IoT systems for handling multiple connections?**

    a. asyncio

    b. threading

    c. multiprocessing

    d. os

107. **When designing an IoT system, what is the purpose of using a Python asyncio event loop?**

    a. To handle file I/O operations

    b. To manage asynchronous tasks

    c. To create graphical user interfaces

    d. To perform numerical computations

108. **Which Python module is used to handle HTTP requests in an IoT system?**

    a. urllib

    b. http.client

    c. requests

    d. http.server

109. **What does the acronym REST stand for in the context of RESTful APIs used in IoT systems?**

    a. Representational State Transfer

    b. Remote State Transfer

    c. Resource State Transfer

    d. Regular State Transfer

110. **Which Python data structure is most suitable for managing an IoT device's configuration settings?**

    a. List

    b. Tuple

    c. Dictionary

    d. Set

111. **In an IoT system, what role does the pyserial library play?**

    a. Network communication

    b. Serial communication

    c. Data analysis

    d. Web scraping

112. **How can you handle JSON data in a Python script for IoT?**

    a. Using the pickle module

    b. Using the json module

    c. Using the csv module

    d. Using the sqlite3 module

113. **Which Python library is used for scheduling tasks in an IoT system?**

    a. schedule

    b. time

    c. datetime

    d. cron

114. **What is the purpose of using the socket library in a Python-based IoT system?**

    a. To create a graphical interface

    b. To handle network communication

    c. To parse JSON data

    d. To perform mathematical calculations

115. **Which Python data type would you use to store a sequence of measurements from an IoT sensor?**

    a. Set

    b. List

    c. Dictionary

    d. Tuple

116. **Which Python library is useful for handling large amounts of data generated by IoT devices?**
    a. Pandas
    b. requests
    c. asyncio
    d. PySerial

117. **What are the requests.get() method work in a Python script?**
    a. Sends data to a server
    b. Retrieves data from a server
    c. Updates data on a server
    d. Deletes data from a server

118. **How can you manage device states in an IoT system using Python?**
    a. By using global variables
    b. By using a state management library
    c. By hardcoding states in the script
    d. By using a file-based database

119. **Which Python construct is typically used for error handling in IoT device communication?**
    a. if-else
    b. try-except
    c. for loop
    d. while loop

120. **In Python, how can you ensure that a specific piece of code runs periodically in an IoT system?**
    a. Using a while loop
    b. Using the schedule library
    c. Using the time.sleep() function
    d. Using asyncio

121. **What does the json.load() function do in Python?**
    a. Converts a JSON string into a Python object
    b. Converts a Python object into a JSON string
    c. Loads JSON data from a file into a Python object
    d. Saves a Python object as a JSON file

122. **Which Python module would you use to handle high-level data storage in an IoT system?**

   a. sqlite3

   b. sys

   c. os

   d. threading

123. **In an IoT system, what does the acronym API stand for?**

   a. Application Programming Interface

   b. Application Protocol Interface

   c. Advanced Programming Interface

   d. Active Programming Interface

124. **Which Python library can be used to visualize data from IoT sensors?**

   a. matplotlib

   b. Flask

   c. requests

   d. NumPy

125. **What is the main use of the RPi.GPIO library in Python for IoT projects?**

   a. Web scraping

   b. Data visualization

   c. Interfacing with hardware

   d. Network communication

126. **Which Python method would you use to parse XML data in an IoT system?**

   a. xml.parser()

   b. xml.etree.ElementTree.parse()

   c. xml.load()

   d. xml.read()

127. **What is the purpose of using async and await keywords in Python for IoT applications?**

   a. To define data structures

   b. To manage asynchronous code

   c. To perform mathematical operations

   d. To create graphical interfaces

128. **Which Python library is used for sending data to a remote server in an IoT system?**
    a. PySerial
    b. Requests
    c. Socket
    d. NumPy

129. **What is the primary function of the socket library in Python for an IoT system?**
    a. To interface with databases
    b. To manage web requests
    c. To handle network connections
    d. To parse JSON data

130. **Which Python function is used to open a file for writing?**
    a. open(filename, 'w')
    b. write(filename)
    c. open_file(filename)
    d. create_file(filename)

131. **Which library is used for performing HTTP requests asynchronously in Python?**
    a. requests
    b. aiohttp
    c. urllib
    d. http.client

132. **In Python, which method is used to write data to a file?**
    a. file.write()
    b. file.append()
    c. file.save()
    d. file.update()

133. **Which of the following is a key feature of the paho-mqtt library in Python for IoT systems?**
    a. Data visualization
    b. MQTT protocol support
    c. Serial communication
    d. Data encryption

134. **What is the primary benefit of using Python's threading module in IoT applications?**

   a. Handling data storage

   b. Improving network security

   c. Running multiple tasks concurrently

   d. Performing mathematical calculations

135. **Which Python library can be used to securely encrypt and decrypt data in IoT systems?**

   a. cryptography

   b. hashlib

   c. os

   d. random

136. **How can you efficiently handle a large stream of real-time data from an IoT device in Python?**

   a. By using synchronous I/O operations

   b. By using asynchronous I/O operations

   c. By storing data in a local file

   d. By using a graphical user interface

137. **Which Python module provides classes for creating and managing threads?**

   a. Threading

   b. Multiprocessing

   c. Asyncio

   d. Queue

138. **What is the purpose of the time.sleep() function in a Python script for an IoT system?**

   a. To pause the execution of the script

   b. To open a file

   c. To read data from a sensor

   d. To establish a network connection

139. **Which method of the socket library is used to bind a socket to a specific address and port?**

   a. socket.connect()

   b. socket.bind()

    c. socket.listen()

    d. socket.accept()

140. How can you efficiently manage configuration settings for an IoT device using Python?

    a. By hardcoding settings in the script

    b. By using a configuration file

    c. By using command-line arguments

    d. By embedding settings in the device firmware

141. What is the role of the requests.post() method in a Python script?

    a. To retrieve data from a server

    b. To send data to a server

    c. To update data on a server

    d. To delete data from a server

142. Which of the following Python libraries is used for high-performance data handling and manipulation in IoT systems?

    a. Pandas

    b. Numpy

    c. Matplotlib

    d. Scikit-learn

143. How can you handle multiple simultaneous connections from IoT devices in Python?

    a. Using synchronous code

    b. Using threading

    c. Using file-based databases

    d. Using synchronous file I/O

144. What is the function of asyncio.run() method in a Python script?

    a. To start an event loop

    b. To execute a synchronous function

    c. To create a new thread

    d. To manage file I/O

145. **Which Python module is commonly used for serial communication with IoT devices?**

    a. Pyserial

    b. Socket

    c. Requests

    d. Asyncio

146. **What does the asyncio.sleep() function do in Python?**

    a. Pauses the execution of the current task asynchronously

    b. Writes data to a file

    c. Connects to a network

    d. Opens a file for reading

147. **Which method in the json module is used to convert a Python dictionary to a JSON string?**

    a. json.load()

    b. json.dumps()

    c. json.dump()

    d. json.loads()

148. **What is the primary purpose of the flask library in a Python-based IoT system?**

    a. Data analysis

    b. Web development and API creation

    c. Serial communication

    d. Image processing

149. **In Python, which library would you use for handling and parsing XML data in an IoT application?**

    a. xml.etree.ElementTree

    b. lxml

    c. BeautifulSoup

    d. xml.parsers.expat

150. **How can you handle real-time data processing efficiently in a Python-based IoT system?**

    a. By using blocking I/O operations

    b. By using non-blocking I/O operations

c. By using synchronous code

d. By using single-threaded operations

151. Which Python library is used for handling JSON data in IoT applications?

a. json

b. csv

c. pickle

d. sqlite3

152. What is the function of the socket.listen() method in Python?

a. To connect to a server

b. To bind a socket to an address

c. To listen for incoming connections

d. To accept a new connection

153. Which Python library helps in creating and managing asynchronous network connections?

a. aiohttp

b. Requests

c. PySerial

d. Pandas

154. In a Python script, what is the purpose of the try block in error handling?

a. To execute code that may raise exceptions

b. To create a new thread

c. To connect to a database

d. To parse JSON data

155. Which Python library is used to parse and manage data from serial ports in IoT projects?

a. pySerial

b. Requests

c. Socket

d. Pandas

156. **What does the asyncio.create_task() function do in Python?**

   a. Creates a new event loop

   b. Schedules a coroutine to run in the event loop

   c. Starts a new thread

   d. Opens a file

157. **Which Python module provides an interface to access system-specific parameters and functions?**

   a. os

   b. sys

   c. datetime

   d. subprocess

158. **What is the purpose of the multiprocessing module in Python for IoT systems?**

   a. To handle network communication

   b. To perform concurrent execution using processes

   c. To handle asynchronous tasks

   d. To create web applications

159. **Which function would you use to read data from a file in Python?**

   a. file.read()

   b. file.load()

   c. file.fetch()

   d. file.get()

160. **In Python, which method is used to parse command-line arguments?**

   a. argparse.ArgumentParser()

   b. sys.argv()

   c. getopt()

   d. configparser()

161. **Which Python library is typically used for high-performance numerical computations in IoT applications?**

   a. NumPy

   b. Pandas

   c. SciPy

   d. Scikit-learn

162. **What is the role of the asyncio.sleep() function in asynchronous Python code?**
    a. To pause the execution of the entire program
    b. To delay the execution of a coroutine without blocking the event loop
    c. To read data from a file
    d. To start a new thread

163. **Which Python method would you use to create a new file if it does not already exist?**
    a. open(filename, 'w')
    b. open(filename, 'r')
    c. open(filename, 'a')
    d. open(filename, 'x')

164. **Which library can be used for real-time data streaming and processing in Python?**
    a. kafka-python
    b. Pandas
    c. NumPy
    d. Matplotlib

165. **What are the requests.put() method in a Python script?**
    a. Retrieves data from a server
    b. Sends data to a server, typically to update resources
    c. Deletes data from a server
    d. Establishes a network connection

166. **In Python, what is the primary use of the pickle module?**
    a. To parse XML data
    b. To serialize and deserialize Python objects
    c. To handle HTTP requests
    d. To manage system configurations

167. **What is the purpose of the threading.Lock() object in Python?**
    a. To manage network connections
    b. To ensure that only one thread executes a block of code at a time
    c. To create asynchronous tasks
    d. To handle file I/O operations

168. **Which Python method is used to handle asynchronous tasks using the asyncio library?**

    a. asyncio.run()

    b. asyncio.create_task()

    c. asyncio.await()

    d. asyncio.start()

169. **Which library would you use for creating a RESTful API server in Python?**

    a. Flask

    b. Requests

    c. Socket

    d. PySerial

170. **In Python, what is the main purpose of the configparser module?**

    a. To handle JSON data

    b. To parse configuration files

    c. To create web applications

    d. To perform numerical computations

171. **What is the function of the os.environ dictionary in Python?**

    a. To manage file paths

    b. To access and manage environment variables

    c. To handle HTTP requests

    d. To parse command-line arguments

172. **Which Python module is commonly used to create and manage network sockets?**

    a. Socket

    b. Requests

    c. asyncio

    d. Multiprocessing

173. **In Python, how can you ensure thread-safe operations when accessing shared resources?**

    a. By using global variables

    b. By using thread synchronization mechanisms like Lock

    c. By using asynchronous I/O

    d. By using file-based data storage

174. **Which Python library can be used to parse and manage CSV data in an IoT application?**

    a. csv

    b. pandas

    c. json

    d. xml

175. **What does the asyncio.gather() function do in Python?**

    a. Starts a new event loop

    b. Waits for multiple asynchronous tasks to complete

    c. Creates a new coroutine

    d. Runs a synchronous function

176. **Which Python library provides support for interacting with HTTP APIs and handling JSON data?**

    a. Requests

    b. json

    c. xml.etree.ElementTree

    d. Numpy

177. **What is the main purpose of the async keyword in Python?**

    a. To define a function as asynchronous

    b. To handle network connections

    c. To create a new thread

    d. To parse JSON data

178. **Which method in the socket library is used to accept an incoming connection request?**

    a. socket.bind()

    b. socket.listen()

    c. socket.accept()

    d. socket.connect()

179. **How can you store and retrieve configuration settings in a Python application for IoT?**

    a. By using environment variables

    b. By using a JSON file

    c. By using a database

    d. All of the above

180. What does the pickle.dump() function do in Python?

    a. Loads data from a file into a Python object

    b. Converts a Python object into a byte stream and writes it to a file

    c. Reads data from a byte stream and loads it into a Python object

    d. Serializes data into JSON format

181. Which Python library is commonly used for creating and managing asynchronous tasks in IoT systems?

    a. asyncio

    b. Threading

    c. Multiprocessing

    d. Socket

182. What is the primary use of the argparse module in Python?

    a. To handle network communication

    b. To parse command-line arguments

    c. To manage asynchronous tasks

    d. To handle file I/O

183. Which method is used to open a file for reading in Python?

    a. open(filename, 'w')

    b. open(filename, 'r')

    c. open(filename, 'a')

    d. open(filename, 'x')

184. What is the primary function of the asyncio.run() method in Python?

    a. To start an event loop and run a coroutine

    b. To create a new thread

    c. To handle file I/O

    d. To parse command-line arguments

185. In Python, what is the purpose of using the yield keyword in a function?

    a. To return a value from a function

    b. To create a generator function that can produce a sequence of values

    c. To pause the execution of a function

    d. To define an asynchronous function

186. **Which Python library can be used for handling and managing large volumes of time-series data from IoT devices?**
    a. Pandas
    b. NumPy
    c. Matplotlib
    d. SQLite3

187. **What is the main advantage of using the aiohttp library for HTTP requests in an IoT system?**
    a. Synchronous processing
    b. Support for asynchronous HTTP requests
    c. Data visualization
    d. File management

188. **Which method in the asyncio library allows you to wait for multiple asynchronous tasks to complete?**
    a. asyncio.run()
    b. asyncio.gather()
    c. asyncio.sleep()
    d. asyncio.create_task()

189. **How do you handle a situation where an IoT device sends data in an incorrect format?**
    a. By ignoring the data
    b. By using try-except blocks to handle exceptions and validate the data
    c. By deleting the data
    d. By restarting the device

190. **What does the asyncio.create_task() function do in an asynchronous Python program?**
    a. Creates and schedules a coroutine to be executed
    b. Starts a new event loop
    c. Waits for all tasks to complete
    d. Handles file I/O operations

191. **Which Python method is used to read all lines from a file into a list?**
    a. file.read()
    b. file.readline()
    c. file.readlines()
    d. file.fetchlines()

192. **What is the purpose of the os.path.join() function in Python?**

    a. To join paths in a cross-platform manner

    b. To open a file for reading

    c. To create a new directory

    d. To split a file path into components

193. **Which Python module provides functions to work with date and time?**

    a. datetime

    b. calendar

    c. time

    d. dateutil

194. **What is the main function of the multiprocessing module in Python?**

    a. To handle network communications

    b. To perform concurrent execution using multiple processes

    c. To create asynchronous tasks

    d. To manage files and directories

195. **Which library is used in Python to handle asynchronous I/O operations efficiently?**

    a. asyncio

    b. Threading

    c. Multiprocessing

    d. Requests

196. **What does the os.system() function do in Python?**

    a. Executes a shell command

    b. Reads system environment variables

    c. Manages file permissions

    d. Handles network connections

197. **How can you handle large data streams from IoT sensors in Python without blocking the main thread?**

    a. By using asynchronous I/O operations

    b. By using synchronous file operations

    c. By using a single-threaded approach

    d. By reading data in chunks synchronously

198. **Which Python method is used to handle command-line arguments?**

    a. argparse.parse_args()

    b. sys.argv()

    c. getopt.getopt()

    d. configparser.read()

199. **What is the role of the requests.head() method in a Python script?**

    a. To send a HEAD request to a server and retrieve headers only

    b. To send a POST request to a server

    c. To send a GET request and retrieve the response body

    d. To send a PUT request and update data on the server

200. **In Python, which library would you use to create a graphical user interface (GUI) for an IoT application?**

    a. tkinter

    b. requests

    c. socket

    d. asyncio

201. **What does the asyncio.Queue() function provide in an asynchronous Python application?**

    a. A way to handle asynchronous tasks

    b. A thread-safe queue for managing tasks and data

    c. A method for creating new threads

    d. A way to manage file I/O operations

202. **Which function in Python allows you to handle incoming HTTP requests asynchronously?**

    a. aiohttp.web.get()

    b. requests.get()

    c. Flask.route()

    d. django.http.HttpResponse()

203. How can you handle a situation where an IoT device is not responding to network requests?

    a. By using retry mechanisms with exponential backoff

    b. By ignoring the device

    c. By restarting the server

    d. By manually resetting the device

204. Which Python method is used to parse JSON data from a string?

    a. json.loads()

    b. json.load()

    c. json.dump()

    d. json.dumps()

205. What is the primary advantage of using aiohttp over requests in an IoT application?

    a. Support for synchronous HTTP requests

    b. Support for asynchronous HTTP requests

    c. Better data visualization

    d. Simpler API for handling files

206. Which Python function is used to read a single line from a file?

    a. file.readline()

    b. file.read()

    c. file.readlines()

    d. file.getline()

207. What is the purpose of the asyncio.Event() object in Python?

    a. To synchronize coroutines by setting and clearing events

    b. To create an asynchronous task

    c. To handle file I/O operations

    d. To manage network connections

208. Which method in the paho-mqtt library is used to publish a message to a topic?

    a. publish_message()

    b. publish()

    c. send()

    d. post()

209. How can you implement a retry mechanism for network requests in Python?

    a. By using a loop with exception handling

    b. By using the asyncio.sleep() function

    c. By using a requests.Session() object

    d. By using a threading.Timer()

210. Which Python module provides support for managing and manipulating environment variables?

    a. os

    b. sys

    c. configparser

    d. argparse

211. What is the function of asyncio.sleep() method in an asynchronous program?

    a. To pause the execution of a coroutine without blocking the event loop

    b. To create a new coroutine

    c. To handle file I/O operations

    d. To start a new thread

212. Which library is used for handling asynchronous tasks in Python and is commonly used in IoT systems?

    a. asyncio

    b. Threading

    c. Multiprocessing

    d. Requests

213. What is the purpose of aiohttp.ClientSession() class in Python?

    a. To manage multiple HTTP requests asynchronously

    b. To create and manage network sockets

    c. To handle file operations

    d. To serialize and deserialize data

214. Which method in the socket library is used to establish a connection to a remote server?

    a. socket.connect()

    b. socket.accept()

    c. socket.bind()

    d. socket.listen()

215. What are requests.get() method work in a Python script?

    a. Sends an HTTP GET request to a server and retrieves the response

    b. Sends an HTTP POST request to a server

    c. Sends an HTTP PUT request to update data on a server

    d. Sends an HTTP DELETE request to remove data from a server

216. How can you handle exceptions that occur during asynchronous operations in Python?

    a. By using try-except blocks within the asynchronous function

    b. By using synchronous error handling

    c. By ignoring the exceptions

    d. By restarting the application

217. Which method in Python is used to write data to a file in append mode?

    a. open(filename, 'w')

    b. open(filename, 'r')

    c. open(filename, 'a')

    d. open(filename, 'x')

218. What does the asyncio.create_task() function do?

    a. Schedules a coroutine to be executed as a task

    b. Creates a new event loop

    c. Manages file operations

    d. Handles network connections

219. Which Python library provides support for handling HTTP requests and responses asynchronously?

    a. aiohttp

    b. requests

    c. urllib

    d. json

220. What is the purpose of using the with statement when working with files in Python?

    a. To ensure that the file is properly closed after its block of code is executed

    b. To create a new file

    c. To open a file for writing

    d. To delete a file

221. **Which method is used to send data over a TCP connection using the socket library in Python?**

    a. socket.send()

    b. socket.write()

    c. socket.sendto()

    d. socket.write_data()

222. **What is the role of the aiohttp.web.Application() class in an asynchronous web server?**

    a. To create a web application and manage routes

    b. To handle HTTP requests and responses

    c. To manage WebSocket connections

    d. To handle file uploads

223. **Which Python module allows you to work with environment variables in a more flexible way?**

    a. dotenv

    b. configparser

    c. argparse

    d. json

224. **How can you ensure that a Python application can handle multiple I/O operations concurrently?**

    a. By using asynchronous programming with asyncio

    b. By using synchronous I/O operations

    c. By using a single-threaded approach

    d. By using blocking calls

225. **Which method from the json module is used to write a Python object to a JSON file?**

    a. json.dump()

    b. json.dumps()

    c. json.load()

    d. json.loads()

226. In Python, what does the asyncio.run() function do?

    a. Executes a coroutine and manages the event loop

    b. Starts a new thread

    c. Opens a file

    d. Handles network connections

227. What is the purpose of multiprocessing.Pool() class in Python?

    a. To handle network communications

    b. To manage a pool of worker processes for concurrent execution

    c. To create asynchronous tasks

    d. To perform file operations

228. Which method is used to set up a server socket to listen for incoming connections?

    a. socket.bind()

    b. socket.listen()

    c. socket.accept()

    d. socket.connect()

229. What does the asyncio.Lock() class provides in asynchronous programming?

    a. A synchronization mechanism to manage access to a shared resource

    b. A way to handle HTTP requests

    c. A method for creating new threads

    d. A way to manage file I/O operations

230. Which library is used for reading and writing data in CSV format in Python?

    a. csv

    b. json

    c. xml.etree.ElementTree

    d. sqlite3

231. How can you handle errors when parsing JSON data in Python?

    a. By using try-except blocks to catch json.JSONDecodeError

    b. By ignoring the errors

    c. By using default values

    d. By using regular expressions

232. **Which method is used to create a new event loop in Python?**

     a. asyncio.new_event_loop()

     b. asyncio.create_event_loop()

     c. asyncio.start_loop()

     d. asyncio.run()

233. **What is the purpose of the asyncio.ensure_future() function in Python?**

     a. To wrap a coroutine or task in a future object

     b. To create a new event loop

     c. To start a new thread

     d. To handle file operations

234. **Which library is commonly used for handling data from sensors and devices in real-time?**

     a. asyncio

     b. kafka-python

     c. numpy

     d. sqlite3

235. **What does the asyncio.run() function replace in modern asynchronous Python code?**

     a. The need for explicit event loop management

     b. The need for threading

     c. The need for multiprocessing

     d. The need for synchronous I/O

236. **Which method in the aiohttp library allows you to handle incoming HTTP POST requests?**

     a. aiohttp.web.post()

     b. aiohttp.web.route()

     c. aiohttp.web.handle_post()

     d. aiohttp.web.request()

237. **What is the purpose of the socket.sendall() method in Python?**

     a. To send data to a remote server, ensuring all data is sent

     b. To send a file to a remote server

     c. To receive data from a remote server

     d. To close the connection

238. **Which method in the asyncio library is used to pause the execution of a coroutine for a specified amount of time?**

    a. asyncio.sleep()

    b. asyncio.wait()

    c. asyncio.pause()

    d. asyncio.delay()

239. **What is the purpose of using the yield keyword in Python?**

    a. To create a generator function that produces values lazily

    b. To return a value from a function

    c. To handle exceptions

    d. To start a new coroutine

240. **Which method is used to handle exceptions in asynchronous Python code?**

    a. Using try-except blocks within coroutines

    b. Using global exception handlers

    c. Ignoring exceptions

    d. Using synchronous exception handling

241. **Which Python module is used to handle XML data?**

    a. xml.etree.ElementTree

    b. json

    c. csv

    d. yaml

242. **What does the asyncio.wait() function do in Python?**

    a. Waits for a set of tasks or coroutines to complete

    b. Creates a new task

    c. Starts a new event loop

    d. Handles file I/O

243. **Which method in the requests library is used to send an HTTP DELETE request?**

    a. requests.delete()

    b. requests.remove()

    c. requests.delete_request()

    d. requests.remove_request()

244. What is the role of asyncio.Event() object in asynchronous programming?

    a. To provide a synchronization primitive that can be set or cleared

    b. To handle HTTP requests

    c. To manage network connections

    d. To handle file operations

245. Which library is used to handle secure network communications in Python?

    a. ssl

    b. socket

    c. aiohttp

    d. multiprocessing

246. What does the aiohttp.web.RouteTableDef() class do?

    a. Defines routing for handling HTTP requests in an asynchronous web application

    b. Manages network connections

    c. Handles file I/O

    d. Manages event loops

247. Which Python module is used for parsing command-line arguments?

    a. argparse

    b. configparser

    c. os

    d. sys

248. What is the purpose of asyncio.shield() function in Python?

    a. To ensure that a given task is not cancelled during its execution

    b. To create a new event loop

    c. To handle file I/O operations

    d. To manage network connections

249. Which method in Python is used to handle binary data in files?

    a. open(filename, 'rb')

    b. open(filename, 'rt')

    c. open(filename, 'w')

    d. open(filename, 'a')

250. **How can you manage shared resources across multiple threads in Python?**

    a. By using synchronization mechanisms like threading.Lock()

    b. By using global variables

    c. By ignoring synchronization

    d. By creating separate processes

Join our Discord space

Join our Discord workspace for latest updates, offers, tech happenings around the world, new releases, and sessions with the authors:

https://discord.bpbonline.com

Answers

Q.No.	Answers	Q.No.	Answers	Q.No.	Answers	Q.No.	Answers	Q.No.	Answers
1	b	31	c	61	d	91	d	121	c
2	c	32	a	62	c	92	d	122	a
3	c	33	c	63	d	93	d	123	a
4	d	34	a	64	a	94	d	124	a
5	c	35	c	65	a	95	b	125	c
6	c	36	a	66	c	96	b	126	b
7	a	37	d	67	d	97	d	127	b
8	b	38	c	68	c	98	b	128	b
9	c	39	d	69	b	99	d	129	c
10	c	40	b	70	b	100	d	130	a
11	a	41	c	71	c	101	b	131	b
12	b	42	d	72	b	102	c	132	a
13	c	43	d	73	d	103	b	133	b
14	a	44	a	74	b	104	c	134	c
15	d	45	c	75	a	105	b	135	a
16	c	46	b	76	d	106	a	136	b
17	d	47	c	77	b	107	b	137	a
18	c	48	d	78	d	108	c	138	a
19	a	49	c	79	a	109	a	139	b
20	d	50	a	80	b	110	c	140	b
21	a	51	d	81	d	111	b	141	b
22	c	52	c	82	b	112	b	142	a
23	c	53	c	83	d	113	a	143	b
24	a	54	c	84	d	114	b	144	a
25	d	55	a	85	c	115	b	145	a
26	d	56	a	86	b	116	a	146	a
27	c	57	c	87	b	117	b	147	b
28	c	58	c	88	b	118	b	148	b
29	c	59	d	89	b	119	b	149	a
30	a	60	c	90	d	120	b	150	b

Q.No.	Answers	Q.No.	Answers	Q.No.	Answers	Q.No.	Answers
151	a	176	a	201	b	226	a
152	c	177	a	202	a	227	b
153	a	178	c	203	a	228	b
154	a	179	d	204	a	229	a
155	a	180	b	205	b	230	a
156	b	181	a	206	a	231	a
157	a	182	b	207	a	232	a
158	b	183	b	208	b	233	a
159	a	184	a	209	a	234	b
160	a	185	b	210	a	235	a
161	a	186	a	211	a	236	b
162	b	187	b	212	a	237	a
163	d	188	b	213	a	238	a
164	a	189	b	214	a	239	a
165	b	190	a	215	a	240	a
166	b	191	c	216	a	241	a
167	b	192	a	217	c	242	a
168	b	193	a	218	a	243	a
169	a	194	b	219	a	244	a
170	b	195	a	220	a	245	a
171	b	196	a	221	a	246	a
172	a	197	a	222	a	247	a
173	b	198	a	223	a	248	a
174	b	199	a	224	a	249	a
175	b	200	a	225	a	250	a

Join our Discord space

Join our Discord workspace for latest updates, offers, tech happenings around the world, new releases, and sessions with the authors:

https://discord.bpbonline.com

CHAPTER 4
Challenges and Future Scope of IoT

Introduction

The **Internet of Things (IoT)** is the next big internet trend. IoT integrates physical devices with online systems to improve connection, automation, and data-driven insights in smart homes, healthcare, and businesses. As with every innovative technology, IoT has drawbacks. IoT's future potential and direction depend on understanding these challenges:

- **Security and privacy**: IoT devices capture massive quantities of personal data and are continually connected, making them appealing cyberattack targets. The variety of gadgets makes conventional security methods challenging to apply.

- **Interoperability**: IoT devices have several manufacturers and different standards, making device-to-device communication difficult. Unified standards are needed for seamless operation.

- **Data management**: IoT devices create massive amounts of data. It is difficult to store, analyze, and derive useful insights from this data. Many IoT gadgets need batteries. Power efficiency and battery longevity are considerations for hard-to-reach or repair devices.

- **Scalability**: As the number of IoT devices rises, the system must scale effectively.

- **Challenges**: IoT requires a quick, reliable, and wide-ranging network. Traditional networks may not work for real-time applications.

- **Economic challenges**: IoT setup costs may be considerable, particularly for companies. Convincing stakeholders of long-term advantages against short-term expenses is difficult.

- **Future IoT scope**: IoT will help build smart cities by improving traffic, waste, energy, and other management. IoT improves patient monitoring, individualized therapies, and medical device integration.

- **Agriculture**: IoT can improve irrigation, soil health, and crop disease prediction, transforming agriculture. Smart grids optimize energy distribution in real time, enhancing efficiency and decreasing waste.

- **Industry 4.0**: IoT would automate and optimize production processes in the next industrial revolution. From inventory management to individualized consumer experiences, IoT will change retail.

- **Environment monitoring**: IoT devices may monitor and analyze environmental data to spot changes or abnormalities early.

- **Transportation**: IoT will enable self-driving automobiles, traffic optimization, and vehicle health monitoring.

- **Integration with other technologies**: AI, ML, Blockchain, and 5G will unleash IoT's full potential.

- **Individualized experiences**: Smarter homes and gadgets will provide individualized user experiences based on preferences and behaviors.

Multiple choice questions

1. **What is one of the major challenges in IoT security?**

    a. Lack of IoT devices

    b. Limited connectivity options

    c. Insufficient cloud storage

    d. Vulnerabilities in IoT devices and networks

2. **Which challenge arises due to the massive amount of data IoT devices generate?**

    a. Limited battery life of devices

    b. Inadequate processing power

    c. Data privacy concerns

    d. Low connectivity options

3. **What is a potential issue caused by the heterogeneity of IoT devices and protocols?**
   a. Easier interoperability
   b. Uniform security measures
   c. Decreased complexity
   d. Difficulty in device integration

4. **Which challenge relates to the continuous need for firmware updates and patches in IoT devices?**
   a. Hardware limitations
   b. Network latency
   c. High power consumption
   d. Maintenance and management

5. **What is a significant concern in IoT deployment in remote or inaccessible areas?**
   a. Data overload
   b. Lack of security protocols
   c. High bandwidth requirements
   d. Limited network coverage

6. **Which challenge is related to the ethical implications of collecting and using data from IoT devices?**
   a. Interoperability issues
   b. Lack of standardization
   c. Data privacy and ethics
   d. Network latency

7. **What does the term IoT interoperability refer to?**
   a. The ease of setting up IoT devices
   b. The ability of IoT devices to communicate and work together
   c. The security of IoT networks
   d. The speed of data transmission in IoT networks

8. **Which challenge arises from ensuring data consistency and accuracy across IoT devices?**
   a. Data privacy concerns
   b. Lack of connectivity options
   c. Data integration difficulties
   d. Limited processing power

9. **Which aspect of IoT raises concerns about potential job displacement due to automation?**

    a. Increased data security

    b. Interoperability challenges

    c. Technological advancements

    d. Employment impact

10. **What does the term IoT scalability refer to?**

    a. The physical size of IoT devices

    b. The ability of IoT devices to work in extreme conditions

    c. The ability of IoT networks to handle a growing number of devices and data

    d. The speed of data transmission in IoT networks and data

11. **Which challenge is related to the sustainability of IoT devices and their impact on the environm ent?**

    a. Rapid technological advancements

    b. Lack of security measures

    c. Excessive energy consumption

    d. High data latency

12. **What is the term used to describe the idea of IoT devices autonomously making decisions without human intervention?**

    a. Automation

    b. Standardization

    c. Virtualization

    d. Autonomy

13. **Which challenge arises due to the diverse regulatory frameworks across regions and countries?**

    a. High connectivity options

    b. Low data traffic

    c. Regulatory compliance

    d. Decreased data security

14. **What does the term IoT standardization refer to?**

    a. The use of unique protocols for each IoT device

    b. The process of automating IoT networks

    c. The establishment of common protocols and guidelines for IoT devices and networks

    d. The use of a single communication technology for all IoT devices

15. **Which challenge is related to the management and analysis of the massive amount of data generated by IoT devices?**

    a. Data privacy concerns

    b. Low data traffic

    c. Network latency

    d. Big data analytics

16. **What is the potential benefit of edge computing in IoT networks?**

    a. Reducing the need for IoT devices

    b. Centralized data processing

    c. Improved data security

    d. Reduced network latency

17. **Which challenge is associated with the reliability and availability of IoT devices and networks?**

    a. Data privacy concerns

    b. Low data traffic

    c. High connectivity options

    d. Downtime and disruptions

18. **What is the term used to describe the scenario where IoT devices form a network and share data without human intervention?**

    a. IoT network

    b. IoT cloud

    c. Machine learning

    d. Machine-to-machine (M2M) communication

19. **Which challenge is related to the lack of universally accepted IoT security standards?**

    a. Reduced data traffic

    b. High data latency

    c. Lack of security measures

    d. Lack of device compatibility

20. **What is the concept of IoT as a service (IoTaaS)?**
    a. Using IoT devices for data storage
    b. Subscribing to an IoT platform to access and manage IoT resources
    c. Creating proprietary IoT protocols
    d. Developing custom IoT devices

21. **Which challenge is associated with the limited lifespan of IoT devices and the subsequent electronic waste?**
    a. Scalability issues
    b. Data privacy concerns
    c. Excessive energy consumption
    d. Sustainability and environmental impact

22. **What is the potential benefit of blockchain technology in the context of IoT?**
    a. Accelerating data transmission
    b. Reducing data traffic
    c. Enhancing data privacy and security
    d. Decreasing data latency

23. **Which challenge arises from the need to provide a continuous and reliable power supply to IoT devices?**
    a. Low data traffic
    b. Energy efficiency
    c. Data latency
    d. Limited battery life

24. **What is the concept of IoT monetization?**
    a. Generating revenue by selling IoT devices
    b. Converting IoT data into valuable insights and profits
    c. Distributing free IoT devices
    d. Enhancing IoT device connectivity

25. **What is the potential challenge associated with the integration of legacy systems with modern IoT technologies?**
    a. Seamless integration
    b. Reduced data traffic

    c. Increased processing power

    d. Compatibility issues

26. **Which challenge is related to the potential misuse of IoT data for unauthorized purposes?**

    a. High data latency

    b. Data privacy concerns

    c. Low data traffic

    d. Inadequate connectivity options

27. **What is the concept of IoT analytics?**

    a. Using IoT devices for real-time analytics

    b. Analyzing data generated by IoT devices to gain insights and make informed decisions

    c. The practice of sharing IoT data without restrictions

    d. Developing IoT-based applications for data analysis

28. **Which challenge is related to the need for seamless integration of IoT devices across different industries and domains?**

    a. High data latency

    b. Lack of connectivity options

    c. Cross-industry interoperability

    d. Inadequate data security

29. **What term describes the potential convergence of AI, IoT, and other technologies to create intelligent systems?**

    a. Artificial Intelligence of Things (AIoT)

    b. Internet of Artificial Intelligence (IoAI)

    c. TechFusion

    d. ConvergentTech

30. **Which challenge arises from managing and securing many endpoints in an IoT network?**

    a. Low data traffic

    b. Device scarcity

    c. Endpoint management and security

    d. Excessive energy consumption

31. **What is the concept of IoT ecosystem?**

    a. A single IoT device

    b. The interconnected network of all IoT devices

    c. The practice of sharing IoT data without restrictions

    d. The idea of using IoT devices for environmental protection

32. **Which challenge is related to the potential lack of standardized communication protocols for IoT devices?**

    a. Inadequate processing power

    b. Device integration

    c. High data latency

    d. Limited battery life

33. **What is the term used to describe the collection of data from various sources for analysis and decision-making in real-time?**

    a. Data aggregation

    b. Real-time analysis

    c. Data correlation

    d. Data fusion

34. **Which challenge is related to the need for better coordination and collaboration among different stakeholders in the IoT ecosystem?**

    a. Limited network coverage

    b. Lack of data traffic

    c. Fragmented ecosystem

    d. Low data latency

35. **What is the potential impact of IoT on urban areas and cities?**

    a. Increased energy consumption

    b. Deterioration of infrastructure

    c. Improved traffic management and city services

    d. Higher pollution levels

36. **Which challenge is related to the potential difficulty in accurately predicting and managing IoT device failures?**

    a. High connectivity options

    b. Inadequate data security

    c. Limited battery life

    d. Predictive maintenance

37. What is the concept of IoT edge computing?

    a. Centralized data processing in cloud servers

    b. Data processing at the physical location of IoT devices

    c. Use of IoT devices for edge detection

    d. Real-time data streaming in IoT networks

38. Which challenge is related to the potential lack of awareness and education about IoT security among users and organizations?

    a. Lack of connectivity options

    b. Inadequate processing power

    c. Limited network coverage

    d. Security awareness and education

39. What is the term used to describe the concept of interconnecting everyday objects and making them smarter through IoT?

    a. Machine-to-machine (M2M)

    b. The Internet of Things (IoT)

    c. Artificial intelligence (AI)

    d. Smart connectivity

40. Which challenge is related to the potential overreliance on cloud services for IoT data storage and processing?

    a. Limited network coverage

    b. Data privacy concerns

    c. High connectivity options

    d. Low data latency

41. What is the concept of IoT data monetization?

    a. Generating revenue by selling IoT devices

    b. Transforming IoT data into valuable insights and profits

    c. Distributing free IoT devices

    d. Improving the connectivity of IoT devices

42. **Which challenge is related to the potential lack of clear ownership and responsibility for IoT data and devices?**

    a. Data overload

    b. Lack of connectivity options

    c. Data privacy concerns

    d. Scalability issues

43. **What term describes the potential growth of IoT applications and services in rural and remote areas?**

    a. Urbanization

    b. Ruralization

    c. Digital divide

    d. Digital inclusion

44. **Which challenge is related to the potential difficulty in managing and updating IoT devices located in hard-to-reach places?**

    a. Low data latency

    b. Limited network coverage

    c. Data privacy concerns

    d. High data traffic

45. **What is the potential challenge related to the massive amount of IoT-generated data and its impact on network bandwidth?**

    a. Reduced data latency

    b. Low data traffic

    c. Increased network capacity

    d. Data congestion

46. **Which challenge arises from the need to balance data storage and processing between edge devices and centralized cloud systems?**

    a. High data latency

    b. Lack of connectivity options

    c. Data overload

    d. Edge-cloud synchronization

47. **What is the concept of IoT security by design?**

    a. Implementing security measures only after deploying IoT devices

    b. Developing IoT devices with security considerations from the beginning

    c. Relying solely on cloud security for IoT networks

    d. Ignoring security in IoT devices

48. **Which challenge is related to the potential lack of standardized data formats and protocols for sharing IoT data?**

    a. Inadequate processing power

    b. High data latency

    c. Data interoperability

    d. Limited battery life

49. **What is the concept of IoT wearables?**

    a. Smart clothing and accessories integrated with IoT technology

    b. IoT devices for tracking weather conditions

    c. IoT devices designed for military applications

    d. IoT devices focused on entertainment purposes

50. **Which challenge is related to the potential misuse of IoT devices for cyberattacks and unauthorized access to networks?**

    a. Lack of connectivity options

    b. Inadequate processing power

    c. Security vulnerabilities

    d. High data latency

51. **What is the term used to describe the integration of IoT with the healthcare industry to monitor and manage patients' health remotely?**

    a. IoT healthcare

    b. e-health

    c. Medical IoT

    d. Remote patient monitoring

52. **Which challenge is related to the potential difficulty in ensuring regulatory compliance for IoT devices that cross international boundaries?**

    a. Low data latency

    b. Lack of connectivity options

    c. Data privacy concerns

    d. Global regulatory compliance

53. **What is the concept of IoT data lake?**

    a. A centralized storage location for IoT devices

    b. The practice of sharing IoT data publicly

    c. An IoT device specifically designed for water monitoring

    d. A repository for storing and analyzing massive amounts of IoT-generated data

54. **Which challenge is related to the potential lack of user trust in IoT devices and data collection practices?**

    a. Limited network coverage

    b. Inadequate processing power

    c. Low data latency

    d. Building user trust and confidence

55. **What is the term used to describe the potential use of IoT in optimizing and enhancing agricultural practices?**

    a. IoT farming

    b. Smart agriculture

    c. Digital farming

    d. Green IoT

56. **Which challenge is related to the potential difficulty in predicting the behavior of complex IoT systems?**

    a. Limited battery life

    b. High data latency

    c. Inadequate data security

    d. System predictability

57. **What is the concept of IoT monetization models?**

    a. The process of transforming IoT data into revenue

    b. Selling IoT devices at a discount

    c. Sharing IoT data for free

    d. Using IoT devices for entertainment purposes

58. **Which challenge is related to the potential interference and congestion in wireless communication channels used by IoT devices?**

    a. Inadequate processing power

    b. Low data traffic

c. Radio frequency interference

d. High data latency

59. **What is the potential benefit of IoT in the energy sector?**

    a. Increased energy consumption

    b. Decreased reliance on renewable energy sources

    c. Improved energy efficiency and resource management

    d. Higher pollution levels

60. **Which challenge is related to the potential need for designing IoT devices resistant to environmental factors like extreme temperatures and humidity?**

    a. High data latency

    b. Limited network coverage

    c. Inadequate processing power

    d. Harsh environment resilience

61. **What is the concept of IoT in logistics?**

    a. Using IoT devices for tracking weather conditions

    b. Integrating IoT technology into supply chain and transportation management

    c. IoT devices for personal navigation

    d. IoT devices for fashion industry applications

62. **Which challenge is related to the potential difficulty in ensuring the secure and seamless connectivity of IoT devices as they move between different networks?**

    a. Limited battery life

    b. High data latency

    c. Roaming and handover management

    d. Data privacy concerns

63. **What is the potential impact of IoT on environmental conservation efforts?**

    a. Increased pollution levels

    b. Depletion of natural resources

    c. Improved monitoring and protection of the environment

    d. Enhanced waste generation

64. **Which challenge is related to the potential lack of clear business models for IoT applications and services?**

    a. Inadequate data security

    b. Low data traffic

    c. Business sustainability

    d. Limited network coverage

65. **What is the term used to describe the integration of IoT with the manufacturing industry to create smart and efficient production processes?**

    a. Smart manufacturing

    b. IoT integration

    c. Digital production

    d. Manufacturing automation

66. **Which challenge is related to the potential need for establishing clear guidelines and regulations for the ethical use of IoT data?**

    a. Data overload

    b. Lack of connectivity options

    c. Ethical data usage

    d. High data latency

67. **What is the concept of IoT in retail?**

    a. Using IoT devices for fashion industry applications

    b. Integrating IoT technology into shopping malls

    c. Utilizing IoT devices for tracking weather conditions

    d. Applying IoT to enhance the retail customer experience

68. **Which challenge is related to the potential difficulty in achieving seamless interoperability between different IoT platforms and ecosystems?**

    a. Limited battery life

    b. Inter-platform connectivity

    c. High data latency

    d. Data privacy concerns

69. **What is the potential benefit of utilizing IoT for transportation and fleet management?**

    a. Increased traffic congestion

    b. Decreased fuel consumption

    c. Higher transportation costs

    d. Reduced vehicle efficiency

70. **Which challenge is related to the potential lack of skilled professionals capable of designing, managing, and securing IoT systems?**

    a. Inadequate processing power

    b. Data privacy concerns

    c. Limited network coverage

    d. Skills gap

71. **What is the term used to describe the integration of IoT devices with household appliances to create smart homes?**

    a. Home automation

    b. IoT household

    c. Smart living

    d. Residential IoT

72. **Which challenge is related to the potential complexity of managing and analyzing heterogeneous IoT data from various sources?**

    a. Data overload

    b. Inadequate connectivity options

    c. Low data latency

    d. Data diversity and integration

73. **What is the concept of IoT in healthcare?**

    a. Applying IoT technology to monitor water quality

    b. Integrating IoT into weather forecasting

    c. Using IoT for tracking animal behavior

    d. Utilizing IoT to enhance medical services and patient care

74. **Which challenge is related to the potential difficulty in ensuring the reliability and accuracy of data generated by IoT sensors and devices?**

    a. High data latency

    b. Data accuracy and reliability

    c. Lack of connectivity options

    d. Excessive energy consumption

75. **What is the potential impact of IoT on the education sector?**

    a. Reduced access to educational resources

    b. Enhanced learning experiences and personalized education

    c. Increased educational costs

    d. Decreased student engagement

76. **Which challenge is related to the potential need for designing IoT devices resistant to cyberattacks and tampering?**

    a. Low data latency

    b. Limited network coverage

    c. Inadequate processing power

    d. Security and tamper resistance

77. **What is the concept of IoT in energy management?**

    a. Using IoT devices for tracking weather conditions

    b. Integrating IoT technology into home energy systems

    c. Utilizing IoT devices for traffic management

    d. Applying IoT to optimize nuclear power plants

78. **Which challenge is related to the potential difficulty in ensuring the accuracy and integrity of IoT-generated data during transmission and storage?**

    a. Inadequate processing power

    b. Data privacy concerns

    c. Data integrity and security

    d. High data latency

79. **What is the potential benefit of using IoT for environmental monitoring and conservation efforts?**

    a. Increased pollution levels

    b. Depletion of natural resources

    c. Enhanced monitoring and protection of ecosystems

    d. Greater energy consumption

80. **Which challenge is related to the potential interference between different wireless communication protocols used by IoT devices?**

    a. Low data latency

    b. Data congestion

    c. Radio frequency interference

    d. Limited battery life

81. **What is the concept of IoT in agriculture?**

    a. Applying IoT technology to track animal behavior

    b. Integrating IoT into weather forecasting

    c. Using IoT devices for water quality monitoring

    d. Utilizing IoT to improve farming practices and crop yield

82. **Which challenge is related to the potential difficulty in addressing legal and liability issues in case of IoT-related incidents or accidents?**

    a. High data latency

    b. Lack of connectivity options

    c. Legal and liability concerns

    d. Inadequate data security

83. **What is the term for integrating IoT devices and technologies into city infrastructure to create smart cities?**

    a. Urban transformation

    b. Digital urbanization

    c. City IoT

    d. Smart cities

84. **Which challenge is related to the potential lack of awareness about the benefits and risks of IoT among consumers and businesses?**

    a. Limited network coverage

    b. Data privacy concerns

    c. Inadequate processing power

    d. Low data latency

85. **What is the potential impact of IoT on the transportation sector?**

    a. Increased traffic congestion

    b. Decreased road safety

    c. Enhanced transportation efficiency and management

    d. Higher transportation costs

86. **Which challenge relates to the potential need to address legal and regulatory issues concerning IoT data ownership and sharing?**

    a. Data overload

    b. Lack of connectivity options

    c. Data ownership and sharing

    d. High data latency

87. **What is the concept of IoT in entertainment?**

    a. Using IoT devices for tracking weather conditions during outdoor events

    b. Integrating IoT technology into amusement park rides

    c. Utilizing IoT devices for wildlife conservation documentaries

    d. Applying IoT to enhance the gaming and media experience

88. **Which challenge is related to the potential difficulty in ensuring user data privacy collected by IoT devices?**

    a. Limited battery life

    b. Data privacy concerns

    c. Low data traffic

    d. Increased network capacity

89. **What is the potential benefit of using IoT for disaster management and response?**

    a. Increased disaster risks

    b. Delayed emergency response

    c. Enhanced situational awareness and response coordination

    d. Higher casualties during disasters

90. **Which challenge is related to the potential need for secure and reliable communication protocols for IoT devices?**

    a. Low data latency

    b. Limited network coverage

    c. Inadequate processing power

    d. Secure communication and protocols

91. **What is the concept of IoT in sports?**

    a. Applying IoT technology to monitor air quality during sports events

    b. Integrating IoT technology into sports equipment and venues

    c. Using IoT devices for tracking animal behavior during sports activities

    d. Utilizing IoT for analyzing historical sports data

92. **Which challenge is related to the potential difficulty in managing and analyzing real-time data streams generated by IoT devices?**

    a. Data overload

    b. Lack of connectivity options

    c. Low data latency

    d. Inadequate processing power

93. **What is the potential impact of IoT on the automotive industry?**

    a. Decreased vehicle connectivity

    b. Increased accidents and safety risks

    c. Enhanced vehicle performance and connectivity

    d. Higher fuel consumption

94. **Which challenge is related to the potential need for ensuring the reliability and availability of IoT devices in critical infrastructure systems?**

    a. High data latency

    b. Limited network coverage

    c. Inadequate processing power

    d. Critical infrastructure resilience

95. **What is the concept of IoT in hospitality?**

    a. Applying IoT technology to track wildlife behavior in resorts

    b. Integrating IoT technology into hotel management systems

    c. Using IoT devices for monitoring ocean tides at beach resorts

    d. Utilizing IoT for optimizing tourism advertising

96. **Which challenge is related to the potential need for establishing global standards and regulations for IoT devices and networks?**

    a. Data privacy concerns

    b. Limited battery life

    c. Local regulatory compliance

    d. High data latency

97. **What is the term used to describe the potential integration of IoT devices with public infrastructure to create smart environments?**

    a. Environmental sensing

    b. Urban transformation

    c. IoT infrastructure

    d. Smart environments

98. **Which challenge is related to the potential difficulty in managing and analyzing historical data collected by IoT devices for trend analysis?**

    a. Data overload

    b. Lack of connectivity options

    c. Low data latency

    d. Historical data analysis

99. **What is the potential impact of IoT on the financial industry?**

    a. Increased financial risks

    b. Decreased customer engagement

    c. Enhanced customer service and fraud detection

    d. Higher interest rates

100. **What is a major challenge of IoT related to data security?**

    a. High data throughput

    b. Secure data storage

    c. Complex user interfaces

    d. Low latency

101. **Which of the following is a key concern regarding IoT device interoperability?**

    a. Network bandwidth

    b. Standardization of communication protocols

    c. Device aesthetics

    d. Energy efficiency

102. **What is one of the primary future trends in IoT technology?**

    a. Decreasing the number of connected devices

    b. Increased use of IPv4 addresses

    c. Greater integration with artificial intelligence

    d. Reduced need for cloud computing

103. **Which factor most affects the scalability of IoT systems?**

    a. Hardware design

    b. Network topology

    c. Software architecture

    d. User interface

104. **What is a significant privacy issue in IoT?**

    a. Data encryption

    b. User data collection without consent

    c. Device update frequency

    d. Network speed

105. **How can edge computing help address IoT challenges?**

    a. By increasing data latency

    b. By centralizing data storage

    c. By processing data closer to the source

    d. By reducing device diversity

106. **What is a common challenge related to IoT network security?**

    a. High device costs

    b. Insufficient data transmission speeds

    c. Vulnerabilities in device firmware

    d. Limited network coverage

107. **Which of the following can help in addressing the challenge of IoT data management?**

    a. Using legacy systems

    b. Implementing robust data analytics

    c. Reducing data collection

    d. Increasing manual data entry

108. **What is a key challenge in the development of IoT standards?**

    a. Simplifying device interfaces

    b. Ensuring backward compatibility

    c. Creating universal standards applicable to all devices

    d. Reducing power consumption

109. What is a potential future development in IoT technology?

   a. Decline in sensor accuracy

   b. Increased use of blockchain for data integrity

   c. Reduced importance of data analytics

   d. Decreased number of smart devices

110. Which challenge is associated with the rapid growth of IoT devices?

   a. Decreased demand for data

   b. Increased energy consumption

   c. Reduced need for connectivity

   d. Improved device performance

111. How can IoT systems address the challenge of managing large amounts of data?

   a. By increasing manual oversight

   b. By utilizing cloud-based storage and processing

   c. By limiting data collection

   d. By reducing device functionality

112. Which technology is expected to enhance IoT security in the future?

   a. Quantum computing

   b. IPv6

   c. 4G LTE

   d. USB 2.0

113. What is a major challenge in ensuring the reliability of IoT systems?

   a. Device aesthetics

   b. Communication protocol failures

   c. User interface complexity

   d. Device size

114. Which approach is being explored to improve IoT device energy efficiency?

   a. Increasing device size

   b. Implementing energy harvesting technologies

   c. Reducing device functionality

   d. Increasing data transmission rates

115. **What is a common challenge in IoT system integration?**
    a. Device compatibility with different operating systems
    b. Lack of cloud storage
    c. High data transmission costs
    d. Limited number of sensors

116. **How does machine learning contribute to the future scope of IoT?**
    a. By simplifying device interfaces
    b. By enabling predictive analytics and automation
    c. By reducing the need for sensors
    d. By eliminating the need for network connectivity

117. **Which of the following is a challenge related to IoT in smart cities?**
    a. Insufficient data collection
    b. Lack of connectivity
    c. Integration of various IoT systems and technologies
    d. High cost of individual devices

118. **What is a key factor in ensuring the longevity of IoT devices?**
    a. Regular firmware updates
    b. Reducing device connectivity
    c. Limiting device functionality
    d. Increasing device size

119. **Which technology is likely to play a significant role in the future of IoT?**
    a. Augmented reality (AR)
    b. Optical discs
    c. Fax machines
    d. Legacy networking protocols

120. **What is a major concern related to IoT data privacy?**
    a. Data transmission speeds
    b. Data storage location and access
    c. Device size
    d. Network latency

121. What is one of the expected benefits of IoT in healthcare?

    a. Reduced data accuracy

    b. Increased manual data entry

    c. Enhanced patient monitoring and care

    d. Decreased connectivity options

122. Which of the following is a challenge associated with IoT device updates?

    a. High data storage costs

    b. Inconsistent update protocols

    c. Reduced device functionality

    d. Increased data transmission rates

123. What is a common issue with IoT device authentication?

    a. Lack of encryption standards

    b. Complexity of user interfaces

    c. Increased data storage

    d. Limited network coverage

124. How can IoT contribute to environmental sustainability in the future?

    a. By increasing energy consumption

    b. By enabling smart energy management and resource monitoring

    c. By reducing the number of sensors

    d. By limiting data collection

125. Which of the following is a challenge in IoT device deployment?

    a. High data encryption standards

    b. Physical device security

    c. Increased data accuracy

    d. Enhanced network coverage

126. What is a significant factor influencing IoT system performance?

    a. Device aesthetics

    b. Network bandwidth and latency

    c. User interface design

    d. Device color

127. **Which technology is expected to improve IoT network reliability?**

    a. 5G networks

    b. Dial-up connections

    c. Analog signals

    d. Bluetooth classic

128. **What is a future challenge for IoT regarding regulations?**

    a. Increasing device costs

    b. Lack of international regulatory frameworks

    c. Reducing data transmission rates

    d. Increasing sensor accuracy

129. **What is a potential application of IoT in agriculture?**

    a. Increased pesticide use

    b. Enhanced crop monitoring and precision farming

    c. Reduced data accuracy

    d. Decreased irrigation efficiency

130. **What is one of the primary challenges in IoT device management?**

    a. Reducing device costs

    b. Ensuring software compatibility

    c. Enhancing device aesthetics

    d. Increasing device size

131. **Which technology is essential for IoT devices to communicate effectively?**

    a. USB 3.0

    b. Network protocols like MQTT or CoAP

    c. Optical fiber cables

    d. HDMI interfaces

132. **What is a major challenge in implementing IoT solutions in industrial settings?**

    a. High data transfer rates

    b. Legacy systems integration

    c. Low power consumption

    d. Device color schemes

133. **Which aspect of IoT presents significant future opportunities in smart homes?**

    a. Increased manual control

    b. Advanced automation and energy management

    c. Reduced connectivity options

    d. Limited device functionality

134. **What challenge does IoT face in terms of global deployment?**

    a. Uniform device design

    b. Regulatory and compliance issues

    c. High-speed data transfer

    d. Device color consistency

135. **How can IoT contribute to improving public safety?**

    a. By increasing manual monitoring tasks

    b. By enabling real-time surveillance and emergency response systems

    c. By reducing data accuracy

    d. By limiting network coverage

136. **What is a key challenge in IoT data privacy regulations?**

    a. Data storage costs

    b. Inconsistent legal frameworks across countries

    c. Network latency

    d. Device energy consumption

137. **Which of the following is a potential benefit of IoT in transportation?**

    a. Decreased vehicle connectivity

    b. Enhanced traffic management and route optimization

    c. Increased fuel consumption

    d. Reduced safety features

138. **What is a significant challenge for IoT in healthcare regarding device interoperability?**

    a. Uniform data encryption

    b. Integration of different health monitoring systems

    c. Reducing device power requirements

    d. Simplifying user interfaces

139. **What is a future trend in IoT related to network infrastructure?**
    a. Decreased reliance on wireless technologies
    b. Expansion of 5G and beyond for improved connectivity
    c. Increased use of wired connections
    d. Reduced network security measures

140. **Which technology can enhance IoT security by providing decentralized verification?**
    a. Blockchain
    b. Satellite communication
    c. Wi-Fi direct
    d. Fiber optics

141. **What is a major challenge in ensuring IoT device longevity?**
    a. Device design aesthetics
    b. Hardware obsolescence and rapid technological advancements
    c. Reduced network coverage
    d. Decreased power efficiency

142. **Which aspect of IoT is crucial for ensuring quality of service in smart grids?**
    a. Device aesthetics
    b. Data accuracy and real-time monitoring
    c. Increased manual control
    d. Reduced energy consumption

143. **What is a common challenge in IoT system deployment in rural areas?**
    a. High data throughput
    b. Limited network infrastructure and connectivity
    c. Increased device cost
    d. Complex user interfaces

144. **What is an emerging solution to address IoT's data privacy concerns?**
    a. Centralized data storage
    b. Advanced encryption and anonymization techniques
    c. Increased manual data management
    d. Reduced data collection

145. **What role does artificial intelligence play in the future of IoT?**

   a. Simplifying device design

   b. Enhancing data analysis and enabling autonomous decision-making

   c. Reducing device connectivity

   d. Increasing manual oversight

146. **Which technology is likely to be integrated with IoT for improved indoor navigation?**

   a. GPS

   b. BLE beacons

   c. Satellite imagery

   d. Analog signals

147. **What is a challenge associated with IoT device scalability?**

   a. Increased data storage requirements

   b. Compatibility with different operating systems and protocols

   c. Reduced data accuracy

   d. Limited sensor capabilities

148. **How can IoT contribute to smart agriculture?**

   a. By reducing data collection

   b. By providing real-time soil monitoring and automated irrigation systems

   c. By increasing pesticide use

   d. By limiting data accuracy

149. **What is a major challenge for IoT in autonomous vehicles?**

   a. Simplifying user interfaces

   b. Ensuring real-time data processing and safety

   c. Reducing device cost

   d. Increasing manual control

150. **Which technology is essential for ensuring low-latency communication in IoT networks?**

   a. 5G networks

   b. Wi-Fi 4

   c. Analog modems

   d. Satellite communication

151. **What is a significant challenge in IoT device manufacturing?**
    a. High device cost
    b. Ensuring compatibility with various standards and protocols
    c. Increased data accuracy
    d. Reduced network coverage

152. **Which of the following is an expected benefit of IoT in the energy sector?**
    a. Increased energy consumption
    b. Enhanced energy management and smart grids
    c. Decreased network reliability
    d. Reduced data storage needs

153. **What is a key factor in addressing the challenge of IoT device security?**
    a. Regular software updates and patch management
    b. Reducing device functionality
    c. Increasing device size
    d. Limiting data collection

154. **Which of the following is a challenge related to IoT in supply chain management?**
    a. Increased data storage costs
    b. Integration with existing systems and technologies
    c. Reduced network coverage
    d. Simplified data collection

155. **How can IoT improve disaster management?**
    a. By decreasing real-time data availability
    b. By enabling early warning systems and real-time monitoring
    c. By limiting device connectivity
    d. By increasing manual data entry

156. **Which technology is likely to enhance IoT device communication range?**
    a. Zigbee
    b. USB 2.0
    c. Infrared
    d. HDMI

157. What is a future challenge related to IoT device lifecycle management?

    a. Decreasing device costs

    b. Managing and updating a growing number of devices

    c. Reducing network latency

    d. Increasing manual oversight

158. Which of the following is a challenge in IoT-based smart grid systems?

    a. High data accuracy

    b. Ensuring secure and reliable data transmission

    c. Increased manual monitoring

    d. Reduced connectivity options

159. How can IoT impact the retail industry?

    a. By increasing manual inventory checks

    b. By enabling real-time inventory management and personalized customer experiences

    c. By reducing data collection

    d. By limiting device functionality

160. Which of the following is a challenge for IoT in the context of smart agriculture?

    a. Reduced sensor accuracy

    b. Integrating diverse agricultural technologies and data sources

    c. Increased manual labor

    d. Limited network infrastructure

161. What is a key factor for improving IoT device performance in industrial environments?

    a. Simplified device interfaces

    b. High durability and reliability under harsh conditions

    c. Increased data collection

    d. Reduced connectivity

162. What challenge does IoT face regarding device updates and patches?

    a. Reduced update frequency

    b. Inconsistent update management and deployment

    c. Increased device cost

    d. Limited data accuracy

163. **Which technology is expected to enhance IoT's ability to handle big data?**

    a. Cloud computing

    b. Fax machines

    c. Analog sensors

    d. USB storage devices

164. **What is a significant concern with the proliferation of IoT devices in terms of data privacy?**

    a. Increased data storage costs

    b. Greater potential for unauthorized data access and breaches

    c. Reduced network coverage

    d. Limited device functionality

165. **How can IoT contribute to the development of smart cities?**

    a. By limiting device integration

    b. By enabling efficient resource management and enhanced public services

    c. By increasing manual processes

    d. By reducing data accuracy

166. **Which aspect of IoT is crucial for improving agricultural productivity?**

    a. Reduced data accuracy

    b. Real-time monitoring and automated systems

    c. Increased manual labor

    d. Limited sensor capabilities

167. **What is a key challenge for IoT in healthcare data management?**

    a. High data encryption standards

    b. Ensuring interoperability and data integration from multiple sources

    c. Reduced data accuracy

    d. Simplified user interfaces

168. **Which of the following technologies is important for IoT in wearable devices?**

    a. Near field communication (NFC)

    b. Dial-up modems

    c. Legacy networking protocols

    d. Optical discs

169. What is a major future trend for IoT in terms of device communication?

    a. Decreased use of wireless communication

    b. Increased use of low-power, wide-area networks (LPWANs)

    c. Reduced data collection capabilities

    d. Simplified device functionality

170. Which of the following presents a challenge for IoT in smart homes?

    a. Increased manual control

    b. Ensuring compatibility between various smart devices

    c. Reduced data accuracy

    d. Decreased network coverage

171. What is a significant challenge in implementing IoT solutions in transportation systems?

    a. Increased data accuracy

    b. Ensuring real-time communication and system integration

    c. Reduced device connectivity

    d. Simplified data management

172. How can IoT benefit the manufacturing industry?

    a. By increasing manual processes

    b. By enabling real-time monitoring and predictive maintenance

    c. By reducing data collection

    d. By limiting device functionality

173. What is a major challenge in IoT system security?

    a. High data transmission speeds

    b. Ensuring end-to-end encryption and secure communication

    c. Reduced network coverage

    d. Increased manual control

174. Which technology is likely to play a key role in the future of IoT in urban environments?

    a. Smart sensors and data analytics

    b. Analog systems

    c. Dial-up modems

    d. Optical storage

175. **What is a challenge for IoT in integrating with existing IT infrastructure?**

    a. High device costs

    b. Compatibility with legacy systems and protocols

    c. Reduced data accuracy

    d. Limited network connectivity

176. **How can IoT improve efficiency in supply chain management?**

    a. By increasing manual tracking processes

    b. By providing real-time tracking and data analysis

    c. By reducing device functionality

    d. By limiting data collection

177. **What is a major concern with IoT devices in terms of physical security?**

    a. Device design aesthetics

    b. Vulnerability to physical tampering and unauthorized access

    c. Increased data accuracy

    d. Reduced connectivity options

178. **Which aspect of IoT is crucial for enhancing consumer experiences in retail?**

    a. Increased manual data entry

    b. Real-time inventory management and personalized offers

    c. Reduced data accuracy

    d. Simplified device interfaces

179. **What is a key challenge in scaling IoT solutions for global deployment?**

    a. Increased device size

    b. Navigating diverse regulatory environments and standards

    c. Reduced data accuracy

    d. Simplified network protocols

180. **Which technology is expected to improve IoT's ability to handle massive data volumes?**

    a. Big data analytics

    b. Dial-up modems

    c. Analog storage solutions

    d. Optical discs

181. **How can IoT contribute to enhancing workplace safety?**

    a. By increasing manual safety checks

    b. By enabling real-time monitoring and automated alerts

    c. By reducing data accuracy

    d. By limiting connectivity options

182. **What is a significant challenge for IoT in the context of data sharing?**

    a. Increased data accuracy

    b. Ensuring secure and compliant data sharing practices

    c. Reduced device functionality

    d. Simplified user interfaces

183. **Which aspect of IoT is important for improving efficiency in smart grids?**

    a. Reduced device connectivity

    b. Real-time data collection and analysis

    c. Increased manual oversight

    d. Limited sensor capabilities

184. **What is a future challenge in IoT device connectivity?**

    a. Increased network speed

    b. Ensuring seamless connectivity across diverse network types

    c. Reduced data accuracy

    d. Simplified device functionality

185. **How can IoT impact the efficiency of smart buildings?**

    a. By increasing manual control of building systems

    b. By automating systems and optimizing energy usage

    c. By reducing data collection

    d. By limiting network connectivity

186. **Which technology is essential for supporting IoT in smart agriculture?**

    a. GPS and remote sensing technologies

    b. Dial-up modems

    c. Optical discs

    d. Analog sensors

187. **What is a major concern with IoT devices in terms of software updates?**

    a. High data transfer speeds

    b. Ensuring timely and secure updates

    c. Reduced device functionality

    d. Limited network coverage

188. **How can IoT benefit the logistics industry?**

    a. By increasing manual tracking

    b. By providing real-time shipment tracking and route optimization

    c. By reducing data accuracy

    d. By limiting connectivity options

189. **What is a significant challenge for IoT in terms of power consumption?**

    a. Increased data accuracy

    b. Managing power-efficient operation for battery-operated devices

    c. Reduced device functionality

    d. Simplified user interfaces

190. **Which aspect of IoT is crucial for enhancing smart healthcare solutions?**

    a. Increased manual data entry

    b. Real-time health monitoring and integration with medical systems

    c. Reduced connectivity options

    d. Limited device functionality

191. **What is a future challenge for IoT regarding data storage?**

    a. Decreasing data storage needs

    b. Managing the growing volume of data generated by IoT devices

    c. Reduced data accuracy

    d. Simplified data management

192. **How can IoT impact the efficiency of energy management in smart grids?**

    a. By increasing manual monitoring

    b. By providing real-time data and automated control systems

    c. By reducing data accuracy

    d. By limiting network connectivity

193. **Which technology is crucial for enhancing IoT security through device authentication?**

    a. Public key infrastructure (PKI)

    b. Analog sensors

    c. Dial-up modems

    d. Optical storage

194. **What is a major challenge for IoT in implementing real-time analytics?**

    a. Increased data accuracy

    b. Ensuring low-latency data processing and analysis

    c. Reduced connectivity options

    d. Simplified user interfaces

195. **How can IoT contribute to improving traffic management in smart cities?**

    a. By increasing manual traffic control

    b. By providing real-time traffic data and optimizing traffic flow

    c. By reducing data accuracy

    d. By limiting network connectivity

196. **Which of the following is a key factor for successful IoT deployment in industrial automation?**

    a. Simplified device interfaces

    b. Integration with existing industrial systems and protocols

    c. Increased manual control

    d. Reduced data collection

197. **What is a significant challenge for IoT in terms of end-user privacy?**

    a. Increased data storage costs

    b. Ensuring users' control over their data and privacy

    c. Reduced device functionality

    d. Simplified data management

198. **Which technology is important for ensuring IoT device communication over long distances?**

    a. LPWAN

    b. USB 2.0

    c. Analog modems

    d. HDMI

199. How can IoT support disaster recovery efforts?

    a. By increasing manual data collection

    b. By providing real-time situational awareness and automated response systems

    c. By reducing device connectivity

    d. By limiting data accuracy

200. What is a challenge in maintaining IoT devices in extreme environments?

    a. Increased data accuracy

    b. Ensuring device durability and reliable performance

    c. Reduced device functionality

    d. Simplified user interfaces

201. How can IoT enhance smart building management?

    a. By increasing manual control of building systems

    b. By enabling automated control of lighting, HVAC, and security systems

    c. By reducing data accuracy

    d. By limiting network connectivity

202. What is a key consideration for IoT in terms of data transmission?

    a. Increasing data collection

    b. Ensuring efficient and secure data transmission protocols

    c. Reduced network coverage

    d. Simplified device interfaces

203. Which technology is important for IoT in managing large-scale sensor networks?

    a. IoT platforms with centralized management

    b. Dial-up modems

    c. Analog sensors

    d. Optical discs

204. What is a future trend in IoT regarding energy efficiency?

    a. Increased energy consumption

    b. Development of energy-harvesting technologies and low-power devices

    c. Reduced device functionality

    d. Limited network coverage

205. **How can IoT impact the field of environmental monitoring?**
    a. By increasing manual data collection efforts
    b. By providing real-time data on environmental conditions and pollution levels
    c. By reducing data accuracy
    d. By limiting network connectivity

206. **What is a challenge in integrating IoT with existing enterprise systems?**
    a. Increased data accuracy
    b. Ensuring compatibility and seamless data exchange
    c. Reduced device functionality
    d. Simplified user interfaces

207. **How can IoT contribute to enhancing public transportation systems?**
    a. By increasing manual scheduling
    b. By providing real-time vehicle tracking and passenger information
    c. By reducing data accuracy
    d. By limiting network connectivity

208. **What is a significant challenge for IoT in terms of regulatory compliance?**
    a. Increased device cost
    b. Navigating varying regulations and standards across different regions
    c. Reduced data accuracy
    d. Simplified device functionality

209. **Which technology is crucial for supporting high-speed IoT data communication?**
    a. 5G networks
    b. Dial-up modems
    c. Analog sensors
    d. Optical storage

210. **What is a challenge related to IoT device interoperability in smart cities?**
    a. Increased device functionality
    b. Ensuring seamless interaction between diverse systems and devices
    c. Reduced data accuracy
    d. Limited network coverage

211. **How can IoT improve operational efficiency in manufacturing?**
    a. By increasing manual processes
    b. By enabling real-time monitoring and predictive maintenance
    c. By reducing data accuracy
    d. By limiting connectivity options

212. **What is a major concern for IoT regarding data sovereignty?**
    a. Increased data storage costs
    b. Ensuring compliance with local data protection laws and regulations
    c. Reduced data accuracy
    d. Simplified data management

213. **Which technology is important for supporting IoT applications in remote areas?**
    a. Satellite communication
    b. Dial-up modems
    c. Optical storage
    d. Analog sensors

214. **How can IoT enhance the efficiency of energy grids?**
    a. By increasing manual monitoring
    b. By providing real-time data and automated control of energy distribution
    c. By reducing data accuracy
    d. By limiting network connectivity

215. **What is a challenge for IoT in terms of device authentication?**
    a. Increased data accuracy
    b. Ensuring robust authentication mechanisms to prevent unauthorized access
    c. Reduced connectivity options
    d. Simplified device functionality

216. **How can IoT contribute to improving customer service in retail?**
    a. By increasing manual inventory checks
    b. By enabling personalized offers and efficient inventory management
    c. By reducing data accuracy
    d. By limiting connectivity options

217. What is a major future trend for IoT in terms of data analytics?

    a. Reduced data processing capabilities

    b. Increased use of artificial intelligence and machine learning for advanced analytics

    c. Simplified data management

    d. Limited data storage

218. What is a primary challenge of integrating IoT devices with AI systems?

    a. High cost of hardware

    b. Limited data storage

    c. Data security and privacy

    d. Lack of network connectivity

219. Which of the following is a significant concern when using AI with IoT devices?

    a. Energy efficiency

    b. Data accuracy

    c. Network latency

    d. Data transmission speed

220. What is a major challenge related to the scalability of IoT systems in AI applications?

    a. Device compatibility

    b. Data processing power

    c. Cost of implementation

    d. User interface design

221. Which of the following issues is related to the interoperability of IoT devices in AI?

    a. Device memory

    b. Different communication protocols

    c. Network bandwidth

    d. Power consumption

222. What is a challenge in ensuring the real-time performance of AI algorithms in IoT applications?

    a. Data storage capacity

    b. Network bandwidth and latency

    c. Device power consumption

    d. User data accessibility

223. **Which aspect of IoT poses a challenge for AI in terms of data management?**

    a. Limited device capabilities

    b. High volume and variety of data

    c. Device upgrade frequency

    d. User interface complexity

224. **In IoT systems, what is a challenge related to AI model training?**

    a. Lack of data

    b. High computational requirements

    c. Device mobility

    d. User interface design

225. **What challenge is associated with deploying AI solutions on resource-constrained IoT devices?**

    a. Data encryption

    b. Limited processing power

    c. High network traffic

    d. Device compatibility

226. **What security challenge is particularly relevant for AI-integrated IoT systems?**

    a. Physical device theft

    b. Insecure communication channels

    c. Software bugs

    d. High energy consumption

227. **What is a challenge of using machine learning models in IoT systems?**

    a. High data transmission rates

    b. Lack of real-time feedback

    c. Model deployment and updates

    d. User interface design

228. **Which of the following is a challenge for AI in handling IoT device-generated data?**

    a. Data encryption methods

    b. Data heterogeneity

    c. User authentication

    d. Device synchronization

229. **What challenge arises when integrating AI with IoT for predictive maintenance?**

    a. Limited sensor accuracy

    b. High data volume

    c. Low network speed

    d. Device compatibility

230. **In the context of IoT, what is a challenge related to AI-driven decision-making?**

    a. Real-time data processing

    b. Device energy consumption

    c. User training requirements

    d. Device location tracking

231. **Which issue is a concern when using AI for anomaly detection in IoT systems?**

    a. Data uniformity

    b. False positives/negatives

    c. Network topology

    d. Device maintenance

232. **What challenge does the diversity of IoT devices pose for AI algorithms?**

    a. Increased cost

    b. Complex integration

    c. Data format standardization

    d. Limited data access

233. **What challenge is related to AI-powered IoT systems in terms of data collection?**

    a. Data transmission reliability

    b. Data redundancy

    c. Data completeness

    d. Data quality

234. **In IoT networks, what is a challenge for AI in maintaining system robustness?**

    a. Network congestion

    b. Device heterogeneity

    c. Energy efficiency

    d. Device location

235. **Which of the following is a challenge for deploying AI in IoT edge devices?**

    a. Limited storage space

    b. High network bandwidth

    c. Device synchronization

    d. Real-time user interaction

236. **What challenge does the large scale of IoT networks present for AI?**

    a. Data encryption

    b. Data integration

    c. Device maintenance

    d. Network security

237. **What challenge is encountered with AI when handling the privacy of data in IoT systems?**

    a. Data redundancy

    b. Data anonymization

    c. Data encryption

    d. Data transmission speed

238. **What is a promising future application of AI in IoT systems?**

    a. Autonomous vehicles

    b. Manual data entry

    c. Traditional computing

    d. Static data analysis

239. **Which technology is expected to enhance AI capabilities in IoT systems in the future?**

    a. 5G networks

    b. Traditional Wi-Fi

    c. Bluetooth 2.0

    d. Ethernet cables

240. **How can AI improve the energy efficiency of IoT devices in the future?**

    a. By increasing device power usage

    b. Through predictive maintenance

    c. By decreasing data processing

    d. By reducing device connectivity

241. What future advancement in AI could benefit IoT security?

a. Improved data encryption methods

b. Static data analysis

c. Manual threat detection

d. Basic firewalls

242. Which future trend in AI could lead to more intelligent IoT systems?

a. Improved hardware constraints

b. Enhanced machine learning algorithms

c. Reduced network speeds

d. Simpler user interfaces

243. What role will edge computing play in the future of AI and IoT?

a. Reducing processing power

b. Centralizing data processing

c. Enhancing real-time data processing

d. Limiting device connectivity

244. How might future AI developments impact IoT device management?

a. Increasing manual oversight

b. Streamlining automated updates

c. Reducing network capabilities

d. Limiting device functionalities

245. Which of the following could be a future challenge in AI-driven IoT systems?

a. Improved data accuracy

b. Increased computational requirements

c. Enhanced device compatibility

d. Simplified data management

246. What future innovation could improve the integration of AI with IoT devices?

a. Enhanced standardization protocols

b. Reduced data collection

c. Lower device processing speeds

d. Increased manual data input

247. **How could AI contribute to the future of IoT in smart cities?**

    a. By reducing network bandwidth

    b. Through advanced traffic management

    c. By increasing manual monitoring

    d. Through limited data analysis

248. **What future development in AI could lead to more effective IoT health monitoring systems?**

    a. Basic data collection

    b. Advanced predictive analytics

    c. Reduced sensor accuracy

    d. Lower data integration

249. **Which future technology is likely to impact AI's role in IoT smart homes?**

    a. Advanced voice recognition systems

    b. Traditional appliance control

    c. Manual temperature adjustment

    d. Basic sensor technology

250. **What is a potential future benefit of AI in IoT for agricultural systems?**

    a. Enhanced manual crop management

    b. Predictive crop yield analytics

    c. Reduced sensor usage

    d. Decreased data collection

251. **Which future trend could drive innovation in AI-powered IoT devices?**

    a. Advanced miniaturization

    b. Reduced data processing capabilities

    c. Decreased connectivity options

    d. Increased manual device operation

252. **How might future advancements in AI affect IoT device communication?**

    a. Enhanced interoperability

    b. Increased manual configuration

    c. Decreased data transmission speeds

    d. Reduced network coverage

253. **What future development could help address data privacy concerns in AI-driven IoT systems?**

    a. Enhanced encryption techniques

    b. Reduced data collection

    c. Simplified data analysis

    d. Manual privacy controls

254. **What future innovation could optimize the performance of AI in IoT networks?**

    a. Increased bandwidth

    b. Reduced device capabilities

    c. Basic network protocols

    d. Lower data processing

255. **What is a potential future application of AI in IoT for environmental monitoring?**

    a. Enhanced pollution tracking

    b. Reduced sensor accuracy

    c. Manual data logging

    d. Decreased real-time analysis

256. **Which future development in AI could help improve IoT energy efficiency?**

    a. Advanced energy management systems

    b. Increased power consumption

    c. Manual energy control

    d. Reduced device connectivity

257. **What future advancement in AI could enhance IoT smart grid systems?**

    a. Predictive load management

    b. Basic power distribution

    c. Reduced data analytics

    d. Manual grid adjustments

258. **How could future AI advancements influence IoT in autonomous systems?**

    a. Improved decision-making algorithms

    b. Reduced sensor reliability

    c. Lower data processing capabilities

    d. Increased manual control

259. **What future development in AI could enhance IoT-based personal assistants?**

   a. Advanced natural language processing

   b. Basic voice recognition

   c. Manual user inputs

   d. Reduced device responsiveness

260. **Which future technology is expected to further the integration of AI with IoT in logistics?**

   a. Autonomous delivery vehicles

   b. Manual route planning

   c. Basic tracking systems

   d. Reduced sensor usage

261. **What future trend in AI could benefit IoT-based financial services?**

   a. Enhanced fraud detection algorithms

   b. Basic transaction processing

   c. Reduced data security measures

   d. Manual data analysis

262. **How might future AI advancements impact IoT in education?**

   a. Personalized learning experiences

   b. Manual grading systems

   c. Reduced digital resources

   d. Basic classroom management

263. **What is a potential future application of AI in IoT for smart transportation systems?**

   a. Improved traffic flow management

   b. Manual vehicle control

   c. Basic route mapping

   d. Reduced sensor accuracy

264. **Which future AI development could aid in the management of IoT-based smart buildings?**

   a. Intelligent building automation systems

   b. Basic manual controls

   c. Reduced sensor integration

   d. Simplified energy usage

265. **What future advancement in AI might address the challenge of IoT data overload?**

    a. Advanced data filtering techniques

    b. Reduced data processing

    c. Manual data handling

    d. Basic storage solutions

266. **How could future AI developments influence IoT in health care?**

    a. Enhanced patient monitoring systems

    b. Manual health record management

    c. Reduced diagnostic capabilities

    d. Basic treatment plans

267. **What future technology could drive innovation in AI-enabled IoT consumer devices?**

    a. Enhanced voice and gesture recognition

    b. Basic user interfaces

    c. Reduced processing speeds

    d. Manual device configuration

Join our Discord space

Join our Discord workspace for latest updates, offers, tech happenings around the world, new releases, and sessions with the authors:

https://discord.bpbonline.com

Answers

Q.No.	Answers	Q.No.	Answers	Q.No.	Answers	Q.No.	Answers	Q.No.	Answers
1	d	31	b	61	b	91	b	121	c
2	c	32	b	62	c	92	a	122	b
3	d	33	d	63	c	93	c	123	a
4	d	34	c	64	c	94	d	124	b
5	d	35	c	65	a	95	b	125	b
6	c	36	d	66	c	96	a	126	b
7	b	37	b	67	d	97	d	127	a
8	c	38	d	68	b	98	d	128	b
9	d	39	b	69	b	99	c	129	b
10	c	40	b	70	d	100	b	130	b
11	c	41	b	71	a	101	b	131	b
12	a	42	c	72	d	102	c	132	b
13	c	43	b	73	d	103	c	133	b
14	c	44	b	74	b	104	b	134	b
15	d	45	d	75	b	105	c	135	b
16	d	46	d	76	d	106	c	136	b
17	d	47	b	77	b	107	b	137	b
18	d	48	c	78	c	108	c	138	b
19	c	49	a	79	c	109	b	139	b
20	b	50	c	80	c	110	b	140	a
21	d	51	d	81	d	111	b	141	b
22	c	52	d	82	c	112	a	142	b
23	d	53	d	83	d	113	b	143	b
24	b	54	d	84	b	114	b	144	b
25	d	55	b	85	c	115	a	145	b
26	b	56	d	86	c	116	b	146	b
27	b	57	a	87	d	117	c	147	b
28	c	58	c	88	b	118	a	148	b
29	a	59	c	89	c	119	a	149	b
30	c	60	d	90	d	120	b	150	a

Q.No.	Answers	Q.No.	Answers	Q.No.	Answers	Q.No.	Answers
151	b	181	b	211	b	241	a
152	b	182	b	212	b	242	b
153	a	183	b	213	a	243	c
154	b	184	b	214	b	244	b
155	b	185	b	215	b	245	b
156	a	186	a	216	b	246	a
157	b	187	b	217	b	247	b
158	b	188	b	218	c	248	b
159	b	189	b	219	b	249	a
160	b	190	b	220	b	250	b
161	b	191	b	221	b	251	a
162	b	192	b	222	b	252	a
163	a	193	a	223	b	253	a
164	b	194	b	224	b	254	a
165	b	195	b	225	b	255	a
166	b	196	b	226	b	256	a
167	b	197	b	227	c	257	a
168	a	198	a	228	b	258	a
169	b	199	b	229	b	259	a
170	b	200	b	230	a	260	a
171	b	201	b	231	b	261	a
172	b	202	b	232	c	262	a
173	b	203	a	233	d	263	a
174	a	204	b	234	b	264	a
175	b	205	b	235	a	265	a
176	b	206	b	236	b	266	a
177	b	207	b	237	b	267	a
178	b	208	b	238	a		
179	b	209	a	239	a		
180	a	210	b	240	b		

CHAPTER 5

Online Simulation Software of IoT

Introduction

The IoT demands comprehensive testing before implementation. Many online simulation tools ease this process and offer a sandbox for IoT development. Developers may construct, test, and simulate IoT devices and interactions without buying hardware using these platforms. Let us look at an overview of IoT online simulation software.

ThingsBoard

This open-source IoT platform offers device administration, telemetry, and analytics. Their live demo lets customers try the app without installing it.

Its features are as follows:

- Data gathering and visualization
- Device and asset management
- Rule engine for data processing and event triggering

Tinkercad

Tinkercad, owned by Autodesk, is a free online simulation program for developing 3D objects and IoT devices like Arduino, and it contains a robust circuit simulator.

Its features are as follows:

- Drag-and-drop tool
- Variety of sensors and microcontrollers

Cisco Packet Tracer

Packet Tracer is a network simulation tool with an IoT module for setting up and testing IoT scenarios.

Its features are as follows:

- Simulate several network protocols
- Physical and mental workplace
- Wide selection of IoT devices and parts

IBM Watson

IBM Watson IoT platform simulator simulates device behavior, cloud data transmission, and application testing.

Its features are as follows:

- Easy virtual device setup
- Visualization and analysis
- Integration with Node-RED for workflow design

myDevices Cayenne

Cayenne is a drag-and-drop IoT project builder for visualizing, monitoring, and controlling real and virtual devices.

Its features are as follows:

- Dashboard widgets for IoT components
- Scheduling and trigger
- Wide device support

Microsoft Azure's

With Microsoft Azure's IoT device simulation, you can construct a customized simulation of millions of devices. It is scalable and can simulate massive IoT networks.

Its features are as follows:

- Scalable to millions of virtual devices
- Custom device scripts and templates
- Integration with Azure IoT Hub

Multiple choice questions

1. **What is the primary purpose of online simulation software for IoT?**

   a. Entertainment purposes

   b. Gaming experiences

   c. Real-time data visualization

   d. Virtual reality experiences

2. **Which of the following statements about online simulation software for IoT is true?**

   a. It requires the installation of software on local machines

   b. It cannot simulate real-world scenarios

   c. It is only accessible to software developers

   d. It allows users to simulate and visualize IoT scenarios over the internet

3. **What type of IoT components can be simulated using online simulation software?**

   a. Hardware only

   b. Software only

   c. Both hardware and software

   d. Networking devices only

4. **Which advantage does online simulation software offer for IoT development and testing?**

   a. Limited scalability

   b. Inflexible environment

   c. Reduced time and cost

   d. Local machine dependency

5. **How does online simulation software enhance collaboration in IoT projects?**

   a. It limits access to a single user

   b. It requires physical presence for collaboration

   c. It enables multiple users to access and work on simulations remotely

   d. It only allows collaboration within a local network

6. **Which aspect of IoT can online simulation software help in understanding better?**

    a. Theoretical concepts only

    b. Networking protocols only

    c. Real-world implementation challenges

    d. Hardware manufacturing processes

7. **What is the primary benefit of using online simulation software for IoT projects before actual deployment?**

    a. It eliminates the need for real hardware

    b. It offers physical testing of devices

    c. It replaces the need for programming skills

    d. It aids in identifying potential issues and optimizations

8. **Which type of users can benefit from online simulation software for IoT projects?**

    a. Hardware manufacturers only

    b. Software developers only

    c. Industry professionals and hobbyists

    d. Network administrators only

9. **How does online simulation software contribute to the learning of IoT concepts?**

    a. It provides real-time IoT device manufacturing

    b. It only supports advanced users

    c. It offers interactive and visual learning experiences

    d. It requires physical access to hardware components

10. **What is the potential drawback of relying solely on online simulation software for IoT testing?**

    a. Lack of real-world data

    b. Expensive subscription fees

    c. Dependence on specific operating systems

    d. Incompatibility with networking protocols

11. **What role does cloud computing play in the functionality of online simulation software for IoT?**

    a. It does not have any connection to cloud computing

    b. It relies on cloud resources to enhance the simulation process

    c. It only supports simulations on local machines

    d. It requires users to set up their own cloud servers

12. **Which aspect of IoT project development can online simulation software help in optimizing?**

    a. Device manufacturing processes

    b. Marketing and sales strategies

    c. Hardware production costs

    d. User interface design

13. **How does online simulation software help in predicting the behavior of IoT devices in real-world scenarios?**

    a. It provides actual physical prototypes for testing

    b. It simulates device interactions with real-world objects and environments

    c. It only works with pre-programmed scenarios

    d. It requires users to have advanced programming skills

14. **What is the potential limitation of using online simulation software for highly complex IoT projects?**

    a. It cannot simulate any IoT projects

    b. It requires additional hardware components

    c. It may lack the necessary complexity and accuracy

    d. It requires a constant internet connection

15. **How can online simulation software assist in troubleshooting IoT applications?**

    a. It can predict all potential issues with 100% accuracy

    b. It provides automatic debugging features

    c. It allows users to simulate and identify possible issues before deployment

    d. It only supports the simulation of software applications

16. **Which of the following statements is true about the accessibility of online simulation software for IoT?**

    a. It is limited to a single user per simulation

    b. It is only available on weekends

    c. It can be accessed by multiple users remotely

    d. It requires physical presence at the simulation center

17. **How does online simulation software help in estimating the resource utilization of IoT devices?**

    a. It cannot estimate resource utilization

    b. It provides exact resource utilization data

    c. It simulates various usage scenarios to estimate resource requirements

    d. It only focuses on network performance

18. **What is the potential advantage of using online simulation software for IoT projects involving large-scale deployments?**

    a. It simplifies the hardware manufacturing process

    b. It requires physical installation of devices for testing

    c. It offers easy scalability for testing a large number of devices

    d. It only supports simulations on local servers

19. **Which challenge can online simulation software for IoT help in addressing during the development phase?**

    a. Identifying the most common programming languages

    b. Reducing the need for any software development

    c. Visualizing data collected from IoT devices

    d. Predicting the stock market trends

20. **How can online simulation software contribute to IoT project planning and decision-making?**

    a. It is not relevant for project planning and decision-making

    b. It replaces the need for any planning or decision-making

    c. It provides real-time manufacturing of IoT devices

    d. It helps in testing different scenarios and making informed choices

21. **Which aspect of IoT implementation can online simulation software assist in optimizing for energy efficiency?**

    a. Device connectivity

    b. Hardware production speed

    c. Data transmission rates

    d. Battery life and power consumption

22. **How does online simulation software contribute to IoT security testing?**
    a. It does not provide any security testing features
    b. It simulates various security breaches to test device vulnerabilities
    c. It only supports physical security tests
    d. It requires physical access to the IoT devices

23. **What is the potential benefit of using online simulation software for IoT in an educational context?**
    a. It limits the exposure of students to IoT concepts
    b. It replaces the need for any theoretical learning
    c. It provides hands-on experience and practical learning opportunities
    d. It focuses exclusively on software development

24. **How can online simulation software assist in testing the scalability of an IoT application?**
    a. It cannot simulate scalability
    b. It generates random data to test scalability
    c. It simulates increasing device numbers and measures performance
    d. It requires the physical setup of numerous devices

25. **Which challenge does online simulation software for IoT help address regarding device communication?**
    a. It does not impact device communication
    b. It enables the simulation of various communication protocols
    c. It only focuses on device hardware design
    d. It simulates communication with actual devices in real time

26. **What is the potential drawback of relying solely on online simulation software for IoT project testing?**
    a. Lack of real-world data
    b. Reduced collaboration opportunities
    c. Limited device compatibility
    d. Excessive hardware requirements

27. **How does online simulation software contribute to evaluating IoT device performance under different network conditions?**

    a. It only supports simulations in ideal network conditions

    b. It cannot simulate network conditions

    c. It simulates various network scenarios to measure device performance

    d. It requires users to configure the network settings manually

28. **What is the potential benefit of using online simulation software for IoT projects regarding cost-effectiveness?**

    a. It increases overall project costs significantly

    b. It eliminates the need for any hardware components

    c. It requires costly subscriptions for cloud services

    d. It reduces the need for physical hardware during testing

29. **How does online simulation software enhance the understanding of IoT architecture and design?**

    a. It only focuses on software design

    b. It replaces the need for understanding architecture

    c. It visualizes the hardware and software interactions in real-time

    d. It does not contribute to understanding IoT design concepts

30. **What is the potential impact of online simulation software on reducing the time-to-market for IoT projects?**

    a. It has no impact on time-to-market

    b. It significantly increases time-to-market due to its complexity

    c. It shortens time-to-market by facilitating testing and optimization

    d. It extends time-to-market by introducing additional layers of complexity

31. **How does online simulation software assist in optimizing IoT device placement and positioning within a given environment?**

    a. It does not impact device placement

    b. It only supports simulations in a fixed position

    c. It simulates device interactions with the environment and aids in optimal placement

    d. It requires physical adjustments to device positions for testing

32. **Which challenge does online simulation software help address when testing IoT applications involving real-time data streaming?**
    a. It does not address real-time data streaming
    b. Simulating large-scale data streams
    c. It only focuses on offline data storage
    d. Simulating ideal network conditions only

33. **What is the potential benefit of using online simulation software for IoT projects regarding geographical reach?**
    a. It limits testing to a specific geographical location
    b. It enables global testing without the need for physical presence
    c. It only supports simulation for one specific country
    d. It does not contribute to geographical testing

34. **How does online simulation software assist in testing the scalability of IoT applications involving cloud services?**
    a. It cannot simulate cloud services
    b. It only supports local simulations
    c. It simulates increasing cloud service demands and measures performance
    d. It requires users to set up cloud environments manually

35. **Which aspect of IoT project development can online simulation software help in optimizing for cost-effectiveness?**
    a. Device manufacturing materials
    b. High-speed data transmission rates
    c. Real-world connectivity challenges
    d. Reduction of hardware production costs

36. **What is the primary advantage of using online simulation software for IoT projects involving remote and inaccessible locations?**
    a. It is not suitable for remote location testing
    b. It replaces the need for any remote testing
    c. It enables simulation and testing of IoT scenarios remotely
    d. It requires physical presence at the remote location

37. **How does online simulation software contribute to IoT project documentation and reporting?**

    a. It does not offer any documentation features

    b. It generates automatic documentation

    c. It only supports software documentation

    d. It aids in creating reports based on simulated scenarios

38. **What is the potential limitation of online simulation software for IoT projects requiring physical interactions and sensor data collection?**

    a. It cannot simulate any physical interactions

    b. It requires advanced robotics knowledge

    c. It simulates physical interactions and sensor data collection accurately

    d. It focuses solely on software interactions

39. **How does online simulation software contribute to understanding the impact of network delays on IoT applications?**

    a. It does not consider network delays

    b. It simulates ideal network conditions only

    c. It simulates various network delay scenarios and measures the impact

    d. It requires manual configuration of network delays

40. **Which challenge can online simulation software help in addressing when testing IoT applications involving a wide range of devices and platforms?**

    a. It cannot address device and platform diversity

    b. Simulating interactions between different devices and platforms

    c. It focuses solely on specific devices and platforms

    d. It requires users to have a deep understanding of device interactions

41. **How does online simulation software contribute to optimizing data flow and processing within an IoT application?**

    a. It has no impact on data flow and processing

    b. It replaces the need for data flow optimization

    c. It simulates data flow and processing scenarios to identify bottlenecks

    d. It requires manual adjustments to data flow and processing

42. **What is the potential impact of using online simulation software for IoT projects on minimizing physical hardware prototypes?**

    a. It requires more physical prototypes

    b. It has no impact on physical prototypes

    c. It eliminates the need for physical prototypes entirely

    d. It increases the complexity of physical prototypes

43. **How does online simulation software contribute to the validation of IoT application logic and behavior?**

    a. It does not contribute to validation

    b. It validates all scenarios automatically

    c. It simulates different scenarios to validate application logic and behavior

    d. It requires users to validate application logic manually

44. **Which challenge can online simulation software help address when testing IoT applications involving high-frequency data updates?**

    a. It cannot address high-frequency data updates

    b. Simulating real-time data updates accurately

    c. It focuses solely on static data

    d. It requires physical data update mechanisms

45. **What is the potential benefit of using online simulation software for IoT projects in terms of early-stage feedback?**

    a. It does not provide early-stage feedback

    b. It replaces the need for any feedback

    c. It enables quick and informed decision-making based on simulated results

    d. It focuses solely on providing late-stage feedback

46. **How does online simulation software assist in identifying potential bottlenecks in IoT applications involving large-scale data processing?**

    a. It does not consider data processing bottlenecks

    b. It simulates scenarios with artificially added bottlenecks

    c. It simulates data processing scenarios and measures performance

    d. It requires users to identify bottlenecks manually

47. **What is the potential limitation of using online simulation software for IoT projects with unique hardware components?**

    a. It cannot simulate any unique hardware components

    b. It requires custom programming for every unique component

    c. It supports the simulation of only standard hardware components

    d. It replaces the need for any hardware components

48. **How does online simulation software contribute to understanding the behavior of IoT applications under varying loads and stress conditions?**

    a. It does not simulate varying loads and stress conditions

    b. It simulates only ideal load conditions

    c. It simulates different load and stress scenarios to measure performance

    d. It requires users to generate stress conditions manually

49. **What is the potential advantage of using online simulation software for IoT projects regarding resource conservation?**

    a. It increases resource consumption

    b. It requires additional resources

    c. It reduces resource consumption by eliminating the need for physical hardware

    d. It requires the physical presence of resources

50. **How does online simulation software contribute to testing IoT applications' responsiveness to user inputs and commands?**

    a. It does not consider user inputs and commands

    b. It simulates user interactions to measure responsiveness

    c. It only focuses on server-side responsiveness

    d. It requires physical user interactions for testing

51. **How does online simulation software assist in understanding the impact of network latency on IoT applications?**

    a. It does not consider network latency

    b. It simulates only ideal network conditions

    c. It simulates varying network latency scenarios to measure application behavior

    d. It focuses solely on hardware components

52. **Which challenge does online simulation software help address when testing IoT applications involving real-time control and feedback loops?**

    a. It does not address real-time control and feedback loops

    b. Simulating real-time interactions and control loops accurately

    c. It only supports offline simulations

    d. It requires users to control feedback loops manually

53. **What is the potential benefit of using online simulation software for IoT projects in reducing the need for physical space and equipment?**

    a. It increases the need for physical space and equipment

    b. It eliminates the need for any physical space

    c. It reduces the physical space and equipment required for testing

    d. It requires users to set up physical spaces manually

54. **How does online simulation software contribute to understanding the behavior of IoT applications during network outages and disruptions?**

    a. It does not consider network disruptions

    b. It simulates only network stability

    c. It simulates network outages and disruptions to evaluate application behavior

    d. It requires manual disconnection of networks

55. **Which aspect of IoT project development can online simulation software help optimize the efficient use of computational resources?**

    a. Device manufacturing processes

    b. Real-time data visualization

    c. Hardware production costs

    d. Device connectivity challenges

56. **How does online simulation software contribute to testing IoT applications' adaptability to changing environmental conditions?**

    a. It does not consider changing environmental conditions

    b. It simulates only stable environmental conditions

    c. It simulates varying environmental conditions to measure application adaptability

    d. It requires users to change the environmental conditions physically

57. **What is the primary advantage of online simulation software for IoT projects involving device interaction testing across time zones?**

    a. It is not suitable for time zone interaction testing

    b. It replaces the need for any time zone interaction testing

    c. It enables simulation of device interactions across different time zones

    d. It requires physical presence in multiple time zones

58. **How does online simulation software contribute to optimizing IoT applications for different device types and models?**

    a. It does not consider device compatibility

    b. It only supports simulation for specific device models

    c. It simulates interactions between different device types and models

    d. It requires users to have a deep understanding of device compatibility

59. **Which challenge can online simulation software help in addressing when testing IoT applications involving constrained devices with limited resources?**

    a. It cannot address constrained device testing

    b. Simulating interactions with constrained devices accurately

    c. It only focuses on devices with abundant resources

    d. It requires users to adjust device resources manually

60. **What is the potential benefit of using online simulation software for IoT projects regarding accessibility for collaboration?**

    a. It limits collaboration to specific individuals

    b. It requires in-person collaboration

    c. It facilitates collaboration among team members regardless of their physical location

    d. It focuses solely on individual work

61. **How does online simulation software contribute to understanding the behavior of IoT applications during peak usage periods?**

    a. It does not consider peak usage scenarios

    b. It simulates only non-peak usage scenarios

    c. It simulates peak usage scenarios to evaluate application behavior

    d. It requires manual user interactions for testing

62. **Which challenge can online simulation software help in addressing when testing IoT applications involving secure data transmission?**

    a. It cannot address secure data transmission testing

    b. Simulating encrypted data transmission accurately

    c. It only focuses on unsecured data transmission

    d. It requires users to encrypt data manually

63. **What is the potential benefit of using online simulation software for IoT projects in reducing environmental impact?**

    a. It increases the environmental impact

    b. It requires more physical hardware components

    c. It reduces the need for physical hardware components and manufacturing processes

    d. It has no impact on the environment

64. **How does online simulation software contribute to optimizing IoT applications for energy-efficient data transmission?**

    a. It does not contribute to energy-efficient data transmission

    b. It only simulates data transmission with high energy consumption

    c. It simulates various data transmission scenarios to measure energy efficiency

    d. It requires users to optimize data transmission manually

65. **Which challenge does online simulation software help address when testing IoT applications involving frequent firmware updates?**

    a. It does not address firmware update testing

    b. Simulating the entire firmware update process accurately

    c. It only supports firmware updates for specific devices

    d. It requires users to manually update the firmware

66. **What is the potential advantage of using online simulation software for IoT projects in minimizing physical hardware maintenance?**

    a. It increases the need for physical hardware maintenance

    b. It eliminates the need for any physical hardware maintenance

    c. It reduces the frequency of physical hardware maintenance

    d. It requires manual physical hardware maintenance

67. **How does online simulation software assist in understanding the behavior of IoT applications during sudden changes in network conditions?**

    a. It does not consider sudden network changes

    b. It simulates only stable network conditions

    c. It simulates abrupt network changes to evaluate application behavior

    d. It requires users to adjust network conditions manually

68. **Which challenge can online simulation software help in addressing when testing IoT applications involving interoperability between different vendors' devices?**

    a. It cannot address device interoperability testing

    b. Simulating interactions between devices from different vendors accurately

    c. It only focuses on devices from a specific vendor

    d. It requires users to adjust devices for interoperability manually

69. **What is the potential benefit of using online simulation software for IoT projects in terms of minimizing the need for physical space for testing setups?**

    a. It increases the need for physical space

    b. It eliminates the need for any physical space

    c. It reduces the physical space required for testing setups

    d. It requires users to manually set up physical spaces

70. **How does online simulation software contribute to testing IoT applications' performance during periods of high data traffic?**

    a. It does not simulate high data traffic scenarios

    b. It simulates data traffic only during low-traffic periods

    c. It simulates high data traffic scenarios to measure application performance

    d. It requires manual generation of data traffic

71. **Which challenge does online simulation software help in addressing when testing IoT applications involving edge computing scenarios?**

    a. It cannot address edge computing scenarios

    b. Simulating interactions between edge devices and cloud services accurately

    c. It only focuses on cloud computing scenarios

    d. It requires users to manually set up edge computing environments

72. **What is the potential advantage of using online simulation software for IoT projects in terms of iterative testing and optimization?**

    a. It hinders iterative testing and optimization

    b. It eliminates the need for any iterative testing

    c. It supports quick and iterative testing cycles for optimization

    d. It requires users to manually optimize without testing

73. **How does online simulation software assist in understanding the behavior of IoT applications under conditions of limited network connectivity?**

    a. It does not consider limited network connectivity

    b. It simulates only ideal network connectivity

    c. It simulates various network connectivity scenarios with limitations

    d. It requires users to manually configure limited network connectivity

74. **Which challenge can online simulation software help in addressing when testing IoT applications involving user interaction across different devices?**

    a. It cannot address cross-device interaction testing

    b. Simulating user interactions across different devices accurately

    c. It only focuses on device-specific interactions

    d. It requires users to manually interact with devices

75. **What is the potential benefit of using online simulation software for IoT projects in terms of reducing the need for physical travel for testing purposes?**

    a. It increases the need for physical travel

    b. It eliminates the need for any travel

    c. It reduces the need for physical travel for testing by enabling remote simulations

    d. It requires users to travel to the simulation center

76. **How does online simulation software contribute to understanding the behavior of IoT applications during sudden power outages?**

    a. It does not consider power outage scenarios

    b. It simulates power outages to evaluate application behavior

    c. It only focuses on power-availability scenarios

    d. It requires users to manually disconnect power

77. **Which challenge does online simulation software help address when testing IoT applications involving device interactions across different communication protocols?**

    a. It cannot address cross-protocol interactions

    b. Simulating interactions between devices using different communication protocols accurately

    c. It only focuses on devices using a single communication protocol

    d. It requires users to manually adjust communication protocols

78. **What is the potential benefit of using online simulation software for IoT projects in terms of reducing the need for physical device setup and configuration?**

    a. It increases the need for physical device setup and configuration

    b. It eliminates the need for any device setup and configuration

    c. It reduces the need for physical device setup and configuration by using virtual simulations

    d. It requires users to manually set up and configure devices

79. **How does online simulation software assist in optimizing IoT applications for data synchronization between devices?**

    a. It does not assist in data synchronization optimization

    b. It only simulates data synchronization in ideal scenarios

    c. It simulates various data synchronization scenarios to measure application behavior

    d. It requires users to manually synchronize data between devices

80. **Which challenge can online simulation software help in addressing when testing IoT applications involving real-world user interactions?**

    a. It cannot address real-world user interaction testing

    b. Simulating real-world user interactions accurately

    c. It only focuses on simulated user interactions

    d. It requires users to manually interact with simulated devices

81. **What is the potential advantage of using online simulation software for IoT projects in terms of risk management?**

    a. It increases project risks

    b. It eliminates all risks

    c. It aids in identifying and mitigating risks through simulated scenarios

    d. It requires users to manually identify and manage risks

82. **How does online simulation software contribute to testing the scalability of IoT applications involving complex data processing algorithms?**

    a. It does not consider data processing scalability

    b. It simulates data processing only for simple algorithms

    c. It simulates complex data processing scenarios to measure scalability

    d. It requires users to manually adjust data processing algorithms

83. **Which challenge does online simulation software help in addressing when testing IoT applications involving real-time data analytics?**

    a. It cannot address real-time data analytics testing

    b. Simulating real-time data analytics accurately

    c. It only focuses on offline data analysis

    d. It requires users to manually analyze data in real time

84. **What is the potential benefit of using online simulation software for IoT projects in terms of avoiding physical device wear and tear?**

    a. It increases physical device wear and tear

    b. It eliminates the need for any physical devices

    c. It reduces physical device wear and tear by using virtual simulations

    d. It requires users to manually wear out devices

85. **How does online simulation software assist in optimizing IoT applications for low-latency data transmission requirements?**

    a. It does not contribute to low-latency optimization

    b. It only simulates high-latency data transmission scenarios

    c. It simulates various low-latency data transmission scenarios to measure application behavior

    d. It requires users to adjust latency settings manually

86. **Which challenge can online simulation software help address when testing IoT applications involving cross-device compatibility?**

    a. It cannot address cross-device compatibility testing

    b. Simulating cross-device compatibility interactions accurately

    c. It only focuses on device-specific compatibility

    d. It requires users to adjust devices for compatibility manually

87. **What is the potential advantage of using online simulation software for IoT projects in terms of rapid experimentation?**

    a. It hinders rapid experimentation

    b. It eliminates the need for any experimentation

    c. It supports quick and iterative experimentation for optimization

    d. It requires users to experiment with simulation manually

88. **How does online simulation software contribute to testing the reliability of IoT applications involving failover mechanisms?**

    a. It does not contribute to failover testing

    b. It only simulates ideal failover scenarios

    c. It simulates failover scenarios to evaluate application reliability

    d. It requires users to trigger failover mechanisms manually

89. **Which challenge does online simulation software help address when testing IoT applications involving real-time sensor data interpretation?**

    a. It cannot address real-time sensor data interpretation testing

    b. Simulating real-time interpretation of sensor data accurately

    c. It only focuses on offline sensor data analysis

    d. It requires users to interpret sensor data in real-time manually

90. **What is the potential benefit of using online simulation software for IoT projects in terms of minimizing physical hardware maintenance costs?**

    a. It increases physical hardware maintenance costs

    b. It eliminates all hardware maintenance costs

    c. It reduces the frequency and cost of physical hardware maintenance by using virtual simulations

    d. It requires users to perform costly hardware maintenance manually

91. **How does online simulation software contribute to optimizing IoT applications for efficient use of cloud resources?**

    a. It does not contribute to cloud resource optimization

    b. It only simulates cloud resource usage in ideal scenarios

    c. It simulates various cloud resource usage scenarios to measure application behavior

    d. It requires users to adjust cloud resource settings manually

92. **Which challenge can online simulation software help address when testing IoT applications involving cross-platform compatibility?**

    a. It cannot address cross-platform compatibility testing

    b. Simulating cross-platform compatibility interactions accurately

    c. It only focuses on interactions within a single platform

    d. It requires users to adjust platforms for compatibility manually

93. **What is the potential advantage of using online simulation software for IoT projects regarding rapid deployment and testing of new features?**

    a. It slows down the deployment and testing of new features

    b. It eliminates the need for new feature deployment and testing

    c. It accelerates the deployment and testing of new features through simulations

    d. It requires users to deploy and test new features manually

94. **How does online simulation software contribute to testing the reliability of IoT applications involving backup and recovery mechanisms?**

    a. It does not contribute to backup and recovery testing

    b. It only simulates backup and recovery in ideal scenarios

    c. It simulates backup and recovery scenarios to evaluate application reliability

    d. It requires users to trigger backup and recovery mechanisms manually

95. **Which challenge does online simulation software help address when testing IoT applications involving complex business logic?**

    a. It cannot address complex business logic testing

    b. Simulating interactions involving complex business logic accurately

    c. It only focuses on simple business logic scenarios

    d. It requires users to adjust business logic manually

96. **What is the potential benefit of using online simulation software for IoT projects in reducing the time required for testing iterations?**

    a. It increases the time required for testing iterations

    b. It eliminates the need for testing iterations

    c. It shortens the time required for testing iterations by enabling quick simulations

    d. It requires users to conduct lengthy testing iterations manually

97. **How does online simulation software contribute to understanding the behavior of IoT applications under conditions of limited computational resources?**

    a. It does not consider limited computational resource scenarios

    b. It simulates only scenarios with abundant computational resources

    c. It simulates various computational resource limitations to measure application behavior

    d. It requires users to adjust computational resource settings manually

98. **Which challenge can online simulation software help address when testing IoT applications involving sensor calibration and accuracy?**

    a. It cannot address sensor calibration and accuracy testing

    b. Simulating accurate sensor calibration and measurements

    c. It only focuses on sensor data without calibration

    d. It requires users to calibrate sensors manually

99. **What is the potential advantage of using online simulation software for IoT projects in terms of fostering innovation and experimentation?**

    a. It inhibits innovation and experimentation

    b. It eliminates the need for innovation and experimentation

    c. It encourages innovation and experimentation by enabling risk-free simulations

    d. It requires users to innovate and experiment without manually simulating

100. **How does online simulation software contribute to understanding the behavior of IoT applications under conditions of varying data quality and accuracy?**

    a. It does not consider varying data quality scenarios

    b. It simulates data with consistent quality and accuracy

    c. It simulates varying data quality scenarios to measure application behavior

    d. It requires users to adjust data quality settings manually

101. **What does NS-3 stand for?**

    a. Network Simulator 3

    b. Network System 3

    c. Network Simulation 3

    d. Network Service 3

102. **Which language is NS-3 primarily written in?**

    a. Python

    b. Java

    c. C++

    d. JavaScript

103. **NS-3 is an open-source tool for simulating what type of systems?**

    a. Operating systems

    b. Network systems

    c. Database systems

    d. File systems

104. **Which organization primarily maintains NS-3?**

    a. NS-3 Consortium

    b. IEEE

    c. W3C

    d. IETF

105. **What is the primary purpose of NS-3 in IoT?**

    a. Web development

    b. Network simulation

    c. Database management

    d. Operating system development

106. **Which component is used in NS-3 to model IoT devices?**

    a. Node

    b. Router

    c. Link

    d. Switch

107. **In NS-3, what does the term 'node' refer to?**

    a. A physical server

    b. A simulation entity representing a network device

    c. A software package

    d. A database entry

108. Which NS-3 module provides support for Internet Protocol version 6 (IPv6)?

    a. ipv4

    b. ipv6

    c. netanim

    d. wifi

109. Which component in NS-3 simulates network traffic generation?

    a. TrafficGenerator

    b. Application

    c. Packet

    d. Link

110. What is the function of the 'Wi-Fi' module in NS-3?

    a. To model cellular networks

    b. To simulate wireless communication

    c. To handle data storage

    d. To manage power consumption

111. How does NS-3 handle mobility models for IoT devices?

    a. Through static positioning only

    b. Using predefined mobility patterns

    c. By randomizing positions

    d. By integrating with GPS systems

112. What is the primary architectural style used by Zetta IoT for its framework?

    a. Event-driven architecture

    b. RESTful APIs

    c. Microservices architecture

    d. Reactive programming

113. In NS-3, how are network protocols generally added to the simulation?

    a. Through external plugins

    b. By modifying source code

    c. Using built-in modules

    d. By configuring XML files

114. **Which NS-3 component is used to visualize simulation results?**
    a. NetAnim
    b. Gnuplot
    c. Wireshark
    d. Doxygen

115. **What does the NS-3 module 'apps' focus on?**
    a. Physical layer simulations
    b. Application layer simulations
    c. Network layer configurations
    d. Transport layer settings

116. **Which method is used to configure parameters in NS-3?**
    a. Configuration files
    b. Command-line arguments
    c. Code modifications
    d. GUI settings

117. **Which type of simulation does NS-3 support?**
    a. Real-time simulation
    b. Batch simulation
    c. Both real-time and batch simulation
    d. No simulation

118. **What is the purpose of the 'trace' functionality in NS-3?**
    a. To log network traffic
    b. To visualize network topologies
    c. To debug code
    d. To analyze simulation results

119. **How are events scheduled in NS-3 simulations?**
    a. Manually by the user
    b. Automatically by the simulator
    c. Using external scheduling software
    d. By configuring system timers

120. **Which NS-3 module is used for simulating cellular networks?**

   a. lte

   b. wifi

   c. internet

   d. mobile

121. **What type of files are used to define the topology in NS-3?**

   a. XML files

   b. JSON files

   c. TXT files

   d. CSV files

122. **Which NS-3 module provides support for Internet of Things (IoT) communication?**

   a. iot

   b. core

   c. wifi

   d. netanim

123. **What kind of user interface does NS-3 offer for simulations?**

   a. Graphical user interface (GUI)

   b. Command-line interface

   c. Web-based interface

   d. Mobile application interface

124. **What is 'pybindgen' used for in NS-3?**

   a. For integrating Python and C++

   b. For generating configuration files

   c. For creating graphical representations

   d. For managing network nodes

125. **Which NS-3 module is responsible for routing protocols?**

   a. routing

   b. core

   c. ipv4

   d. apps

126. **How does NS-3 support integration with real-world data?**

    a. Through API interfaces

    b. By importing datasets directly

    c. Via external plugins

    d. NS-3 does not support integration

127. **What does 'NetAnim' provide in NS-3 simulations?**

    a. Data analysis tools

    b. Network animation visualization

    c. Protocol debugging

    d. Hardware integration

128. **Which NS-3 module simulates wireless sensor networks?**

    a. sensors

    b. wifi

    c. netanim

    d. iot

129. **In NS-3, how is a custom protocol typically added?**

    a. By modifying existing modules

    b. Through scripting in Python

    c. By developing new modules

    d. Using configuration files

130. **Which tool is commonly used with NS-3 for packet analysis?**

    a. Gnuplot

    b. Wireshark

    c. Excel

    d. Matlab

131. **How are random variables typically managed in NS-3 simulations?**

    a. Through external libraries

    b. Using built-in random number generators

    c. By manually inputting values

    d. NS-3 does not support randomness

132. **Which module in NS-3 is responsible for managing network protocols like TCP/UDP?**

   a. net

   b. apps

   c. core

   d. ipv4

133. **What is the primary output format of NS-3 simulation results?**

   a. XML

   b. JSON

   c. CSV

   d. Binary

134. **Which NS-3 feature helps in debugging and optimizing simulations?**

   a. Profiling tools

   b. Trace files

   c. Code coverage tools

   d. Static analysis tools

135. **What is the role of the 'internet' module in NS-3?**

   a. Simulates physical layer communication

   b. Manages internet layer protocols

   c. Configures wireless settings

   d. Analyzes simulation data

136. **Which module would you use in NS-3 for simulating Bluetooth networks?**

   a. Bluetooth

   b. Wi-Fi

   c. LTE

   d. IoT

137. **How does NS-3 ensure the accuracy of simulations?**

   a. By validating with real-world data

   b. Through peer reviews of the simulation models

   c. By using advanced debugging tools

   d. NS-3 does not ensure accuracy

138. **What type of network topologies can be simulated using NS-3?**

    a. Only linear topologies

    b. Only hierarchical topologies

    c. Various topologies, including mesh and star

    d. Only point-to-point topologies

139. **Which module in NS-3 is used for network visualization?**

    a. visualization

    b. netanim

    c. gnuplot

    d. trace

140. **What does the 'core' module in NS-3 handle?**

    a. Network applications

    b. Core network functionalities and basic protocols

    c. Wireless settings

    d. Simulation results

141. **How does NS-3 support cross-layer design?**

    a. By allowing modules to interact with each other

    b. By segregating functionality into separate files

    c. By using fixed protocol stacks

    d. NS-3 does not support cross-layer design

142. **Which simulation scenario is not typically supported by NS-3?**

    a. Large-scale ad-hoc networks

    b. Real-time system simulations

    c. Internet traffic modeling

    d. Hardware-in-the-loop simulations

143. **What is the NS-3 'wave' module used for?**

    a. Simulating vehicular networks

    b. Managing Wi-Fi connections

    c. Modeling satellite communication

    d. Analyzing waveforms

144. How can users contribute to the development of NS-3?

    a. By submitting code patches

    b. By using the software only

    c. By participating in surveys

    d. By writing documentation

145. Which component is essential for running NS-3 simulations?

    a. A Python interpreter

    b. A C++ compiler

    c. A Java runtime environment

    d. A database management system

146. What is the primary advantage of using NS-3 over NS-2?

    a. NS-3 is more user-friendly

    b. NS-3 offers better performance and modularity

    c. NS-3 has a more extensive set of protocols

    d. NS-3 supports real-time simulations

147. What is the function of the 'visualizer' in NS-3?

    a. To manage simulation parameters

    b. To visualize and analyze network behavior

    c. To simulate network protocols

    d. To generate network topologies

148. Which module in NS-3 is used for modeling network delays?

    a. delay

    b. core

    c. network

    d. wifi

149. How does NS-3 handle high-fidelity simulations?

    a. By using detailed models and accurate parameters

    b. Through simplified models to speed up simulations

    c. By limiting the number of nodes in simulations

    d. By ignoring real-world data

150. **Which module in NS-3 is designed for simulating vehicular networks?**

    a. vehicular

    b. wave

    c. lte

    d. wifi

151. **What does MIMIC stand for in the context of IoT simulation?**

    a. Mobile Internet Management and Integration Control

    b. Multi-layered Integrated Management and Intelligent Control

    c. Multi-purpose Internet and IoT Controller

    d. Management Information Monitoring and Integrated Control

152. **Which company develops the MIMIC IoT Simulator?**

    a. Cisco Systems

    b. Techtopia Inc

    c. Auvik Networks

    d. GNS3 Technologies

153. **What is the primary function of the MIMIC IoT Simulator?**

    a. Network traffic analysis

    b. Network configuration management

    c. Simulation of network devices and IoT environments

    d. Database management

154. **Which protocol does MIMIC IoT Simulator primarily support for IoT device simulation?**

    a. HTTP

    b. MQTT

    c. SNMP

    d. FTP

155. **MIMIC IoT Simulator is typically used for which type of testing?**

    a. Performance testing

    b. Security testing

    c. Network simulation and monitoring

    d. Software development

156. What type of visualization does MIMIC IoT Simulator offer?

    a. 3D network topology maps

    b. Real-time data graphs and charts

    c. Interactive network simulations

    d. Detailed device logs

157. Which of the following is a key feature of MIMIC IoT Simulator?

    a. Real-time network monitoring

    b. Customizable device templates

    c. Cloud-based simulation

    d. Integrated software development environment

158. Can MIMIC IoT Simulator be integrated with other network management tools?

    a. Yes, it supports integration with various network management tools

    b. No, it operates independently

    c. Only with Cisco tools

    d. Only with open-source tools

159. What type of devices can be simulated using MIMIC IoT Simulator?

    a. Only IoT sensors

    b. Routers and switches

    c. End-user devices and servers

    d. A wide range of network devices, including IoT devices

160. Which feature in MIMIC IoT Simulator allows for the simulation of network failures?

    a. Fault Injection

    b. Device Simulation

    c. Traffic Analysis

    d. Performance Monitoring

161. What type of user interface does MIMIC IoT Simulator provide?

    a. Command-line interface

    b. Web-based graphical user interface (GUI)

    c. Text-based interface

    d. API-only interface

162. **Which programming language is used for scripting in the MIMIC IoT Simulator?**

    a. Python

    b. JavaScript

    c. Java

    d. Ruby

163. **How does MIMIC IoT Simulator handle scalability?**

    a. It scales by adding more hardware resources

    b. It scales by adding more virtual devices

    c. It does not support scalability

    d. It scales through cloud integration

164. **Which aspect of IoT networks does MIMIC IoT Simulator focus on?**

    a. IoT device manufacturing

    b. IoT device software development

    c. IoT network simulation and management

    d. IoT data storage

165. **Does MIMIC IoT Simulator support multi-vendor device simulation?**

    a. Yes, it supports multi-vendor device simulation

    b. No, it supports only single-vendor devices

    c. It supports only devices from specific vendors

    d. It requires custom configurations for each vendor

166. **What kind of scenarios can be tested using MIMIC IoT Simulator?**

    a. Network traffic scenarios

    b. IoT device interaction scenarios

    c. Network performance scenarios

    d. All of the above

167. **Which network layer protocols can be simulated using MIMIC IoT Simulator?**

    a. Only application layer protocols

    b. Only transport layer protocols

    c. Multiple network layer protocols

    d. Only Data link layer protocols

168. **Can MIMIC IoT Simulator be used for educational purposes?**

    a. Yes, it is commonly used for educational purposes

    b. No, it is intended only for commercial use

    c. Only in advanced research environments

    d. Only by network professionals

169. **Which type of network topologies can be simulated with MIMIC IoT Simulator?**

    a. Only linear topologies

    b. Only star topologies

    c. Various topologies, including mesh and hybrid

    d. Only point-to-point topologies

170. **What is the role of the MIMIC IoT Simulator's API?**

    a. To integrate with third-party applications

    b. To manage network configurations

    c. To generate simulation reports

    d. To monitor network traffic

171. **Which types of devices can be simulated in the MIMIC IoT Simulator's virtual network?**

    a. Only routers and switches

    b. Only IoT sensors

    c. A variety of network devices, including IoT devices

    d. Only end-user devices

172. **Does MIMIC IoT Simulator support real-time simulation?**

    a. Yes, it supports real-time simulation

    b. No, it only supports batch simulations

    c. It supports simulation in a paused state

    d. Real-time simulation is only available in the professional version

173. **Which type of simulation can be performed with MIMIC IoT Simulator?**

    a. Static network simulation

    b. Dynamic network simulation

    c. Both static and dynamic network simulation

    d. Only static network simulation

174. **What is a key advantage of using MIMIC IoT Simulator over physical testing?**

  a. Higher cost

  b. Greater flexibility and scalability

  c. Increased hardware requirements

  d. Limited to basic scenarios

175. **Can MIMIC IoT Simulator simulate network congestion?**

  a. Yes, it can simulate network congestion

  b. No, it cannot simulate congestion

  c. Only partially

  d. Only in specific network scenarios

176. **Which type of network traffic can be simulated using MIMIC IoT Simulator?**

  a. Only HTTP traffic

  b. Only IoT-specific traffic

  c. Various types of network traffic including IoT and general traffic

  d. Only TCP traffic

177. **What type of reporting does MIMIC IoT Simulator offer?**

  a. Performance reports

  b. Error logs

  c. Detailed simulation reports

  d. All of the above

178. **Which feature allows MIMIC IoT Simulator to simulate multiple IoT devices?**

  a. Device templates

  b. Device virtualization

  c. Device management

  d. Device emulation

179. **How does MIMIC IoT Simulator support network protocol testing?**

  a. By providing pre-built protocol stacks

  b. By allowing custom protocol configuration

  c. Through external protocol testing tools

  d. Only for standard protocols

180. **What is a common use case for MIMIC IoT Simulator?**

    a. Hardware debugging

    b. Network design and testing

    c. Application development

    d. Cloud service management

181. **Does MIMIC IoT Simulator support automation?**

    a. Yes, it supports automation through scripting

    b. No, it requires manual configuration

    c. Only in the professional version

    d. Automation is not supported

182. **Which of the following is a limitation of MIMIC IoT Simulator?**

    a. Limited protocol support

    b. High cost of licensing

    c. Limited scalability

    d. Limited device types

183. **Can MIMIC IoT Simulator be used for multi-site network simulation?**

    a. Yes, it supports multi-site network simulation

    b. No, it only supports single-site simulation

    c. Only with specific configurations

    d. Multi-site simulation is not supported

184. **Which file format is commonly used for importing and exporting network configurations in MIMIC IoT Simulator?**

    a. XML

    b. JSON

    c. CSV

    d. YAML

185. **What kind of network environments can MIMIC IoT Simulator replicate?**

    a. Only enterprise networks

    b. Only residential networks

    c. Various network environments including enterprise, residential, and industrial

    d. Only industrial networks

186. **How does MIMIC IoT Simulator assist in training and development?**

   a. By providing real-world scenarios for hands-on practice

   b. By offering online training modules

   c. Through interactive tutorials

   d. By providing documentation only

187. **Which of the following is a benefit of using MIMIC IoT Simulator?**

   a. Real-time hardware feedback

   b. High cost of implementation

   c. Cost-effective network simulation

   d. Limited protocol support

188. **Can MIMIC IoT Simulator simulate network security features?**

   a. Yes, it can simulate network security features

   b. No, it cannot simulate security features

   c. Only basic security features

   d. Security simulation is only available in the enterprise version

189. **Which of the following best describes MIMIC IoT Simulator's architecture?**

   a. Client-server architecture

   b. Peer-to-peer architecture

   c. Cloud-based architecture

   d. Hybrid architecture

190. **What kind of support is available for MIMIC IoT Simulator users?**

   a. Community forums only

   b. Professional support and documentation

   c. No support available

   d. Support is limited to email only

191. **Which network simulation features are included in MIMIC IoT Simulator?**

   a. Device emulation

   b. Traffic simulation

   c. Network protocol simulation

   d. All of the above

192. How does MIMIC IoT Simulator handle device and network state changes?

    a. Through real-time updates

    b. By requiring manual input

    c. Only during initialization

    d. Through scheduled updates

193. Which user roles are typically involved in using MIMIC IoT Simulator?

    a. Network engineers and administrators

    b. Software developers only

    c. End-users only

    d. Database administrators

194. Can MIMIC IoT Simulator simulate traffic from multiple IoT devices simultaneously?

    a. Yes, it can simulate traffic from multiple devices

    b. No, it can only simulate one device at a time

    c. Only in batch mode

    d. Only with advanced configurations

195. What type of documentation is available for MIMIC IoT Simulator?

    a. Online user guides and manuals

    b. Printed manuals only

    c. Video tutorials only

    d. Limited documentation

196. Which of the following is not a typical application of MIMIC IoT Simulator?

    a. Network performance testing

    b. IoT device development

    c. Network security analysis

    d. Financial forecasting

197. How often is MIMIC IoT Simulator updated?

    a. Annually

    b. Biannually

    c. Regularly, with periodic updates

    d. Only on demand

198. What type of license is typically associated with MIMIC IoT Simulator?

    a. Open-source license

    b. Commercial license

    c. Academic license

    d. Freeware license

199. Which of the following best describes MIMIC IoT Simulator's scalability?

    a. Scalable to meet various network sizes and complexities

    b. Limited to small network simulations

    c. Scalable only through cloud integration

    d. Not scalable

200. How does MIMIC IoT Simulator support network reliability testing?

    a. By simulating network failures and recovery scenarios

    b. By providing real-time network data

    c. By analyzing network performance metrics

    d. By offering detailed device configuration options

201. What is the primary purpose of the Cooja Simulator?

    a. To compile C code

    b. To simulate wireless sensor networks

    c. To design hardware circuits

    d. To manage databases

202. Which programming language is commonly used to write code for the Cooja Simulator?

    a. Python

    b. C

    c. Java

    d. JavaScript

203. What is the name of the network protocol suite used in Cooja simulations?

    a. TCP/IP

    b. Zigbee

    c. 6LoWPAN

    d. MQTT

204. Cooja is primarily used to simulate which type of network?

    a. Cellular networks

    b. Local area networks (LANs)

    c. Wireless sensor networks

    d. Satellite networks

205. Which tool is used to visualize the simulation in Cooja?

    a. Wireshark

    b. Graphical user interface (GUI)

    c. Command line interface (CLI)

    d. Text Editor

206. What does the Cooja Simulator window allow you to do?

    a. Edit code

    b. Manage network traffic

    c. Observe simulation progress and node interactions

    d. Generate reports

207. Which Contiki OS component is typically used with Cooja?

    a. uIP

    b. Rime

    c. IPv6

    d. TelosB

208. In Cooja, what is the role of a node?

    a. To represent a physical device in the simulation

    b. To store data

    c. To compile code

    d. To run a database

209. What type of graphical representation does Cooja provide for nodes?

    a. Bar charts

    b. Network maps

    c. Heat maps

    d. Scatter plots

210. **Which feature in Cooja helps in debugging simulations?**
    a. Logger
    b. Profiler
    c. Trace Analyzer
    d. Event Viewer

211. **Which file format is used for saving Cooja simulation configurations?**
    a. cooja
    b. xml
    c. json
    d. cfg

212. **What is the default simulation time unit in Cooja?**
    a. Seconds
    b. Microseconds
    c. Milliseconds
    d. Hours

213. **Which type of sensor is not typically simulated in Cooja?**
    a. Temperature sensor
    b. Humidity sensor
    c. GPS sensor
    d. Heart rate sensor

214. **What is the role of Contiki OS in Cooja simulations?**
    a. To provide network routing algorithms
    b. To offer a real-time operating system for simulation nodes
    c. To handle user interfaces
    d. To manage hardware drivers

215. **What does the Send button do in the Cooja simulation interface?**
    a. Compiles code
    b. Transmits data from one node to another
    c. Saves the simulation state
    d. Starts the simulation

216. In Cooja, how can you add a new node to the simulation?

    a. By importing a node configuration file

    b. By dragging and dropping from the toolbar

    c. By using the Add Node option in the menu

    d. By modifying the simulation script

217. What type of simulation models can Cooja use?

    a. Single-node models

    b. Multi-node models

    c. Hybrid models

    d. Static models

218. Which component is essential for configuring node behavior in Cooja?

    a. Node Configuration File

    b. Network Simulator

    c. Logger Module

    d. Time Manager

219. What is the purpose of the Simulation tab in Cooja?

    a. To start and stop simulations

    b. To edit node configurations

    c. To analyze simulation results

    d. To manage network settings

220. What does the Log window in Cooja display?

    a. Simulation errors and warnings

    b. Real-time network traffic

    c. Node configuration parameters

    d. Code compilation results

221. What is the function of the Network Setup option in Cooja?

    a. To configure the physical layout of nodes

    b. To define network protocols and parameters

    c. To install the Contiki OS

    d. To set up data logging

222. **How can you observe data transmission between nodes in Cooja?**

    a. By using the network graph

    b. By examining the node logs

    c. By visualizing the node's console output

    d. By analyzing the simulation timeline

223. **What type of environment does Cooja primarily simulate?**

    a. Urban environments

    b. Laboratory environments

    c. Wireless sensor networks

    d. Server environments

224. **Which feature in Cooja allows for a detailed examination of network traffic?**

    a. Network Analyzer

    b. Packet Sniffer

    c. Traffic Monitor

    d. Data Logger

225. **What is the role of the Radio tab in Cooja?**

    a. To set up radio transmission parameters

    b. To adjust the display settings

    c. To configure node storage

    d. To manage user accounts

226. **Which feature in Cooja helps in simulating different radio conditions?**

    a. Radio Propagation Model

    b. Radio Signal Strength Indicator

    c. Radio Frequency Analyzer

    d. Network Interference Simulator

227. **What does the Execution window in Cooja allow you to do?**

    a. Monitor node performance

    b. Edit code in real-time

    c. Visualize simulation results

    d. Control simulation speed

228. Which Cooja tool helps in visualizing the position of nodes in a simulation?

a. Node Map

b. Network Graph

c. Simulation Dashboard

d. Position Tracker

229. What is the Simulation Speed feature in Cooja used for?

a. To adjust how quickly simulation time progresses

b. To compile simulation scripts faster

c. To increase the performance of the simulation

d. To reduce the simulation's memory usage

230. How can you save the state of a Cooja simulation?

a. By using the Save State option

b. By exporting the simulation data

c. By capturing a screenshot

d. By creating a backup file

231. Which type of nodes does Cooja support?

a. Virtual nodes

b. Physical nodes

c. Hybrid nodes

d. All of the above

232. What is the primary advantage of using Cooja for IoT simulations?

a. Real-time hardware interaction

b. Flexibility in simulating large networks

c. Cost-effectiveness

d. High computational power

233. What type of output can you expect from Cooja's simulation results?

a. Graphical visualizations

b. Raw data logs

c. Statistical summaries

d. Both A and B

234. **Which component in Cooja is used to simulate network traffic?**

    a. Traffic Generator

    b. Network Emulator

    c. Packet Sender

    d. Node Communication Module

235. **What does the Debugging feature in Cooja help with?**

    a. Identifying and fixing simulation errors

    b. Optimizing node performance

    c. Enhancing network security

    d. Configuring network protocols

236. **How can you simulate different node behaviors in Cooja?**

    a. By altering node scripts

    b. By adjusting simulation parameters

    c. By using predefined node models

    d. All of the above

237. **What does the Node Manager feature in Cooja do?**

    a. Oversees node configurations and statuses

    b. Manages network settings

    c. Analyzes node performance

    d. Coordinates simulation start and stop

238. **Which simulation feature allows you to view packet exchanges between nodes?**

    a. Packet Viewer

    b. Network Monitor

    c. Communication Log

    d. Data Inspector

239. **In Cooja, what is the role of the Console window?**

    a. To display real-time node outputs

    b. To edit simulation parameters

    c. To configure network settings

    d. To visualize node locations

240. What does the Event Log in Cooja record?

    a. Simulation errors and warnings

    b. Node interaction events

    c. Configuration changes

    d. System performance metrics

241. Which type of network topology can be simulated in Cooja?

    a. Star topology

    b. Mesh topology

    c. Tree topology

    d. All of the above

242. What feature in Cooja helps to analyze the energy consumption of nodes?

    a. Energy Monitor

    b. Power Consumption Analyzer

    c. Battery Status Viewer

    d. Resource Usage Tracker

243. Which type of simulation result can be visualized in Cooja?

    a. Node battery life

    b. Packet delivery ratio

    c. Signal strength

    d. All of the above

244. What does the Simulation Dashboard in Cooja display?

    a. Overall simulation progress and statistics

    b. Detailed node configuration

    c. Network traffic patterns

    d. Compilation errors

245. How can you change the simulation environment in Cooja?

    a. By modifying simulation parameters

    b. By importing different environment models

    c. By adjusting node behaviors

    d. By reconfiguring network settings

246. Which feature in Cooja allows for detailed analysis of network performance?

    a. Network Analyzer

    b. Performance Monitor

    c. Traffic Inspector

    d. Data Logger

247. What is the purpose of the Packet Sniffer in Cooja?

    a. To capture and analyze network packets

    b. To generate random packet traffic

    c. To simulate packet loss

    d. To optimize packet routing

248. Which Cooja feature can be used to simulate various communication protocols?

    a. Protocol Simulator

    b. Communication Model Editor

    c. Network Protocol Manager

    d. Protocol Configuration Tool

249. What is a common use case for the Cooja Simulator in IoT research?

    a. Testing new IoT applications

    b. Evaluating network protocols

    c. Analyzing energy consumption

    d. All of the above

250. Which of the following is not a typical output format from a Cooja simulation?

    a. Graphical plots

    b. Code snippets

    c. Log files

    d. Network statistics

251. What does IoTNetSim primarily simulate?

    a. Web applications

    b. IoT networks

    c. Cloud computing

    d. Database systems

252. **Which protocol is commonly simulated by IoTNetSim for IoT communication?**

    a. HTTP

    b. FTP

    c. MQTT

    d. SMTP

253. **IoTNetSim is most suitable for which of the following tasks?**

    a. Hardware design

    b. Software development

    c. Network simulation

    d. User interface design

254. **Which of the following is a key feature of IoTNetSim?**

    a. Real-time video streaming

    b. Network topology visualization

    c. Financial modeling

    d. Text processing

255. **IoTNetSim supports simulations for which type of network devices?**

    a. Smartphones

    b. IoT devices

    c. Servers

    d. Routers

256. **In IoTNetSim, what does the term 'network topology' refer to?**

    a. The structure of hardware components

    b. The layout of network nodes and connections

    c. The design of user interfaces

    d. The configuration of databases

257. **Which network topology is commonly simulated for IoT networks in IoTNetSim?**

    a. Star topology

    b. Mesh topology

    c. Ring topology

    d. Bus topology

258. **What does 'node density' refer to in IoTNetSim simulations?**

    a. The number of nodes per unit area

    b. The memory capacity of each node

    c. The processing power of each node

    d. The distance between nodes

259. **Which IoTNetSim feature allows users to test various node distributions?**

    a. Node placement configuration

    b. Data packet size

    c. Power consumption

    d. Bandwidth allocation

260. **In IoTNetSim, what does 'node mobility' affect?**

    a. The physical size of the nodes

    b. The speed at which nodes move

    c. The network's communication stability

    d. The energy consumption of nodes

261. **What is the primary purpose of the MQTT protocol in IoTNetSim simulations?**

    a. File transfer

    b. Messaging and communication

    c. Web page rendering

    d. Email delivery

262. **Which protocol does IoTNetSim use for low-power, low-bandwidth scenarios?**

    a. CoAP

    b. HTTP

    c. FTP

    d. SNMP

263. **In IoTNetSim, which protocol is suitable for real-time data streaming?**

    a. TCP

    b. UDP

    c. HTTP

    d. FTP

264. **How does IoTNetSim handle protocol efficiency in simulations?**

    a. By measuring transmission speeds only

    b. By analyzing protocol overhead and latency

    c. By counting the number of protocols used

    d. By simulating hardware performance

265. **Which of the following is not a communication protocol typically simulated in IoTNetSim?**

    a. MQTT

    b. CoAP

    c. BLE

    d. SNMP

266. **What aspect of IoT security is commonly tested in IoTNetSim?**

    a. Encryption algorithms

    b. Physical security measures

    c. User authentication processes

    d. Firewall configurations

267. **Which security protocol is often simulated in IoTNetSim to ensure secure communication?**

    a. SSL/TLS

    b. SSH

    c. IPsec

    d. WEP

268. **How does IoTNetSim help with privacy concerns in simulations?**

    a. By masking user identities

    b. By analyzing data encryption methods

    c. By providing anonymization tools

    d. By simulating user behavior

269. **Which type of attack is IoTNetSim used to simulate in IoT networks?**

    a. Denial of service (DoS)

    b. SQL injection

    c. Phishing

    d. Ransomware

270. **What is one of the primary goals of testing security protocols in IoTNetSim?**

    a. To improve hardware performance

    b. To ensure data integrity and confidentiality

    c. To enhance user interface design

    d. To optimize software compatibility

271. **Which metric is used to measure the efficiency of data transmission in IoTNetSim?**

    a. Packet loss rate

    b. Node battery life

    c. User satisfaction

    d. Storage capacity

272. **In IoTNetSim, what does 'latency' refer to?**

    a. The time taken to process a request

    b. The delay in data packet delivery

    c. The frequency of network disruptions

    d. The rate of data loss

273. **How is 'throughput' defined in IoTNetSim simulations?**

    a. The number of nodes in the network

    b. The amount of data transmitted per unit time

    c. The time taken to establish a connection

    d. The distance covered by data packets

274. **Which factor does not directly affect the performance of an IoT network in IoTNetSim?**

    a. Network topology

    b. Node density

    c. Device color

    d. Communication protocol

275. **What performance issue is indicated by a high packet loss rate in IoTNetSim?**

    a. Efficient network operation

    b. Poor network connectivity

    c. Fast data processing

    d. Low energy consumption

276. **Which scenario might IoTNetSim simulate to test network reliability?**

    a. Device failure

    b. Software updates

    c. User interface changes

    d. Cloud storage usage

277. **In IoTNetSim, which scenario helps evaluate network scalability?**

    a. Adding more nodes to the network

    b. Changing network colors

    c. Adjusting node shapes

    d. Altering user preferences

278. **What is a common scenario for testing network congestion in IoTNetSim?**

    a. Increasing data transmission rates

    b. Decreasing node battery life

    c. Reducing node mobility

    d. Improving data encryption

279. **Which scenario would be used to test the impact of node mobility in IoTNetSim?**

    a. Stationary nodes with fixed positions

    b. Nodes moving randomly within a defined area

    c. Nodes with static data rates

    d. Nodes with constant communication intervals

280. **How does IoTNetSim simulate environmental factors in its scenarios?**

    a. By altering node hardware

    b. By adjusting network topology

    c. By modeling temperature and humidity effects

    d. By changing user interfaces

281. **What advanced feature does IoTNetSim offer for analyzing network performance?**

    a. Real-time traffic analysis

    b. Hardware stress testing

    c. Code debugging

    d. User experience testing

282. **Which feature of IoTNetSim allows for the testing of energy consumption?**

    a. Energy modeling tools

    b. Node placement adjustments

    c. Data encryption settings

    d. User interface modifications

283. **What does the 'network emulation' feature in IoTNetSim enable?**

    a. Testing software compatibility

    b. Simulating real-world network conditions

    c. Designing hardware components

    d. Evaluating user behavior

284. **How can IoTNetSim help in optimizing network protocols?**

    a. By providing protocol comparison tools

    b. By changing hardware configurations

    c. By offering user training sessions

    d. By modifying application code

285. **Which advanced feature of IoTNetSim aids in evaluating the impact of different traffic patterns?**

    a. Traffic pattern simulation

    b. Device color adjustments

    c. Interface customization

    d. Data storage configuration

286. **Which programming language is commonly used for customizing simulations in IoTNetSim?**

    a. JavaScript

    b. Python

    c. HTML

    d. SQL

287. **What type of data does IoTNetSim typically generate for analysis?**

    a. Text files

    b. Graphs and charts

    c. Video files

    d. Audio files

288. **Which user role is primarily responsible for configuring simulations in IoTNetSim?**

    a. Network administrator

    b. Software developer

    c. Data analyst

    d. End user

289. **How can IoTNetSim users share simulation results with colleagues?**

    a. By exporting data files

    b. By sending email attachments

    c. By using social media

    d. By posting on forums

290. **What is the primary purpose of using a simulation tool like IoTNetSim?**

    a. To design physical hardware

    b. To test and optimize network performance

    c. To create marketing materials

    d. To develop user interfaces

291. **What should a user do if they encounter simulation errors in IoTNetSim?**

    a. Restart the software

    b. Consult the documentation

    c. Contact customer support

    d. Update the hardware

292. **Which resource is typically available for troubleshooting IoTNetSim issues?**

    a. User manual

    b. Online forums

    c. Technical support team

    d. All of the above

293. **What is the first step in diagnosing a simulation performance issue in IoTNetSim?**

    a. Check the simulation settings

    b. Upgrade the computer hardware

    c. Change the simulation software

    d. Reinstall the operating system

294. **Where can users find updates and patches for IoTNetSim?**

    a. The official website

    b. Social media channels

    c. User forums

    d. Email newsletters

295. **What is a common reason for slow performance in IoTNetSim simulations?**

    a. High network traffic

    b. Insufficient system resources

    c. Incorrect simulation parameters

    d. Outdated software versions

296. **What type of license is often required to use IoTNetSim for commercial purposes?**

    a. Free trial

    b. Academic license

    c. Professional license

    d. Open-source license

297. **How can users obtain a license for IoTNetSim?**

    a. By contacting the vendor

    b. By downloading from a public repository

    c. By participating in a beta program

    d. By requesting a free demo

298. **Which of the following might be a benefit of using an academic license for IoTNetSim?**

    a. Reduced cost

    b. Unlimited access

    c. Full commercial use rights

    d. Extended support

299. **What is typically included in a professional license for IoTNetSim?**

    a. Limited features

    b. Basic technical support

    c. Full feature set and advanced support

    d. Community forum access only

300. Which organization is likely to offer IoTNetSim licenses?

    a. Academic institutions

    b. Software development companies

    c. Government agencies

    d. IoTNetSim's official website or authorized vendors

301. What is IoTIFY primarily used for?

    a. Web development

    b. IoT simulation and testing

    c. Game development

    d. Cloud storage

302. Which type of simulation does IoTIFY support?

    a. Traffic simulation

    b. Social media simulation

    c. IoT device and network simulation

    d. Virtual reality simulation

303. Which of the following can be simulated using IoTIFY?

    a. IoT devices

    b. IoT networks

    c. Both A and B

    d. None of the above

304. IoTIFY is designed to support which type of testing?

    a. Load testing

    b. Functional testing

    c. Performance testing

    d. All of the above

305. Which protocol is commonly used in IoTIFY simulations?

    a. HTTP

    b. MQTT

    c. FTP

    d. POP3

306. **IoTIFY allows the creation of simulations for how many devices at once?**

   a. 10

   b. 100

   c. 1,000

   d. Thousands

307. **Which feature is crucial for visualizing data in IoTIFY?**

   a. Graphs and charts

   b. Text logs

   c. Audio output

   d. Virtual reality

308. **In IoTIFY, what does a 'scenario' typically represent?**

   a. A device's physical location

   b. A specific use case or environment for simulation

   c. A software bug

   d. A network protocol

309. **Which of the following can IoTIFY simulate in terms of network behavior?**

   a. Latency

   b. Bandwidth

   c. Packet loss

   d. All of the above

310. **What type of user interface does IoTIFY offer?**

   a. Command-line interface

   b. Graphical user interface

   c. Text-based interface

   d. Audio-based interface

311. **IoTIFY's device simulation supports which types of devices?**

   a. Only sensors

   b. Only actuators

   c. Both sensors and actuators

   d. None of the above

312. How does IoTIFY help in performance testing?

    a. By simulating high load conditions

    b. By generating random errors

    c. By creating user interfaces

    d. By managing databases

313. Which of the following is not a common use case for IoTIFY?

    a. IoT device integration testing

    b. Network security auditing

    c. Real-time data visualization

    d. Game development

314. IoTIFY can be used to test which of the following scenarios?

    a. Device communication failures

    b. Network congestion

    c. Data integrity

    d. All of the above

315. What type of data can IoTIFY handle during simulations?

    a. Real-time data

    b. Historical data

    c. Simulated data

    d. All of the above

316. Which of the following protocols is not natively supported by IoTIFY?

    a. MQTT

    b. CoAP

    c. HTTP

    d. POP3

317. Which IoTIFY feature allows you to observe the behavior of devices in a network?

    a. Device emulation

    b. Network simulation

    c. Data visualization

    d. All of the above

318. **What kind of scalability does IoTIFY offer?**
    a. Only small-scale simulations
    b. Only medium-scale simulations
    c. Large-scale simulations with thousands of devices
    d. No scalability

319. **Which of the following is an advantage of using IoTIFY for IoT testing?**
    a. Ability to test real devices in real environments
    b. Cost-effective testing with simulated environments
    c. Limited scalability
    d. Only supports outdated protocols

320. **How does IoTIFY handle network conditions during simulations?**
    a. It ignores network conditions
    b. It provides a predefined set of network conditions
    c. It simulates various network conditions like latency and packet loss
    d. It requires manual network configuration

321. **What is the primary benefit of using IoTIFY for data visualization?**
    a. Real-time graphical representation of data
    b. Static text-based data output
    c. Audio feedback
    d. Virtual reality experience

322. **Which user roles can benefit from IoTIFY?**
    a. Developers
    b. Testers
    c. Network engineers
    d. All of the above

323. **What type of testing environment does IoTIFY provide?**
    a. Virtual environment
    b. Physical environment
    c. Hybrid environment
    d. No testing environment

324. How does IoTIFY facilitate the testing of IoT solutions?

    a. By providing real devices for testing

    b. By offering a simulated environment to model and test IoT systems

    c. By replacing physical sensors with software

    d. By directly connecting to live networks

325. What does IoTIFY's 'Scenario Builder' feature allow users to do?

    a. Build physical devices

    b. Create and configure test scenarios

    c. Write code for device firmware

    d. Manage databases

326. Which type of analytics is commonly used in IoTIFY simulations?

    a. Predictive analytics

    b. Prescriptive analytics

    c. Descriptive analytics

    d. All of the above

327. In IoTIFY, how can users simulate different device behaviors?

    a. By adjusting device settings manually

    b. By using predefined behavior models

    c. By programming device firmware

    d. By connecting to live devices

328. Which of the following does not represent a benefit of IoTIFY?

    a. Cost-effective testing

    b. Ability to test large-scale IoT networks

    c. Real-time device interaction

    d. Customizable testing scenarios

329. What does IoTIFY use to simulate different network topologies?

    a. Network diagrams

    b. Virtual network models

    c. Physical network hardware

    d. Network configuration scripts

330. **Which component is not typically part of an IoTIFY simulation setup?**

    a. Simulation engine

    b. Data visualization tools

    c. Physical network hardware

    d. Device emulators

331. **How does IoTIFY manage simulated device data?**

    a. Through a cloud storage service

    b. By storing data locally

    c. Using an in-built data management system

    d. By sending data to a remote server

332. **Which of the following is a key feature of IoTIFY for testing device communication?**

    a. Real device connectivity

    b. Emulation of device communication protocols

    c. Manual configuration of network settings

    d. Physical network setup

333. **What type of reports can IoTIFY generate after a simulation?**

    a. Performance reports

    b. Error logs

    c. Network traffic reports

    d. All of the above

334. **IoTIFY supports which of the following for data integration?**

    a. API integration

    b. Database integration

    c. File-based integration

    d. All of the above

335. **Which protocol's characteristics are often modeled in IoTIFY simulations?**

    a. HTTP

    b. MQTT

    c. FTP

    d. SMTP

336. What is one of the primary purposes of IoTIFY's 'Network Simulator'?

    a. To test network security

    b. To simulate network traffic patterns

    c. To create network hardware

    d. To configure network switches

337. Which of the following is not a common simulation parameter in IoTIFY?

    a. Device type

    b. Network bandwidth

    c. Device firmware version

    d. Physical location of devices

338. IoTIFY's 'Device Emulator' can simulate which of the following?

    a. Sensor readings

    b. Actuator responses

    c. Device failures

    d. All of the above

339. How does IoTIFY assist in identifying bottlenecks in an IoT system?

    a. By providing real-time alerts

    b. By simulating different system loads and conditions

    c. By monitoring physical devices

    d. By generating error logs only

340. Which of the following is an example of a simulated environment in IoTIFY?

    a. A virtual smart home

    b. A real-world factory floor

    c. An actual hospital network

    d. A physical smart city

341. What is the role of 'Scenario Builder' in IoTIFY?

    a. To construct physical devices

    b. To design and customize simulation scenarios

    c. To write device firmware

    d. To manage real-time data streams

342. Which kind of data does IoTIFY typically visualize?

    a. Network traffic data

    b. Device performance data

    c. Simulation results

    d. All of the above

343. How does IoTIFY contribute to improving IoT system reliability?

    a. By providing real devices for testing

    b. By offering simulations to identify and address issues before deployment

    c. By monitoring live systems

    d. By replacing physical devices

344. Which type of simulation model is not typically supported by IoTIFY?

    a. Sensor models

    b. Actuator models

    c. Physical device models

    d. Network behavior models

345. IoTIFY's 'data visualization' tools are used for:

    a. Displaying real-time simulation metrics

    b. Designing user interfaces

    c. Writing simulation scripts

    d. Configuring physical network equipment

346. Which type of network topology can be simulated in IoTIFY?

    a. Star topology

    b. Mesh topology

    c. Hybrid topology

    d. All of the above

347. What does IoTIFY use to model the behavior of IoT devices?

    a. Physical hardware

    b. Virtual emulators

    c. Manual input

    d. Live device data

348. Which of the following is an IoTIFY simulation feature for network analysis?

    a. Real-time traffic monitoring

    b. Historical data review

    c. Network topology configuration

    d. All of the above

349. What type of feedback can IoTIFY provide during simulations?

    a. Real-time performance feedback

    b. Simulation error reports

    c. Device status updates

    d. All of the above

350. Which aspect of IoTIFY helps in scalability testing?

    a. Device emulator configurations

    b. Network Simulator capacity

    c. Data visualization tools

    d. Scenario building

Join our Discord space

Join our Discord workspace for latest updates, offers, tech happenings around the world, new releases, and sessions with the authors:

https://discord.bpbonline.com

Answer

Q.No.	Answers	Q.No.	Answers	Q.No.	Answers	Q.No.	Answers	Q.No.	Answers
1	c	34	c	67	c	100	c	133	c
2	d	35	d	68	b	101	a	134	b
3	c	36	c	69	c	102	c	135	b
4	c	37	d	70	c	103	b	136	a
5	c	38	a	71	b	104	a	137	b
6	c	39	c	72	c	105	b	138	c
7	d	40	b	73	c	106	a	139	b
8	c	41	c	74	b	107	b	140	b
9	c	42	c	75	c	108	b	141	a
10	a	43	c	76	b	109	b	142	d
11	b	44	b	77	b	110	b	143	a
12	a	45	c	78	c	111	b	144	a
13	b	46	c	79	c	112	c	145	b
14	c	47	a	80	b	113	c	146	b
15	c	48	c	81	c	114	a	147	b
16	c	49	c	82	c	115	b	148	a
17	c	50	b	83	b	116	b	149	a
18	c	51	c	84	c	117	c	150	b
19	c	52	b	85	c	118	a	151	d
20	d	53	c	86	b	119	b	152	c
21	d	54	c	87	c	120	a	153	c
22	b	55	b	88	c	121	a	154	b
23	c	56	c	89	b	122	a	155	c
24	c	57	c	90	c	123	b	156	c
25	b	58	c	91	c	124	a	157	b
26	a	59	b	92	b	125	a	158	a
27	c	60	c	93	c	126	a	159	d
28	d	61	c	94	c	127	b	160	a
29	c	62	b	95	b	128	d	161	b
30	c	63	c	96	c	129	c	162	a
31	c	64	c	97	c	130	b	163	b
32	b	65	b	98	b	131	b	164	c
33	b	66	c	99	c	132	d	165	a

Q.No.	Answers	Q.No.	Answers	Q.No.	Answers	Q.No.	Answers	Q.No.	Answers
166	d	203	c	240	b	277	a	314	d
167	c	204	c	241	d	278	a	315	d
168	a	205	b	242	b	279	b	316	d
169	c	206	c	243	d	280	c	317	d
170	a	207	b	244	a	281	a	318	c
171	c	208	a	245	a	282	a	319	b
172	a	209	b	246	a	283	b	320	c
173	c	210	a	247	a	284	a	321	a
174	b	211	a	248	b	285	a	322	d
175	a	212	c	249	d	286	b	323	a
176	c	213	d	250	b	287	b	324	b
177	d	214	b	251	b	288	a	325	b
178	b	215	b	252	c	289	a	326	c
179	b	216	c	253	c	290	b	327	b
180	b	217	b	254	b	291	b	328	c
181	a	218	a	255	b	292	d	329	b
182	a	219	a	256	b	293	a	330	c
183	a	220	a	257	b	294	a	331	c
184	a	221	b	258	a	295	b	332	b
185	c	222	b	259	a	296	c	333	d
186	a	223	c	260	c	297	a	334	d
187	c	224	b	261	b	298	a	335	b
188	a	225	a	262	a	299	c	336	b
189	a	226	a	263	b	300	d	337	d
190	b	227	a	264	b	301	b	338	d
191	d	228	a	265	d	302	c	339	b
192	a	229	a	266	a	303	c	340	a
193	a	230	a	267	a	304	d	341	b
194	a	231	a	268	b	305	b	342	d
195	a	232	b	269	a	306	d	343	b
196	d	233	d	270	b	307	a	344	c
197	c	234	a	271	a	308	b	345	a
198	b	235	a	272	b	309	d	346	d
199	a	236	d	273	b	310	b	347	b
200	a	237	a	274	c	311	c	348	d
201	b	238	c	275	b	312	a	349	d
202	b	239	a	276	a	313	d	350	b

CHAPTER 6
Offline Simulation Software of IoT

Introduction

As the IoT ecosystem has grown, comprehensive simulation environments are needed to test and verify IoT systems. Many developers and enterprises choose offline simulation software over Internet solutions for flexibility and security. Here is a complete study of offline IoT simulation software:

A modular, component-based C++ simulation toolkit and framework, OMNeT++ is mainly used for constructing network simulators.

Its features are as follows:

- Combining hierarchical models
- Designing networks using a GUI
- Development environment integration

The discrete-event network simulator NS-3 is primarily used for research and teaching.

Its features are as follows:

- Protocol implementation in practice
- Python/C++ development
- Comprehensive documentation and community assistance

Simulink/MATLAB

MATLAB is a powerful technical computer language, whereas Simulink supports multidomain simulation and model-based design. They provide a complete IoT simulation.

Its features are as follows:

- Effective visualization tools
- Signal processing and communications libraries abound
- Connection to real-time testing devices

Contiki

Contiki, an open-source OS for IoT devices, includes a simulator called Cooja to mimic networks of devices.

Its features are as follows:

- Small, low-cost, low-power microcontrollers
- Simulation of multilevel networks
- Real-time OS functions

Ptolemy II

Ptolemy II provides a visual platform for creating complex systems, including IoT. UC Berkeley develops it.

Its features are as follows:

- Design by components
- Visual syntax (AO class definitions)
- Wide range of preset parts

LabVIEW

National Instruments' LabVIEW is a graphical programming environment for system design and IoT simulations.

Its features are as follows:

- Drag-and-drop UI
- Numerous application toolkits
- FPGA and real-time modules support

IoTify

IoTify is a cloud-based IoT simulation tool with an offline version for local simulations.

Its features are as follows:

- Network stress testing
- Simulation of device behaviour
- Integration with key IoT clouds

Multiple choice questions

1. **What is the purpose of using offline simulation software in IoT projects?**

    a. To replace physical devices entirely.

    b. To simulate real-time data transmission.

    c. To avoid the need for simulation altogether.

    d. To simulate IoT scenarios without physical hardware.

2. **Which challenge does offline simulation software help in addressing when testing IoT applications involving constrained devices with limited resources?**

    a. It cannot address constrained device testing.

    b. Simulating interactions with constrained devices accurately.

    c. It only focuses on devices with abundant resources.

    d. It requires users to manually adjust device resources.

3. **How does offline simulation software contribute to understanding the behavior of IoT applications during network outages and disruptions?**

    a. It does not consider network disruptions.

    b. It simulates network outages and disruptions to evaluate application behavior.

    c. It only focuses on network stability.

    d. It requires manual disconnection of networks.

4. **What is the primary advantage of using offline simulation software for IoT projects involving real-world user interactions?**

    a. It is not suitable for real-world user interaction testing.

    b. It replaces the need for any real-world user interactions.

    c. It enables realistic simulation of user interactions without physical devices.

    d. It requires users to manually interact with physical devices.

5. **Which aspect of IoT project development can offline simulation software help in optimizing for efficient resource utilization?**

   a. Device manufacturing processes

   b. Real-time data visualization

   c. Hardware production costs

   d. Device connectivity challenges

6. **How does offline simulation software contribute to testing IoT applications' responsiveness to user inputs and commands?**

   a. It does not consider user inputs and commands.

   b. It simulates user interactions to measure responsiveness.

   c. It only focuses on server-side responsiveness.

   d. It requires manual interactions for testing.

7. **What is the potential advantage of using offline simulation software for IoT projects in terms of iterative testing and optimization?**

   a. It hinders iterative testing and optimization.

   b. It eliminates the need for any iterative testing.

   c. It supports quick and iterative testing cycles for optimization.

   d. It requires users to manually optimize without testing.

8. **How does offline simulation software assist in understanding the behavior of IoT applications during network latency variations?**

   a. It does not consider network latency variations.

   b. It simulates ideal network conditions only.

   c. It simulates varying network latency scenarios to measure application behavior.

   d. It requires manual configuration of network latency.

9. **Which challenge can offline simulation software help in addressing when testing IoT applications involving real-time control and feedback loops?**

   a. It does not address real-time control and feedback loops.

   b. Simulating real-time interactions and control loops accurately.

   c. It only supports offline simulations.

   d. It requires users to manually control feedback loops.

10. **What is the potential benefit of using offline simulation software for IoT projects in terms of minimizing physical hardware prototypes?**

    a. It requires more physical prototypes.

    b. It has no impact on physical prototypes.

    c. It eliminates the need for physical prototypes entirely.

    d. It increases the complexity of physical prototypes.

11. **How does offline simulation software contribute to understanding the behavior of IoT applications during peak usage periods?**

    a. It does not simulate peak usage scenarios.

    b. It simulates peak usage scenarios to evaluate application behavior.

    c. It only focuses on non-peak usage scenarios.

    d. It requires manual user interactions for testing.

12. **Which challenge does offline simulation software help in addressing when testing IoT applications involving secure data transmission?**

    a. It cannot address secure data transmission testing.

    b. Simulating encrypted data transmission accurately.

    c. It only focuses on unsecured data transmission.

    d. It requires users to encrypt data manually.

13. **What is the potential advantage of offline simulation software for IoT projects to reduce the need for physical device setup and configuration?**

    a. It increases the need for physical device setup and configuration.

    b. It eliminates the need for any device setup and configuration.

    c. It reduces the need for physical device setup and configuration by using virtual simulations.

    d. It requires users to set up and configure devices manually.

14. **How does offline simulation software contribute to optimizing IoT applications for different device types and models?**

    a. It does not consider device compatibility.

    b. It only supports simulation for specific device models.

    c. It simulates interactions between different device types and models.

    d. It requires users to have a deep understanding of device compatibility.

15. **Which challenge can offline simulation software help in addressing when testing IoT applications involving cross-platform compatibility?**

    a. It cannot address cross-platform compatibility testing.

    b. Simulating cross-platform compatibility interactions accurately.

    c. It only focuses on interactions within a single platform.

    d. It requires users to adjust platforms for compatibility manually.

16. **What is the potential benefit of using offline simulation software for IoT projects regarding risk management?**

    a. It increases project risks.

    b. It eliminates all risks.

    c. It aids in identifying and mitigating risks through simulated scenarios.

    d. It requires users to identify and manage risks manually.

17. **How does offline simulation software contribute to testing the reliability of IoT applications involving backup and recovery mechanisms?**

    a. It does not contribute to backup and recovery testing.

    b. It simulates backup and recovery scenarios to evaluate application reliability.

    c. It only focuses on ideal scenarios without backup and recovery.

    d. It requires users to manually trigger backup and recovery mechanisms.

18. **Which challenge can offline simulation software help in addressing when testing IoT applications involving frequent firmware updates?**

    a. It does not address firmware update testing.

    b. Simulating the entire firmware update process accurately.

    c. It only supports firmware updates for specific devices.

    d. It requires users to update firmware manually.

19. **What is the potential advantage of offline simulation software for IoT projects in minimizing physical hardware maintenance?**

    a. It increases the need for physical hardware maintenance.

    b. It eliminates the need for any physical hardware maintenance.

    c. It reduces the frequency of physical hardware maintenance.

    d. It requires manual physical hardware maintenance.

20. **How does offline simulation software contribute to testing IoT applications' performance during periods of high data traffic?**

    a. It does not simulate high data traffic scenarios.

    b. It simulates data traffic only during low-traffic periods.

    c. It simulates high-data traffic scenarios to measure application performance.

    d. It requires manual generation of data traffic.

21. **Which challenge does offline simulation software help address when testing IoT applications involving interoperability between different vendors' devices?**

    a. It cannot address device interoperability testing.

    b. Simulating interactions between devices from different vendors accurately.

    c. It only focuses on devices from a specific vendor.

    d. It requires users to adjust devices for interoperability manually.

22. **What is the potential benefit of using offline simulation software for IoT projects regarding rapid deployment and testing of new features?**

    a. It slows down the deployment and testing of new features.

    b. It eliminates the need for new feature deployment and testing.

    c. It accelerates the deployment and testing of new features through simulations.

    d. It requires users to deploy and test new features manually.

23. **How does offline simulation software assist in understanding the behavior of IoT applications under conditions of varying data quality and accuracy?**

    a. It does not consider varying data quality scenarios.

    b. It simulates data with consistent quality and accuracy.

    c. It simulates varying data quality scenarios to measure application behavior.

    d. It requires users to adjust data quality settings manually.

24. **Which challenge can offline simulation software help in addressing when testing IoT applications involving energy-efficient data transmission?**

    a. It cannot address energy-efficient data transmission testing.

    b. Simulating various data transmission scenarios to measure energy efficiency.

    c. It only focuses on data transmission with high energy consumption.

    d. It requires users to optimize data transmission manually.

25. **What is the potential advantage of using offline simulation software for IoT projects to minimize the need for physical travel for testing purposes?**

    a. It increases the need for physical travel.

    b. It eliminates the need for any travel.

    c. It reduces the need for physical travel for testing by enabling offline simulations.

    d. It requires users to travel to the simulation centre.

26. **How does offline simulation software contribute to optimizing IoT applications for low-latency data transmission requirements?**

    a. It does not contribute to low-latency optimization.

    b. It only simulates data transmission with high latency.

    c. It simulates various low-latency data transmission scenarios to measure application behavior.

    d. It requires users to manually adjust latency settings.

27. **Which challenge can offline simulation software help in addressing when testing IoT applications involving device interactions across different communication protocols?**

    a. It cannot address cross-protocol interactions.

    b. Simulating interactions between devices using different communication protocols accurately.

    c. It only focuses on devices using a single communication protocol.

    d. It requires users to adjust communication protocols manually.

28. **What is the potential benefit of using offline simulation software for IoT projects in terms of fostering innovation and experimentation?**

    a. It inhibits innovation and experimentation.

    b. It eliminates the need for innovation and experimentation.

    c. It encourages innovation and experimentation through risk-free simulations.

    d. It requires users to manually innovate and experiment without simulation.

29. **How does offline simulation software contribute to testing the reliability of IoT applications involving failover mechanisms?**

    a. It does not contribute to failover testing.

    b. It simulates ideal failover scenarios only.

    c. It simulates failover scenarios to evaluate application reliability.

    d. It requires users to manually trigger failover mechanisms.

30. **Which challenge does offline simulation software help in addressing when testing IoT applications involving real-time sensor data interpretation?**

    a. It cannot address real-time sensor data interpretation testing.

    b. Simulating real-time interpretation of sensor data accurately.

    c. Only focuses on offline sensor data analysis.

    d. It requires users to manually interpret sensor data in real time.

31. **What is the potential advantage of using offline simulation software for IoT projects in optimising energy-efficient data transmission?**

    a. It increases energy consumption during simulation.

    b. It eliminates the need for energy-efficient optimization.

    c. It simulates various energy-efficient data transmission scenarios.

    d. It requires users to optimize data transmission manually.

32. **How does offline simulation software assist in understanding the behavior of IoT applications during sudden power outages?**

    a. It does not consider power outage scenarios.

    b. It simulates power outages to evaluate application behavior.

    c. It only focuses on power-availability scenarios.

    d. It requires users to manually disconnect power.

33. **Which challenge can offline simulation software help in addressing when testing IoT applications involving cross-device compatibility?**

    a. It cannot address cross-device compatibility testing.

    b. Simulating cross-device compatibility interactions accurately.

    c. It only focuses on device-specific compatibility.

    d. It requires users to manually adjust devices for compatibility.

34. **What is the potential benefit of using offline simulation software for IoT projects in terms of reducing the time required for testing iterations?**

    a. It increases the time required for testing iterations.

    b. It eliminates the need for testing iterations.

    c. It shortens the time required for testing iterations by enabling offline simulations.

    d. It requires users to manually conduct lengthy testing iterations.

35. **How does offline simulation software contribute to testing IoT applications involving real-time analytics?**

    a. It does not contribute to real-time analytics testing.

    b. It simulates real-time data analysis accurately.

    c. It only focuses on offline data analytics.

    d. It requires manual data analysis for testing.

36. **Which challenge does offline simulation software help address when testing IoT applications involving sensor calibration and accuracy?**

    a. It cannot address sensor calibration and accuracy testing.

    b. Simulating accurate sensor calibration and measurements.

    c. It only focuses on sensor data without calibration.

    d. It requires users to calibrate sensors manually.

37. **What is the potential advantage of using offline simulation software for IoT projects in terms of minimizing physical device wear and tear?**

    a. It increases physical device wear and tear.

    b. It eliminates the need for any physical devices.

    c. It reduces physical device wear and tear by using virtual simulations.

    d. It requires users to wear out devices manually.

38. **How does offline simulation software contribute to understanding the behavior of IoT applications during sudden changes in network conditions?**

    a. It does not consider sudden network changes.

    b. It simulates only stable network conditions.

    c. It simulates abrupt network changes to evaluate application behavior.

    d. It requires users to adjust network conditions manually.

39. **Which challenge can offline simulation software help in addressing when testing IoT applications involving edge computing scenarios?**

    a. It cannot address edge computing scenarios.

    b. Simulating interactions between edge devices and cloud services accurately.

    c. It only focuses on cloud computing scenarios.

    d. It requires users to set up edge computing environments manually.

40. **What is the potential benefit of using offline simulation software for IoT projects in terms of minimizing physical space requirements for testing setups?**

    a. It increases the need for physical space.

    b. It eliminates the need for any physical space.

    c. It reduces the physical space required for testing setups.

    d. It requires users to manually set up physical spaces.

41. **How does offline simulation software contribute to optimizing IoT applications for efficient utilization of cloud resources?**

    a. It does not contribute to cloud resource optimization.

    b. It only simulates cloud resource usage in ideal scenarios.

    c. It simulates various cloud resource usage scenarios to measure application behavior.

    d. It requires users to adjust cloud resource settings manually.

42. **Which challenge can offline simulation software help in addressing when testing IoT applications involving real-time data synchronization?**

    a. It cannot address real-time data synchronization testing.

    b. Simulating real-time data synchronization accurately.

    c. It only focuses on offline data synchronization.

    d. It requires users to synchronize data manually.

43. **What is the potential advantage of using offline simulation software for IoT projects in terms of reducing the need for physical travel for testing purposes?**

    a. It increases the need for physical travel.

    b. It eliminates the need for any travel.

    c. It reduces the need for physical travel for testing by enabling offline simulations.

    d. It requires users to travel to the simulation center.

44. **How does offline simulation software contribute to testing the scalability of IoT applications involving complex data processing algorithms?**

    a. It does not consider data processing scalability.

    b. It simulates data processing only for simple algorithms.

    c. It simulates complex data processing scenarios to measure scalability.

    d. It requires users to adjust data processing algorithms manually.

45. **Which challenge does offline simulation software help address when testing IoT applications involving energy-efficient communication protocols?**

    a. It cannot address energy-efficient protocol testing.

    b. Simulating various communication protocols to measure energy efficiency.

    c. It only focuses on high-energy-consumption protocols.

    d. It requires users to manually adjust communication protocols.

46. **What is the primary purpose of using offline simulation software for IoT projects involving complex network topologies?**

    a. To avoid the need for network topologies.

    b. To simulates simplified network topologies.

    c. To simulate and evaluate complex network topologies.

    d. To eliminate the complexity of network topologies.

47. **How does offline simulation software contribute to optimizing IoT applications for optimal utilization of device resources?**

    a. It does not contribute to device resource optimization.

    b. It only simulates scenarios with resource over utilization.

    c. It simulates various resource utilization scenarios to measure application behavior.

    d. It requires users to adjust resource settings manually.

48. **Which challenge can offline simulation software help address when testing IoT applications involving secure device authentication?**

    a. It cannot address secure device authentication testing.

    b. Simulating secure device authentication accurately.

    c. It only focuses on unauthenticated devices.

    d. It requires users to authenticate devices manually.

49. **Which programming language is primarily used to develop IoT solutions with Particle?**

    a. Python

    b. C++

    c. JavaScript

    d. Java

50. **How does offline simulation software assist in understanding the behavior of IoT applications during dynamic changes in data volume and velocity?**

    a. It does not consider changes in data volume and velocity.

    b. It simulates only static data volume and velocity scenarios.

    c. It simulates dynamic changes in data volume and velocity to measure application behavior.

    d. It requires users to manually adjust data volume and velocity settings.

51. **What is the potential advantage of using offline simulation software for IoT projects in terms of optimizing the utilization of edge computing resources?**

    a. It increases the consumption of edge computing resources.

    b. It eliminates the need for any edge computing resources.

    c. It simulates various edge computing scenarios to measure resource utilization.

    d. It requires users to optimize edge computing resource usage manually.

52. **How does offline simulation software contribute to testing the reliability of IoT applications involving device interactions in isolated environments?**

    a. It does not consider isolated environment testing.

    b. It simulates isolated environment scenarios to evaluate application behavior.

    c. It only focuses on non-isolated environment interactions.

    d. It requires users to set up isolated environments manually.

53. **Which challenge can offline simulation software help in addressing when testing IoT applications involving data synchronization across multiple geographies?**

    a. It cannot address multi-geography data synchronization testing.

    b. Simulating data synchronization across multiple geographies accurately.

    c. It only focuses on local data synchronization.

    d. It requires users to manually synchronize data across geographies.

54. **What is the primary purpose of using offline simulation software for IoT projects involving predictive maintenance scenarios?**

    a. To eliminate the need for predictive maintenance.

    b. To simulate ideal predictive maintenance scenarios.

    c. To simulate and evaluate predictive maintenance scenarios.

    d. To minimize the complexity of predictive maintenance.

55. **How does offline simulation software contribute to testing the security of IoT applications involving encryption and decryption mechanisms?**

    a. It does not contribute to encryption and decryption testing.

    b. It simulates secure communication scenarios to measure security behavior.

    c. It only focuses on unsecured communication scenarios.

    d. It requires users to encrypt manually and decrypt data.

56. **Which challenge can offline simulation software help in addressing when testing IoT applications involving resource allocation and load balancing?**

    a. It cannot address resource allocation and load-balancing testing.

    b. Simulating accurate resource allocation and load balancing scenarios.

    c. It only focuses on resource overallocation.

    d. It requires users to allocate resources manually.

57. **What is the potential benefit of using offline simulation software for IoT projects in terms of minimizing the risk of real-world device failures during testing?**

    a. It increases the risk of device failures.

    b. It eliminates the need for device failure testing.

    c. It reduces the risk of real-world device failures during testing through virtual simulations.

    d. It requires users to trigger device failures manually.

58. **How does offline simulation software contribute to understanding the behavior of IoT applications during sudden changes in user behavior?**

    a. It does not consider changes in user behavior.

    b. It simulates sudden changes in user behavior to evaluate application behavior.

    c. It only focuses on stable user behavior scenarios.

    d. It requires users to manually change their behavior.

59. **Which aspect of IoT project development can offline simulation software help in optimizing for efficient use of computational resources?**

    a. Network topology design

    b. Energy-efficient communication

    c. Device firmware updates

    d. Sensor data accuracy

60. **What is the primary benefit of using offline simulation software for IoT projects involving machine learning algorithms?**

   a. It eliminates the need for machine learning algorithms.

   b. It simulates ideal machine-learning scenarios.

   c. It simulates and evaluates machine learning algorithms' behavior.

   d. It reduces the complexity of machine learning algorithms.

61. **How does offline simulation software contribute to optimizing IoT applications for low-latency communication between devices?**

   a. It does not contribute to low-latency communication optimization.

   b. It simulates low-latency communication scenarios to measure application behavior.

   c. It only focuses on high-latency communication.

   d. It requires users to adjust communication latency manually.

62. **Which challenge can offline simulation software help in addressing when testing IoT applications involving real-time data aggregation and analysis?**

   a. It cannot address real-time data aggregation and analysis testing.

   b. Simulating real-time data aggregation and analysis accurately.

   c. It only focuses on offline data aggregation and analysis.

   d. It requires users to manually aggregate and analyze data.

63. **What is the potential advantage of using offline simulation software for IoT projects in terms of minimizing the need for physical hardware prototypes?**

   a. It requires more physical prototypes.

   b. It has no impact on physical prototypes.

   c. It eliminates the need for physical prototypes entirely.

   d. It increases the complexity of physical prototypes.

64. **How does offline simulation software contribute to testing the scalability of IoT applications involving cloud-based data storage and retrieval?**

   a. It does not consider cloud scalability scenarios.

   b. It simulates cloud data storage and retrieval only for small-scale scenarios.

   c. It simulates cloud scalability scenarios to measure application behavior.

   d. It requires users to manually adjust cloud scalability settings.

65. **Which challenge does offline simulation software help in addressing when testing IoT applications involving real-time data visualization?**

    a. It cannot address real-time data visualization testing.

    b. Simulating real-time data visualization accurately.

    c. It only focuses on offline data visualization.

    d. It requires users to manually visualize data in real time.

66. **What is the potential benefit of using offline simulation software for IoT projects in terms of enhancing the testing of fault tolerance mechanisms?**

    a. It reduces fault tolerance testing effectiveness.

    b. It eliminates the need for fault tolerance testing.

    c. It enhances fault tolerance testing through simulated fault scenarios.

    d. It requires users to introduce faults manually.

67. **How does offline simulation software assist in understanding the behavior of IoT applications during variations in network bandwidth?**

    a. It does not consider network bandwidth variations.

    b. It simulates varying network bandwidth scenarios to measure application behavior.

    c. It only focuses on stable network bandwidth conditions.

    d. It requires users to adjust network bandwidth manually.

68. **Which challenge can offline simulation software help in addressing when testing IoT applications involving reliable data storage and retrieval mechanisms?**

    a. It cannot address reliable data storage and retrieval testing.

    b. Simulating reliable data storage and retrieval scenarios accurately.

    c. It only focuses on unreliable data storage and retrieval.

    d. It requires users to manually store and retrieve data.

69. **What is the potential advantage of using offline simulation software for IoT projects in terms of minimizing the time required for testing various scenarios?**

    a. It increases the time required for scenario testing.

    b. It eliminates the need for scenario testing.

    c. It reduces the time required for scenario testing by enabling simulations.

    d. It requires users to manually test scenarios without simulation.

70. **How does offline simulation software contribute to testing the resilience of IoT applications during sudden spikes in user activity?**

    a. It does not consider spikes in user activity.

    b. It simulates user activity spikes to evaluate application resilience.

    c. It only focuses on user activity during normal scenarios.

    d. It requires users to simulate spikes in user activity manually.

71. **Which challenge does offline simulation software help address when testing IoT applications involving real-time location tracking?**

    a. It cannot address real-time location tracking testing.

    b. Simulating real-time location tracking accurately.

    c. It only focuses on offline location tracking.

    d. It requires users to manually track locations in real time.

72. **What is the potential benefit of using offline simulation software for IoT projects in terms of minimizing the need for physical hardware setup for testing?**

    a. It increases the need for physical hardware setup.

    b. It eliminates the need for any physical hardware setup.

    c. It reduces the need for physical hardware setup by using virtual simulations.

    d. It requires users to set up physical hardware manually.

73. **How does offline simulation software contribute to testing IoT applications involving adaptive learning algorithms?**

    a. It does not contribute to adaptive learning algorithm testing.

    b. It simulates only fixed learning algorithms.

    c. It simulates and evaluates adaptive learning algorithm behavior.

    d. It requires users to manually adjust learning algorithms.

74. **Which challenge can offline simulation software help in addressing when testing IoT applications involving seamless device handoff between networks?**

    a. It cannot address seamless device handoff testing.

    b. Simulating seamless device handoff accurately.

    c. It only focuses on non-seamless device handoff scenarios.

    d. It requires users to manually perform device handoffs.

75. **What is the primary purpose of using offline simulation software for IoT projects involving data aggregation from various sources?**

    a. To avoid the need for data aggregation.

    b. To simulate ideal data aggregation scenarios.

    c. To simulate and evaluate data aggregation scenarios.

    d. To simplify the complexity of data aggregation.

76. **How does offline simulation software contribute to understanding the behavior of IoT applications during sudden changes in environmental conditions?**

    a. It does not consider changes in environmental conditions.

    b. It simulates sudden changes in environmental conditions to evaluate application behavior.

    c. It only focuses on stable environmental conditions.

    d. It requires users to change environmental conditions manually.

77. **Which challenge does offline simulation software help address when testing IoT applications involving real-time analytics and decision-making?**

    a. It cannot address real-time analytics and decision-making testing.

    b. Simulating real-time analytics and decision-making accurately.

    c. It only focuses on offline analytics and decision-making.

    d. It requires users to manually perform real-time analytics and decision-making.

78. **What is the potential advantage of using offline simulation software for IoT projects in terms of minimizing the need for physical device recalibration?**

    a. It increases the need for device recalibration.

    b. It eliminates the need for any device recalibration.

    c. It reduces the frequency of device recalibration by using virtual simulations.

    d. It requires users to recalibrate devices manually.

79. **How does offline simulation software assist in optimizing IoT applications for energy-efficient data storage and retrieval mechanisms?**

    a. It does not assist in energy-efficient data storage and retrieval optimization.

    b. It simulates energy-efficient data storage and retrieval scenarios to measure application behavior.

    c. It only focuses on energy-intensive data storage and retrieval.

    d. It requires users to manually adjust data storage and retrieval mechanisms.

80. **Which challenge can offline simulation software help address when testing IoT applications involving seamless integration with existing IT systems?**

    a. It cannot address integration testing with existing IT systems.

    b. Simulating seamless integration accurately with existing IT systems.

    c. It only focuses on isolated application scenarios.

    d. It requires users to integrate systems manually.

81. **What is the potential benefit of using offline simulation software for IoT projects in terms of minimizing the risk of data privacy breaches during testing?**

    a. It increases the risk of data privacy breaches.

    b. It eliminates the need for data privacy testing.

    c. It reduces the risk of data privacy breaches during testing through simulated scenarios.

    d. It requires users to breach data privacy manually.

82. **How does offline simulation software contribute to understanding the behavior of IoT applications during sudden changes in communication protocols?**

    a. It does not consider changes in communication protocols.

    b. It simulates sudden changes in communication protocols to evaluate application behavior.

    c. It only focuses on stable communication protocol scenarios.

    d. It requires users to manually adjust communication protocols.

83. **Which aspect of IoT project development can offline simulation software help in optimizing for enhanced security mechanisms?**

    a. Device connectivity

    b. Data transmission speed

    c. Resource allocation

    d. Secure communication protocols

84. **What is the primary benefit of using offline simulation software for IoT projects involving dynamic reconfiguration of device networks?**

    a. It eliminates the need for dynamic reconfiguration testing.

    b. It simulates ideal dynamic reconfiguration scenarios.

    c. It simulates and evaluates dynamic reconfiguration behavior.

    d. It simplifies the complexity of dynamic reconfiguration.

85. **How does offline simulation software contribute to optimizing IoT applications for optimal utilization of cloud resources during traffic peaks?**

    a. It does not contribute to cloud resource optimization during traffic peaks.

    b. It simulates cloud resource usage only during low-traffic periods.

    c. It simulates cloud resource usage during traffic peaks to measure application behavior.

    d. It requires users to adjust cloud resource settings manually.

86. **Which challenge can offline simulation software help in addressing when testing IoT applications involving seamless integration with legacy systems?**

    a. It cannot address integration with legacy systems.

    b. Simulating seamless integration with legacy systems accurately.

    c. It only focuses on integration with modern systems.

    d. It requires users to integrate legacy systems manually.

87. **What is the potential advantage of using offline simulation software for IoT projects in terms of reducing the need for physical travel for testing purposes?**

    a. It increases the need for physical travel.

    b. It eliminates the need for any travel.

    c. It reduces the need for physical travel for testing by enabling offline simulations.

    d. It requires users to travel to the simulation center.

88. **How does offline simulation software contribute to testing the reliability of IoT applications involving device interactions with intermittent connectivity?**

    a. It does not contribute to intermittent connectivity testing.

    b. It simulates intermittent connectivity scenarios to evaluate application behavior.

    c. It only focuses on continuous connectivity scenarios.

    d. It requires users to manually disconnect devices intermittently.

89. **Which challenge does offline simulation software help address when testing IoT applications involving real-time response to critical events?**

    a. It cannot address real-time response testing.

    b. Simulating real-time response accurately to critical events.

    c. It only focuses on non-critical event response.

    d. It requires users to trigger critical events manually.

90. **What is the potential benefit of using offline simulation software for IoT projects in terms of reducing the need for physical device configuration for testing?**

    a. It increases the need for physical device configuration.

    b. It eliminates the need for any device configuration.

    c. It reduces the need for physical device configuration through virtual simulations.

    d. It requires users to manually configure devices.

91. **How does offline simulation software contribute to understanding the behavior of IoT applications during sudden changes in device traffic patterns?**

    a. It does not consider changes in device traffic patterns.

    b. It simulates sudden changes in device traffic patterns to evaluate application behavior.

    c. It only focuses on stable device traffic patterns.

    d. It requires users to manually adjust device traffic patterns.

92. **Which aspect of IoT project development can offline simulation software help in optimizing for data integrity and security during transmission?**

    a. Device compatibility

    b. Energy-efficient communication

    c. Device firmware updates

    d. Encryption mechanisms

93. **What is the primary purpose of using offline simulation software for IoT projects involving real-time event detection and response?**

    a. To avoid the need for real-time event detection and response.

    b. To simulate ideal real-time event scenarios.

    c. To simulate and evaluate real-time event detection and response scenarios.

    d. To minimize the complexity of real-time event detection.

94. **How does offline simulation software contribute to optimizing IoT applications for efficient utilization of sensor data for decision-making?**

    a. It does not contribute to sensor data utilization optimization.

    b. It simulates sensor data utilization scenarios to measure application behavior.

    c. It only focuses on sensor data storage.

    d. It requires users to adjust sensor data utilization settings manually.

95. **Which challenge can offline simulation software help address when testing IoT applications involving seamless device handover between access points?**

    a. It cannot address seamless device handover testing.

    b. Simulating seamless device handover accurately between access points.

    c. It only focuses on non-seamless device handover scenarios.

    d. It requires users to perform device handovers manually.

96. **What is the potential advantage of using offline simulation software for IoT projects in terms of reducing the need for physical device maintenance during testing?**

    a. It increases the need for physical device maintenance.

    b. It eliminates the need for any physical device maintenance.

    c. It reduces the frequency of physical device maintenance by using virtual simulations.

    d. It requires users to manually maintain physical devices.

97. **How does offline simulation software contribute to testing the scalability of IoT applications involving data aggregation across distributed devices?**

    a. It does not consider data aggregation scalability testing.

    b. It simulates data aggregation across a few distributed devices only.

    c. It simulates data aggregation scalability scenarios to measure application behavior.

    d. It requires users to manually aggregate data across distributed devices.

98. **Which challenge does offline simulation software help address when testing IoT applications involving real-time communication between devices and cloud services?**

    a. It cannot address real-time communication testing.

    b. Simulating real-time communication accurately between devices and cloud services.

    c. It only focuses on non-real-time communication scenarios.

    d. It requires users to establish communication manually.

99. **What is the potential benefit of using offline simulation software for IoT projects in terms of reducing the need for physical device deployment for testing?**

    a. It increases the need for physical device deployment.

    b. It eliminates the need for any physical device deployment.

    c. It reduces the need for physical device deployment through virtual simulations.

    d. It requires users to manually deploy physical devices.

100. **How does offline simulation software assist in optimizing IoT applications for low-latency response to user commands?**

    a. It does not assist in low-latency response optimization.

    b. It simulates low-latency response scenarios to measure application behavior.

    c. It only focuses on high-latency response scenarios.

    d. It requires users to manually adjust response latency.

101. **Which MATLAB function is used to create a Simulink model?**

    a. sim

    b. new_system

    c. open_system

    d. add_block

102. **In Simulink, which block is commonly used for data visualization?**

    a. Gain

    b. Scope

    c. MATLAB function

    d. Sum

103. **What does the 'From Workspace' block in Simulink do?**

    a. Imports data from a file

    b. Sends data to the workspace

    c. Retrieves data from the MATLAB workspace

    d. Transmits data to a remote server

104. **Which Simulink block is used to interface with hardware for real-time simulation?**

    a. Transfer function

    b. Real-time workshop

    c. S-function

    d. Data store memory

105. **In MATLAB, which function is used to convert Simulink models into executable code for embedded systems?**

    a. codegen

    b. sim

    c. rtwbuild

    d. compile

106. What is the primary purpose of the Simulink 'Constant' block?

    a. To generate a constant value

    b. To simulate a variable value

    c. To integrate with a constant input

    d. To provide a time-varying signal

107. Which MATLAB toolbox provides support for IoT communications?

    a. Communications system toolbox

    b. Instrument control toolbox

    c. Simulink real-time

    d. Control system toolbox

108. In Simulink, which block would you use to model a digital filter?

    a. Discrete filter

    b. Transfer function

    c. Fir filter

    d. Sum

109. How can you implement a custom algorithm in Simulink?

    a. By using the 'MATLAB Function' block

    b. By using the 'Simulink Function' block

    c. By creating a new subsystem

    d. By modifying the block parameters

110. Which block in Simulink is used for signal routing and switching?

    a. Demux

    b. Mux

    c. Switch

    d. Selector

111. In Simulink, which block can be used to integrate a mathematical equation into a model?

    a. Sum

    b. Product

    c. Math function

    d. Integrator

112. **What is the function of the 'Embedded MATLAB Function' block in Simulink?**
    a. To execute MATLAB code in real-time
    b. To create custom graphical blocks
    c. To design block parameters
    d. To model system dynamics

113. **Which block in Simulink would you use to model a continuous-time system?**
    a. Integrator
    b. Derivative
    c. Sum
    d. Scope

114. **What tool in MATLAB is used for real-time simulation and testing of models?**
    a. Simulink real-time
    b. Stateflow
    c. MATLAB coder
    d. Simulink coder

115. **Which Simulink feature is used for model-based design and simulation of control systems?**
    a. Stateflow
    b. Simulink coder
    c. Control system toolbox
    d. Real-time workshop

116. **In MATLAB, which command is used to open a Simulink model?**
    a. open
    b. load_system
    c. sim
    d. view

117. **Which MATLAB function is used to simulate a Simulink model?**
    a. simulate
    b. run_model
    c. sim
    d. execute

118. In Simulink, what does the 'Scope' block display?

    a. Parameter values

    b. Input data

    c. Simulation results as waveforms

    d. Block configuration options

119. What is the purpose of the 'Data Store Memory' block in Simulink?

    a. To store simulation results

    b. To share data between different parts of the model

    c. To manage real-time data acquisition

    d. To control block parameters

120. Which MATLAB toolbox provides support for wireless communication systems?

    a. Communications system toolbox

    b. DSP system toolbox

    c. Aerospace blockset

    d. Image processing toolbox

121. Which Simulink block is used to model a simple mathematical operation, such as addition or subtraction?

    a. Math function

    b. Gain

    c. Sum

    d. Product

122. What is the primary use of the 'MATLAB Function' block in Simulink?

    a. To visualize simulation data

    b. To execute custom MATLAB code within a Simulink model

    c. To define system parameters

    d. To create a subsystem

123. Which Simulink block is used for converting continuous signals to discrete signals?

    a. Discrete transfer function

    b. Zero-order hold

    c. Sample and hold

    d. Digital filter

124. What does the 'To Workspace' block do in Simulink?

    a. Sends simulation results to a file

    b. Imports data from the MATLAB workspace

    c. Exports simulation data to the MATLAB workspace

    d. Integrates with real-time systems

125. In Simulink, what is the purpose of the 'S-Function' block?

    a. To create custom block functionalities

    b. To execute system-level simulations

    c. To display signal values

    d. To perform system integration

126. Which Simulink tool is used to generate C/C++ code from a Simulink model?

    a. Simulink coder

    b. MATLAB coder

    c. Stateflow

    d. Real-time workshop

127. Which block is used in Simulink to model a system with multiple inputs and outputs?

    a. Multiport switch

    b. Mux

    c. Demux

    d. Bus creator

128. How can you visualize the frequency response of a system in MATLAB?

    a. Using the bode function

    b. Using the plot function

    c. Using the freqz function

    d. Using the impulse function

129. Which Simulink block can be used to model a PID controller?

    a. PID controller

    b. Transfer function

    c. State-space

    d. MATLAB function

130. **What feature in Simulink allows for automatic code generation for embedded systems?**

 a. Simulink real-time

 b. Simulink coder

 c. Embedded coder

 d. HDL coder

131. **What is an essential feature of Particle's offline simulation software?**

 a. Device-to-device communication testing

 b. Cloud-based analytics

 c. Real-time manufacturing cost analysis

 d. Hardware prototyping with 3D models

132. **In Simulink, what does the 'Clock' block provide?**

 a. A real-time system clock signal

 b. The current simulation time

 c. System clock frequency

 d. Simulation speed

133. **What is the role of the 'Integrator' block in Simulink?**

 a. To compute the derivative of a signal

 b. To compute the integral of a signal

 c. To simulate discrete systems

 d. To add a signal to another

134. **Which block is used to apply a gain to a signal in Simulink?**

 a. Gain

 b. Sum

 c. Product

 d. Constant

135. **What does the 'Data Store Read' block do in Simulink?**

 a. Writes data to the data store

 b. Reads data from the data store

 c. Creates a data store

 d. Initializes data for simulation

136. **Which block in Simulink is used to model a discrete transfer function?**

    a. Discrete transfer function

    b. Transfer function

    c. Discrete filter

    d. Discrete state-space

137. **In MATLAB, which function is used to design digital filters?**

    a. filter

    b. designfilt

    c. fdatool

    d. fir1

138. **What does the 'Scope' block in Simulink do?**

    a. Performs mathematical operations

    b. Displays simulation results in graphical form

    c. Stores data for post-processing

    d. Executes MATLAB functions

139. **Which Simulink block can you use to send data to an external device?**

    a. To workspace

    b. From workspace

    c. Serial receive

    d. UDP send

140. **In Simulink, which block is used to create a state machine model?**

    a. Stateflow

    b. State-space

    c. Memory

    d. Transfer function

141. **What does the 'Mux' block in Simulink do?**

    a. Multiplies signals

    b. Merges multiple signals into a vector

    c. Separates signals

    d. Filters signals

142. **Which MATLAB toolbox is essential for designing and simulating communication systems?**

    a. Communications system toolbox

    b. Signal processing toolbox

    c. Image processing toolbox

    d. Control system toolbox

143. **In Simulink, which block is used to generate random numbers?**

    a. Random number

    b. Uniform random number

    c. Gaussian random number

    d. Signal generator

144. **What is the purpose of the 'Rate Transition' block in Simulink?**

    a. To convert signal rates between different rates

    b. To change signal amplitudes

    c. To simulate different time steps

    d. To integrate signals

145. **Which Simulink feature allows you to simulate the performance of a system in real time?**

    a. Simulink coder

    b. Simulink real-time

    c. Stateflow

    d. Simulink design verifier

146. **Which MATLAB function would you use to analyze the stability of a control system?**

    a. bode

    b. pzmap

    c. step

    d. nyquist

147. **In Simulink, how can you model a system with variable sample time?**

    a. Using a Rate Transition block

    b. Using a Variable Step Solver

    c. Using a Fixed-Step Solver

    d. Using a Sample and Hold block

148. Which block in Simulink can be used to model a random walk process?

    a. Random Number

    b. Random Walk

    c. Signal Generator

    d. Discrete Random Number

149. Which type of IoT hardware is most commonly supported by Particle's platform?

    a. Microcontrollers

    b. Edge servers

    c. Smartphones

    d. Sensors

150. Which Simulink block is used to apply a mathematical transformation to input signals?

    a. Math Function

    b. Gain

    c. Transfer Function

    d. Product

151. In MATLAB, which function is used to generate a time vector for simulation?

    a. linspace

    b. timevector

    c. tspan

    d. logspace

152. Which Simulink block allows for complex number calculations?

    a. Complex Math

    b. Complex Gain

    c. Complex Signal

    d. Complex Arithmetic

153. What does the 'Compare To Constant' block do in Simulink?

    a. Compares a signal to a constant value

    b. Generates a constant value for comparison

    c. Stores comparison results

    d. Changes the constant value based on input

154. **Which MATLAB function is used to create and manage Simulink models programmatically?**

    a. sim

    b. open_system

    c. new_system

    d. add_block

155. **In Simulink, which block is used for modeling and simulating discrete-time systems?**

    a. Discrete Transfer Function

    b. Transfer Function

    c. Discrete State-Space

    d. Zero-Order Hold

156. **Which block in Simulink is used for interfacing with external data acquisition systems?**

    a. Data Acquisition

    b. External Input

    c. Analog Input

    d. External Mode

157. **What is the purpose of the 'Bus Selector' block in Simulink?**

    a. To create a bus object

    b. To select specific elements from a bus

    c. To merge signals into a bus

    d. To split a signal into multiple buses

158. **Which MATLAB function is used to design and analyze filters?**

    a. fdatool

    b. filter

    c. designfilt

    d. freqz

159. **In Simulink, which block is used to represent a system with multiple state variables?**

    a. State-Space

    b. Transfer Function

    c. Stateflow

    d. MATLAB Function

160. **Which MATLAB toolbox is useful for modeling and simulation of mechanical systems?**
    a. Simscape Multibody
    b. Simulink Coder
    c. Aerospace Blockset
    d. Vehicle Network Toolbox

161. **What does the 'Subsystem' block do in Simulink?**
    a. Defines a hierarchical structure within a model
    b. Performs data acquisition
    c. Analyzes simulation results
    d. Creates a custom block

162. **Which block in Simulink is used to simulate the effect of a delay in the system?**
    a. Delay
    b. Transport Delay
    c. Memory
    d. Unit Delay

163. **In MATLAB, which function is used to visualize the response of a linear time-invariant (LTI)system?**
    a. step
    b. impulse
    c. bode
    d. nyquist

164. **What is the purpose of the 'Sine Wave' block in Simulink?**
    a. To generate a sine wave signal
    b. To analyze sine wave frequency
    c. To filter sine wave signals
    d. To convert a sine wave to a cosine wave

165. **Which Simulink block is used to create a real-time communication link with external hardware?**
    a. Serial Send
    b. UDP Send
    c. External Mode
    d. Analog Input

166. **Which MATLAB function is used to simulate a system with predefined initial conditions?**

     a. ode45

     b. sim

     c. lsim

     d. initial

167. **What is a major limitation of Particle's offline simulation software?**

     a. It cannot simulate multiple devices simultaneously.

     b. It requires a constant internet connection.

     c. It does not support debugging tools.

     d. It cannot integrate with Particle's cloud platform.

168. **Which Simulink feature allows you to validate the functionality of a model before implementation?**

     a. Simulink Design Verifier

     b. Simulink Coder

     c. Simulink Real-Time

     d. Stateflow

169. **In MATLAB, which function is used to determine the poles and zeros of a transfer function?**

     a. pole

     b. zero

     c. pzmap

     d. bode

170. **Which Simulink block allows for modeling of systems with complex number inputs?**

     a. Complex Arithmetic

     b. Complex Math

     c. Complex Gain

     d. Complex Signal

171. **In Simulink, which block is used to model a system with a time delay?**

     a. Delay

     b. Transport Delay

     c. Memory

     d. Unit Delay

172. **Which MATLAB function is used to create a new Simulink model programmatically?**

    a. new_system

    b. create_system

    c. open_system

    d. build_model

173. **What does the 'Bus Creator' block in Simulink do?**

    a. Merges signals into a bus

    b. Splits a bus into individual signals

    c. Creates a bus object

    d. Analyzes bus data

174. **Which Simulink block can be used to simulate a continuous-time integrator?**

    a. Integrator

    b. Transfer Function

    c. Sum

    d. State-Space

175. **In MATLAB, which function is used to plot the impulse response of a system?**

    a. impulse

    b. step

    c. bode

    d. nyquist

176. **What is the main advantage of using Particle's offline simulation during the development phase?**

    a. It speeds up deployment to production.

    b. It ensures devices are connected to the cloud at all times.

    c. It reduces dependency on hardware during initial testing.

    d. It simplifies user interface design for IoT applications.

177. **Which MATLAB function is used to create a frequency response plot for a system?**

    a. bode

    b. step

    c. impulse

    d. nyquist

178. What does the 'Scope' block in Simulink help with?

    a. Visualizing signal data

    b. Performing mathematical operations

    c. Defining system parameters

    d. Creating custom blocks

179. Which Simulink block is used to model a discrete-time state-space system?

    a. Discrete State-Space

    b. State-Space

    c. Transfer Function

    d. MATLAB Function

180. In Simulink, which block is used to separate signals from a bus?

    a. Bus Selector

    b. Demux

    c. Mux

    d. Bus Creator

181. Which MATLAB function is used to design a low-pass filter?

    a. designfilt

    b. lowpass

    c. butter

    d. filter

182. What does the 'Signal Generator' block in Simulink produce?

    a. Random signals

    b. Sine, square, and triangular waves

    c. Filtered signals

    d. Frequency-modulated signals

183. In MATLAB, which function is used to simulate the output of a linear system?

    a. lsim

    b. sim

    c. step

    d. impulse

184. **Which block in Simulink is used for asynchronous communication with hardware?**

    a. Serial Receive

    b. UDP Receive

    c. Data Acquisition

    d. External Mode

185. **What is the purpose of the 'Transfer Function' block in Simulink?**

    a. To represent a system's dynamics in the Laplace domain

    b. To integrate signals

    c. To apply gain to signals

    d. To filter noise

186. **Which Simulink block can be used to merge multiple signals into a single vector?**

    a. Mux

    b. Bus Creator

    c. Selector

    d. Demux

187. **In Simulink, which block would you use to model a linear time-invariant system with differential equations?**

    a. Transfer Function

    b. State-Space

    c. Stateflow

    d. MATLAB Function

188. **Which MATLAB function is used to plot the step response of a system?**

    a. step

    b. impulse

    c. bode

    d. nyquist

189. **What is the role of Particle Workbench in offline simulation?**

    a. It manages cloud integrations for IoT devices.

    b. It provides a local development environment with simulation capabilities.

    c. It serves as a hardware design tool for IoT prototypes.

    d. It enables real-time monitoring of deployed IoT devices.

190. **Which Simulink feature allows you to test model behavior under varying conditions?**
   a. Parameter Sweep
   b. Model Checker
   c. Design Verifier
   d. External Mode

191. **In MATLAB, which function is used to plot the Nyquist plot for a system?**
   a. nyquist
   b. bode
   c. step
   d. impulse

192. **What does the 'Unit Delay' block in Simulink do?**
   a. Delays the input signal by one sample period
   b. Integrates the input signal
   c. Computes the derivative of the input signal
   d. Applies a gain to the input signal

193. **Which MATLAB function is used to analyze the frequency response of a digital filter?**
   a. freqz
   b. bode
   c. step
   d. impulse

194. **What does the 'Subsystem' block in Simulink allow you to do?**
   a. Group related blocks together
   b. Define external system interfaces
   c. Create a new Simulink model
   d. Analyze system performance

195. **Which block in Simulink is used to define a fixed constant input to a system?**
   a. Constant
   b. Gain
   c. Step
   d. Square Wave

196. **In Simulink, which block can be used to visualize real-time simulation data?**

    a. Scope

    b. Display

    c. Data Store Memory

    d. To Workspace

197. **Which MATLAB function is used to determine the poles of a transfer function?**

    a. pole

    b. zero

    c. pzmap

    d. bode

198. **What is the purpose of the 'Memory' block in Simulink?**

    a. To store the previous value of a signal

    b. To perform mathematical operations

    c. To define system constants

    d. To analyze signal data

199. **Which block in Simulink allows for the modeling of a linear system with feedback?**

    a. Feedback

    b. Transfer Function

    c. Sum

    d. State-Space

200. **What is Contiki?**

    a. A web development framework

    b. An operating system for IoT devices

    c. A cloud computing service

    d. A database management system

201. **Which programming language is primarily used for developing applications in Contiki?**

    a. Java

    b. C

    c. Python

    d. JavaScript

202. What does the Contiki operating system primarily target?

    a. High-performance computing systems

    b. Embedded systems and low-power devices

    c. Desktop applications

    d. Mobile applications

203. Which of the following is a key feature of Contiki?

    a. Graphical user interface support

    b. Real-time operating system capabilities

    c. Support for high-definition graphics

    d. Extensive database management

204. What is the purpose of the Rime stack in Contiki?

    a. To provide a user interface framework

    b. To handle low-level hardware operations

    c. To provide a communication stack for low-power wireless networks

    d. To manage file systems

205. Which protocol is used by Contiki for network communication in low-power wireless networks?

    a. HTTP

    b. CoAP

    c. MQTT

    d. FTP

206. Which programming tool does Contiki provide for network simulation?

    a. NS-3

    b. OMNeT++

    c. Cooja

    d. GNS3

207. What type of devices does Contiki support?

    a. Only smartphones

    b. Only high-performance servers

    c. Low-power wireless devices and sensors

    d. Desktop computers

208. **What is the primary goal of Contiki's 'uIP' stack?**
    a. To provide a web development environment
    b. To implement a lightweight IP stack for small devices
    c. To manage user interfaces
    d. To handle complex database operations

209. **Which of the following is a key benefit of using Contiki in IoT applications?**
    a. High power consumption
    b. Extensive GUI support
    c. Low memory footprint
    d. High-end graphics processing

210. **Which module in Contiki handles the scheduling of tasks and events?**
    a. The Rime stack
    b. The Protothread library
    c. The uIP stack
    d. The Cooja simulator

211. **In Contiki, what is the role of the 'Contiki OS Scheduler'?**
    a. To manage hardware resources
    b. To schedule and manage tasks and events
    c. To handle network communications
    d. To provide database connectivity

212. **What is the function of Contiki's 'Power Management' module?**
    a. To handle data encryption
    b. To manage energy consumption and sleep modes
    c. To provide graphical output
    d. To manage file storage

213. **Which of the following is a primary characteristic of the Contiki operating system?**
    a. High computational overhead
    b. Large codebase
    c. Lightweight and modular design
    d. Extensive hardware requirements

214. **Which network protocol is supported by Contiki for low-power IoT devices?**

    a. TCP/IP

    b. IPv4

    c. 6LoWPAN

    d. HTTP

215. **What type of operating system is Contiki classified as?**

    a. Batch processing OS

    b. Real-time OS

    c. Multi-user OS

    d. Time-sharing OS

216. **In Contiki, what does the term 'Protothreads' refer to?**

    a. A library for file management

    b. A framework for web development

    c. A lightweight, stackless thread library

    d. A graphics processing unit

217. **What does Contiki's 'uIP' stack stand for?**

    a. Unified IP stack

    b. Ultra-light IP stack

    c. Universal IP stack

    d. Uniform IP stack

218. **Which feature of Contiki helps to simulate networks for IoT applications?**

    a. The Rime stack

    b. The Contiki OS Scheduler

    c. The Cooja simulator

    d. The uIP stack

219. **What is the primary focus of Contiki's 'Rime' stack?**

    a. High-speed internet connections

    b. Wireless communication in low-power networks

    c. High-definition video streaming

    d. Desktop application support

220. **Which file system is commonly used with Contiki?**

    a. NTFS

    b. FAT32

    c. LFS (LittleFS)

    d. EXT4

221. **Which tool is used for developing and debugging Contiki applications?**

    a. Eclipse

    b. Visual Studio Code

    c. GNU Compiler Collection (GCC)

    d. CodeBlocks

222. **What is the purpose of Contiki's 'lib' directory?**

    a. To store source code for user applications

    b. To provide libraries and utilities for Contiki applications

    c. To handle graphical user interfaces

    d. To manage network configurations

223. **What is Contiki's 'Cooja' used for?**

    a. Writing applications in Java

    b. Compiling source code

    c. Simulating wireless sensor networks

    d. Managing power consumption

224. **Which protocol does Contiki use for multicast communication?**

    a. IPv4

    b. 6LoWPAN

    c. UDP

    d. ICMP

225. **What does Contiki's 'Netstack' refer to?**

    a. A network stack implementation for Contiki

    b. A library for handling graphical output

    c. A file system management tool

    d. A power management system

226. **Which of the following is a key advantage of using Contiki for IoT development?**

    a. Large memory footprint

    b. High energy consumption

    c. Scalability and low power consumption

    d. Complex configuration

227. **What kind of devices is Contiki optimized for?**

    a. High-performance computing devices

    b. Large server farms

    c. Resource-constrained, low-power devices

    d. High-end gaming consoles

228. **In Contiki, what is the role of the 'contiki-conf.h' file?**

    a. To configure network settings

    b. To handle application-specific settings

    c. To include project-specific configurations and settings

    d. To manage user permissions

229. **Which communication protocol is not natively supported by Contiki?**

    a. CoAP

    b. MQTT

    c. XMPP

    d. HTTP

230. **What is the default communication range of Contiki's wireless network stack?**

    a. 10 meters

    b. 50 meters

    c. 100 meters

    d. 1 kilometer

231. **Which module in Contiki provides a lightweight implementation of the IPv6 protocol?**

    a. uIP

    b. 6LoWPAN

    c. Rime

    d. LwIP

232. Which file extension is used for Contiki configuration files?

    a. .conf

    b. .cfg

    c. .cont

    d. .h

233. What is the purpose of Contiki's 'net/ip' directory?

    a. To handle network communication and IP stack implementations

    b. To store source code for IP-based applications

    c. To manage hardware interfaces

    d. To configure user settings

234. Which Contiki feature allows for the simulation of radio communications and network protocols?

    a. Contiki OS Scheduler

    b. Cooja Simulator

    c. Protothreads

    d. Rime Stack

235. In Contiki, what does the 'uIP' stack handle?

    a. Low-level hardware communication

    b. Lightweight IP and TCP/IP protocols

    c. Graphical user interface elements

    d. File system operations

236. Which protocol is used by Contiki to facilitate efficient communication in low-power, low-data-rate networks?

    a. CoAP

    b. FTP

    c. SMTP

    d. Telnet

237. Which component of Particle's ecosystem is typically bypassed in offline simulations?

    a. Particle CLI

    b. Particle Cloud

    c. Particle Workbench

    d. Particle Devices

238. **Which Contiki component is responsible for handling data encryption and security?**

    a. uIP

    b. Contiki's security libraries

    c. Rime stack

    d. Protothreads

239. **What is a key reason developers use offline simulation software for IoT?**

    a. To simulate real-world device interactions without internet dependency

    b. To reduce hardware costs in production

    c. To automate deployment to production

    d. To manage device fleets remotely

240. **What does the 'Contiki' project primarily focus on?**

    a. High-performance computing

    b. Embedded systems and IoT applications

    c. Desktop applications

    d. High-definition video streaming

241. **What is the main purpose of the Contiki 'sys' directory?**

    a. To handle network communication

    b. To manage system-level operations and utilities

    c. To provide graphical user interface components

    d. To store application-specific data

242. **Which of the following protocols is used by Contiki for lightweight messaging and data exchange?**

    a. SMTP

    b. MQTT

    c. POP3

    d. IMAP

243. **What type of simulation environment is Cooja?**

    a. A 3D graphics simulation tool

    b. A network simulation environment for wireless sensor networks

    c. A real-time operating system

    d. A hardware design tool

244. **Which Contiki feature provides support for building and managing real-time applications?**

   a. Protothreads

   b. uIP stack

   c. Cooja

   d. Rime stack

245. **In Contiki, what does the term '6LoWPAN' stand for?**

   a. 6 Low-power Wide Area Network

   b. 6 Low-power Wireless Personal Area Network

   c. 6 Low-power Wireless Access Network

   d. 6 Low-power Wide Protocol Area Network

246. **What is the typical use case for Contiki's 'Rime' stack?**

   a. High-speed internet communication

   b. Low-power, low-bandwidth sensor networks

   c. High-definition video processing

   d. Real-time graphics rendering

247. **Which file contains the main configuration settings for a Contiki application?**

   a. Makefile

   b. main.c

   c. project-conf.h

   d. contiki-conf.h

248. **Which of the following is not a feature of Contiki?**

   a. Support for low-power devices

   b. Real-time operating system capabilities

   c. Extensive graphical user interface support

   d. Network simulation with Cooja

249. **Offline simulation tools are most effective during which phase of IoT development?**

   a. Deployment phase

   b. Prototyping and testing phase

   c. Production phase

   d. Maintenance phase

250. **Which file in Contiki contains the main settings for building applications?**

    a. Makefile

    b. main.c

    c. project-conf.h

    d. contiki-conf.h

251. **What is the primary limitation of offline simulation in IoT development?**

    a. Inability to test cloud-based integrations

    b. Limited support for debugging tools

    c. Lack of firmware customization options

    d. Restricted compatibility with development boards

252. **Which directory in Contiki contains the source code for various network protocols?**

    a. /core

    b. /net

    c. /sys

    d. /apps

253. **What does Contiki's 'uIP' stack handle in terms of networking?**

    a. Low-power Bluetooth communication

    b. Lightweight TCP/IP stack for small devices

    c. High-speed internet connections

    d. Real-time graphics rendering

254. **What type of network does Contiki's 'Rime' stack primarily support?**

    a. Cellular networks

    b. High-speed Ethernet

    c. Low-power wireless networks

    d. Satellite networks

255. **Which directory contains the source code for Contiki's protothreads?**

    a. /core

    b. /sys

    c. /apps

    d. /net

256. **In Contiki, which file extension is commonly used for configuration files specific to a project?**

   a. .conf

   b. .cfg

   c. .h

   d. .c

257. **What does Contiki's 'sys/etimer.c' file provide?**

   a. Event timer management

   b. Network protocol implementation

   c. Power management

   d. File system operations

258. **Which of the following protocols is not typically used with Contiki?**

   a. CoAP

   b. 6LoWPAN

   c. Zigbee

   d. HTTP

259. **What is the main advantage of Contiki's protothreads compared to traditional threading models?**

   a. More complex scheduling

   b. High memory usage

   c. Low memory overhead and stackless threads

   d. Extensive graphical support

260. **What is the main purpose of Contiki's 'sys/etimer.h' header file?**

   a. To manage energy consumption

   b. To provide network stack configurations

   c. To handle event timers and delays

   d. To manage user interface elements

261. **Which protocol does Contiki use for low-power and low-bandwidth networks that provides header compression and fragmentation?**

   a. IPv4

   b. 6LoWPAN

   c. Zigbee

   d. BLE

262. **Which Contiki component provides a lightweight, non-blocking input/output library?**

    a. uIP

    b. Protothreads

    c. Rime

    d. Netstack

263. **What is the role of the 'contiki-main.c' file in a Contiki application?**

    a. To configure network settings

    b. To define the main entry point of the application

    c. To manage user interface elements

    d. To provide library functions

264. **Which Contiki directory contains example applications?**

    a. /core

    b. /sys

    c. /apps

    d. /net

265. **What does Contiki's 'Rime' stack support for communication?**

    a. Wireless Sensor Networks (WSNs)

    b. Cellular networks

    c. High-speed wired networks

    d. High-definition video streaming

266. **In Contiki, which file would you edit to add or modify an application-specific configuration?**

    a. contiki-conf.h

    b. project-conf.h

    c. Makefile

    d. main.c

267. **What is the primary use case of Contiki's 'uIP' stack?**

    a. To handle high-speed Ethernet connections

    b. To provide a lightweight TCP/IP stack for small embedded systems

    c. To manage graphical user interfaces

    d. To perform complex data analysis

268. **Which of the following is a feature of Contiki's 'Cooja' simulator?**

    a. Support for 3D modeling

    b. Real-time simulation of wireless sensor networks

    c. High-performance server simulation

    d. Video editing tools

269. **In Contiki, which module is used for creating and managing events?**

    a. Event handling module

    b. Protothreads

    c. Netstack

    d. Rime

270. **Which directory in Contiki contains core operating system functionalities and abstractions?**

    a. /apps

    b. /sys

    c. /net

    d. /core

271. **What is the main role of Contiki's 'lib/list.h' file?**

    a. To handle file system operations

    b. To provide list data structures and operations

    c. To manage network configurations

    d. To support graphical user interfaces

272. **Which Contiki feature is used to simulate the behavior of wireless networks with nodes and communication protocols?**

    a. Contiki OS Scheduler

    b. Cooja Simulator

    c. Protothreads

    d. Rime Stack

273. **What is the primary purpose of the 'Makefile' in a Contiki project?**

    a. To configure network settings

    b. To manage source code files

    c. To define build instructions and compile the application

    d. To handle user interface elements

274. Which of the following is a primary component of Contiki's network stack for low-powerdevices?

    a. Rime

    b. uIP

    c. 6LoWPAN

    d. All of the above

275. Which file would you modify to include additional libraries in a Contiki project?

    a. project-conf.h

    b. Makefile

    c. contiki-conf.h

    d. main.c

276. Which directory in Contiki contains files for various network protocols and implementations?

    a. /sys

    b. /apps

    c. /net

    d. /core

277. In Contiki, what is the purpose of the 'sys/clock.h' file?

    a. To handle event timers

    b. To manage system clock and timekeeping

    c. To configure network settings

    d. To provide graphical outputs

278. What does the 'net/rime' directory in Contiki typically include?

    a. Files related to low-power communication protocols

    b. Network stack configuration files

    c. Application-specific source code

    d. User interface components

279. Which file in Contiki is responsible for defining the system-wide configuration settings?

    a. project-conf.h

    b. contiki-conf.h

    c. Makefile

    d. main.c

280. **What is Ptolemy II primarily used for?**

    a. Web development

    b. Data analysis

    c. Modeling and simulation of systems

    d. Database management

281. **Which programming language is primarily used to implement Ptolemy II?**

    a. Python

    b. Java

    c. C++

    d. MATLAB

282. **Ptolemy II is known for its support in which type of modeling?**

    a. Relational modeling

    b. Object-oriented modeling

    c. Component-based modeling

    d. Hierarchical and concurrent modeling

283. **Which feature is a core component of Ptolemy II for simulation?**

    a. Data visualization

    b. System analysis

    c. Graphical user interface for designing models

    d. Automated testing

284. **In Ptolemy II, what does the term actor refer to?**

    a. A software component that performs computation

    b. A database entity

    c. A user interface element

    d. A network protocol

285. **LabVIEW is developed by which company?**

    a. Microsoft

    b. National Instruments

    c. IBM

    d. Oracle

286. **LabVIEW is primarily used for.**

    a. Web development

    b. Embedded system design

    c. System design and data acquisition

    d. Text processing

287. **In LabVIEW, what is the primary interface for designing a system?**

    a. Block diagram

    b. Flowchart

    c. UML diagram

    d. Circuit diagram

288. **Which language is LabVIEW based on for creating its graphical programs?**

    a. G language

    b. Java

    c. C#

    d. Python

289. **Which feature in LabVIEW is used to communicate with IoT devices?**

    a. VI Server

    b. DataSocket

    c. Network streams

    d. Web services

290. **Ptolemy II is an example of which type of system modeling approach?**

    a. Event-based

    b. Dataflow-based

    c. Object-oriented

    d. Class-based

291. **What is a key feature of the Ptolemy II software architecture?**

    a. Distributed processing

    b. Modular design

    c. Relational database management

    d. Direct hardware interfacing

292. **Which of the following is a core concept in Ptolemy II?**

    a. Model-View-Controller

    b. Actor-Oriented Design

    c. Client-Server Model

    d. Layered Architecture

293. **Ptolemy II's director is responsible for.**

    a. Defining the model's behavior

    b. Executing the model's components

    c. Designing the model's user interface

    d. Managing data storage

294. **Which of the following best describes a composite actor in Ptolemy II?**

    a. An actor that performs multiple types of operations

    b. An actor that encapsulates other actors

    c. An actor that interacts with external databases

    d. An actor that manages user interfaces

295. **In LabVIEW, what does a Virtual Instrument (VI) refer to?**

    a. A physical instrument used for measurements

    b. A software module that performs specific tasks

    c. A programming language

    d. A hardware interface

296. **LabVIEW's Front Panel is used for.**

    a. Programming the logic

    b. Designing the graphical user interface

    c. Configuring network settings

    d. Debugging code

297. **Which protocol is commonly used in LabVIEW for communication with IoT devices?**

    a. HTTP

    b. FTP

    c. Modbus

    d. SNMP

298. LabVIEW's DAQ stands for.

    a. Data Acquisition

    b. Digital Analysis Queue

    c. Dynamic Application Query

    d. Data Authentication Quality

299. Which LabVIEW feature allows for the creation of custom functions?

    a. SubVIs

    b. Libraries

    c. Modules

    d. Plugins

300. What is the role of the token in Ptolemy II's dataflow model?

    a. It represents a data packet sent over a network

    b. It signifies a unit of data passed between actors

    c. It is a software license key

    d. It is a time synchronization signal

301. In Ptolemy II, what does the Director component manage?

    a. System resources

    b. The execution order of actors

    c. User interface elements

    d. External device communication

302. Which type of model does Ptolemy II use to describe the flow of data between components?

    a. Entity-Relationship Model

    b. Petri Nets

    c. Dataflow Model

    d. Finite State Machine

303. What is an actor in the context of Ptolemy II?

    a. A hardware component

    b. A software module that processes data

    c. A user interface element

    d. A network protocol

304. Ptolemy II supports which of the following model abstractions?

    a. Real-time modeling

    b. Object-oriented modeling

    c. Synchronous and asynchronous modeling

    d. Hierarchical file management

305. Which of the following is used to simulate hardware in LabVIEW?

    a. Simulation Toolkit

    b. Virtual Instruments (VIs)

    c. Software Simulation Package

    d. Hardware Abstraction Layer

306. LabVIEW's Block Diagram is used to.

    a. Design the physical layout of hardware

    b. Write and compile code

    c. Create and manage graphical representations of system logic

    d. Configure network settings

307. Which LabVIEW feature is used to create real-time data visualization?

    a. Front Panel Indicators

    b. Block Diagram Controls

    c. Data Acquisition Toolkit

    d. User Interface Designer

308. LabVIEW's DataSocket is used for.

    a. Data visualization

    b. Data transfer and sharing over networks

    c. System configuration

    d. Debugging code

309. In LabVIEW, what is a Case Structure?

    a. A way to handle different cases or conditions in a program

    b. A data type for case-sensitive operations

    c. A hardware abstraction layer

    d. A network communication protocol

310. **How can Ptolemy II be integrated with LabVIEW for IoT applications?**

    a. By using a shared database

    b. By exchanging data through a web service

    c. By directly embedding LabVIEW code in Ptolemy II models

    d. By exporting and importing data files between both systems

311. **What is a common use case for combining Ptolemy II and LabVIEW in IoT applications?**

    a. Simulating IoT device behavior and controlling hardware through LabVIEW

    b. Managing database transactions

    c. Developing web interfaces

    d. Performing text analysis

312. **In a combined Ptolemy II and LabVIEW system, how might Ptolemy II handle real-time data from LabVIEW?**

    a. By using direct hardware interfacing

    b. By processing data via external APIs

    c. By utilizing network communication protocols

    d. By storing data in a shared file system

313. **What is the benefit of using Ptolemy II for modeling when integrating with LabVIEW for IoT?**

    a. Enhanced hardware control

    b. Improved data visualization

    c. Comprehensive system modeling and simulation capabilities

    d. Simplified user interface design

314. **Which data format might be used for interoperability between Ptolemy II and LabVIEW systems?**

    a. XML

    b. JSON

    c. CSV

    d. Binary

315. **In Ptolemy II, which design pattern is commonly used to model concurrent systems?**

    a. Observer Pattern

    b. Singleton Pattern

    c. Actor Model

    d. Decorator Pattern

316. What does the term modal model refer to in Ptolemy II?

    a. A model that operates under different modes of operation

    b. A graphical user interface model

    c. A database schema model

    d. A file management model

317. Which Ptolemy II component handles communication between different parts of the model?

    a. Communication Director

    b. Data Manager

    c. Actor

    d. Port

318. What type of system does Ptolemy II's Synchronous Dataflow (SDF) model best represent?

    a. Event-driven systems

    b. Time-triggered systems

    c. Data-driven systems

    d. Resource-constrained systems

319. Which of the following is a primary advantage of using Ptolemy II for system design?

    a. Built-in hardware support

    b. Integrated simulation and model analysis tools

    c. Direct data acquisition

    d. Comprehensive cloud integration

320. What is the purpose of LabVIEW's Shared Variable feature?

    a. To share data between different VIs running on the same computer

    b. To handle network communications

    c. To interface with external hardware

    d. To manage user interface elements

321. Which LabVIEW toolkit provides functions for communicating with web services?

    a. Web services toolkit

    b. Internet Protocol toolkit

    c. HTTP toolkit

    d. Network communication toolkit

322. How does LabVIEW handle data acquisition from sensors?

    a. Through direct hardware connections only

    b. Via simulated data only

    c. By using the data acquisition (DAQ) hardware and drivers

    d. Through cloud-based APIs

323. What is a key benefit of using LabVIEW's graphical programming approach?

    a. Enhanced debugging capabilities

    b. Simplified program visualization and design

    c. Faster code execution

    d. Direct integration with multiple programming languages

324. Which LabVIEW feature allows users to create reusable code components?

    a. SubVIs

    b. Control design toolkit

    c. Simulation module

    d. Data management toolkit

325. What is a common method for integrating Ptolemy II with LabVIEW for real-time applications?

    a. Using a middleware platform

    b. Employing data exchange formats such as XML or JSON

    c. Directly embedding Ptolemy II models in LabVIEW

    d. Utilizing shared network drives for data exchange

326. When integrating Ptolemy II with LabVIEW, what role does a gateway often play?

    a. It provides a direct data feed from Ptolemy II to LabVIEW.

    b. It serves as an intermediary for data transformation and communication.

    c. It manages user authentication between systems.

    d. It controls system hardware directly.

327. **How can LabVIEW's data acquisition capabilities be utilized within a Ptolemy II model?**

    a. By exporting data from LabVIEW to Ptolemy II for simulation

    b. By directly embedding LabVIEW code in Ptolemy II models

    c. By using LabVIEW to generate data for Ptolemy II to process

    d. By creating a direct Data link between LabVIEW and Ptolemy II for real-time analysis

328. **What is the primary purpose of using Ptolemy II for modeling in an IoT application that also involves LabVIEW?**

    a. To develop a detailed simulation of system behavior before implementing in LabVIEW

    b. To replace LabVIEW's hardware with Ptolemy II's virtual hardware

    c. To simplify LabVIEW's graphical user interface

    d. To manage network communication protocols

329. **Which of the following is a challenge when integrating Ptolemy II with LabVIEW for IoT applications?**

    a. Ensuring compatibility between the graphical programming languages

    b. Handling data synchronization between simulation and real-time execution

    c. Managing user interface design across different platforms

    d. Directly coding the models in LabVIEW's native language

330. **What does Ptolemy II's actor model enable in system design?**

    a. Visual data representation

    b. Encapsulation and modularity of components

    c. Direct control of hardware components

    d. User interface design

331. **Which feature in Ptolemy II allows for hierarchical modeling?**

    a. Composite actors

    b. Data tokens

    c. Model views

    d. Port connections

332. **Ptolemy II's dataflow model is most suitable for which kind of system?**

   a. Event-driven systems

   b. Data-parallel processing systems

   c. File management systems

   d. User interface design systems

333. **Which of the following is not a supported domain in Ptolemy II?**

   a. Continuous

   b. Discrete event

   c. Hybrid

   d. Relational database

334. **How does Ptolemy II handle system integration?**

   a. By providing APIs for direct hardware control

   b. By using model transformations and inter-domain communication

   c. By creating web-based interfaces

   d. By managing user authentication

335. **What is the function of LabVIEW's event structure?**

   a. To manage data acquisition

   b. To handle and respond to different events in a program

   c. To create user interface elements

   d. To configure network settings

336. **In LabVIEW, what does the queue function help manage?**

   a. Hardware resources

   b. Data flow between different VIs

   c. User interface components

   d. Network communications

337. **Which of the following is a common use of LabVIEW's file I/O functions?**

   a. To interface with external hardware

   b. To perform network operations

   c. To read from and write to files

   d. To create user interface designs

338. **What does LabVIEW's cluster data type allow users to do?**

    a. Manage collections of related data

    b. Create user-defined control elements

    c. Design hardware interfaces

    d. Implement network protocols

339. **Which of the following LabVIEW features supports creating custom user interfaces?**

    a. Front panel

    b. Block diagram

    c. DataSocket

    d. VI server

340. **What is a common method for exchanging data between Ptolemy II and LabVIEW?**

    a. Using shared database systems

    b. Through intermediary data formats like XML or JSON

    c. By embedding Ptolemy II models directly in LabVIEW

    d. Via direct hardware connections

341. **Which type of data model is often used in Ptolemy II to handle complex IoT scenarios?**

    a. Dataflow model

    b. Object-oriented model

    c. Relational model

    d. Document model

342. **When using LabVIEW for IoT applications with Ptolemy II, what is a key consideration?**

    a. Ensuring compatibility of graphical programming environments

    b. Configuring network security protocols

    c. Developing custom hardware interfaces

    d. Managing user authentication systems

343. **How can Ptolemy II and LabVIEW interact in a real-time IoT system?**

    a. By using LabVIEW to control Ptolemy II simulations

    b. By Ptolemy II managing the real-time data processing while LabVIEW handles the visualization

    c. By directly integrating Ptolemy II code in LabVIEW

    d. By exchanging data through web services or APIs

344. What is one advantage of using LabVIEW's graphical programming for IoT projects?

    a. Enhanced support for textual programming languages

    b. Simplified visualization and debugging of complex systems

    c. Direct database integration

    d. Improved hardware compatibility

345. In a Ptolemy II and LabVIEW integrated system, what role might a middleware layer play?

    a. Facilitating communication between the two systems

    b. Directly controlling hardware devices

    c. Performing data analysis

    d. Creating user interfaces

346. What is the main purpose of using mock data in offline IoT simulations?

    a. To replace physical sensors and actuators during tests

    b. To enhance the performance of IoT devices

    c. To establish secure communication protocols

    d. To validate cloud-based data storage

347. What challenge might arise when integrating LabVIEW with Ptolemy II for an IoT system?

    a. Ensuring real-time synchronization of data between systems

    b. Configuring hardware interfaces

    c. Developing graphical user interfaces

    d. Handling network security

348. Which LabVIEW feature might be used to interface with Ptolemy II models running on a remote server?

    a. Network streams

    b. Shared variables

    c. DataSocket

    d. Web services

349. For efficient data exchange between Ptolemy II and LabVIEW, which approach might be used?

    a. Using data export/import files

    b. Implementing direct API calls

    c. Utilizing middleware for data translation

    d. Embedding models within each other's environments

350. In Ptolemy II, what does the term continuous time domain refer to?

    a. A model that handles discrete events

    b. A model that simulates continuous signals and systems

    c. A data storage mechanism

    d. A graphical user interface component

351. What is the main function of ports in Ptolemy II?

    a. To manage user interface elements

    b. To provide connections for data flow between actors

    c. To handle external device communication

    d. To manage system resources

352. Which feature in Ptolemy II allows users to define custom behaviors for system components?

    a. Custom Actors

    b. Directories

    c. Event Listeners

    d. Database Interfaces

353. In Ptolemy II, how does the discreet event domain function?

    a. It processes continuous signals in real-time

    b. It models systems with discrete changes or events

    c. It handles data acquisition from external sensors

    d. It provides a graphical interface for system design

354. What is the main purpose of the INET framework in OMNeT++?

    a. To provide a graphical interface for IoT devices

    b. To simulate communication protocols like TCP, UDP, and IPv6

    c. To connect OMNeT++ simulations with real-world IoT devices

    d. To manage IoT device firmware

355. **Which LabVIEW feature is used to create a user-defined data type?**

    a. Enum

    b. Cluster

    c. Array

    d. Queue

356. **What is the function of LabVIEW's state machine design pattern?**

    a. To manage different states or conditions in a system

    b. To simulate hardware components

    c. To handle file I/O operations

    d. To design graphical user interfaces

357. **How does LabVIEW's NI-DAQ system contribute to IoT applications?**

    a. By providing network management tools

    b. By offering hardware interfaces for data acquisition

    c. By enabling software simulation of systems

    d. By creating user interfaces for applications

358. **Which LabVIEW module is specifically designed for simulation and control systems?**

    a. Control Design and Simulation Module

    b. Real-Time Module

    c. Data Acquisition Module

    d. Vision Development Module

359. **What does LabVIEW's property node allow users to do?**

    a. Access and modify properties of controls and indicators

    b. Create custom data types

    c. Perform network communications

    d. Manage system resources

360. **Which method can be used to visualize Ptolemy II simulation results in LabVIEW?**

    a. By exporting data from Ptolemy II and importing it into LabVIEW

    b. By directly embedding LabVIEW code in Ptolemy II models

    c. By using LabVIEW to simulate Ptolemy II models

    d. By creating a custom middleware to handle data exchange and visualization

361. **What is one benefit of using Ptolemy II for modeling when working with LabVIEW for IoT applications?**

    a. Improved hardware integration

    b. Advanced simulation and modeling capabilities

    c. Enhanced user interface design

    d. Direct network communication

362. **Which feature might be used to synchronize data between Ptolemy II and LabVIEW in real-time?**

    a. Shared Variables

    b. Network Streams

    c. DataSocket

    d. Web Services

363. **How can LabVIEW handle data generated by Ptolemy II models?**

    a. By using LabVIEW's real-time data processing capabilities

    b. By embedding Ptolemy II models directly into LabVIEW

    c. By creating data exchange files that can be read by LabVIEW

    d. By directly accessing the Ptolemy II simulation engine

364. **Which of the following is a typical use case for OMNeT++ in IoT research?**

    a. Simulating device hardware performance

    b. Modeling wireless sensor networks (WSNs)

    c. Designing IoT-specific operating systems

    d. Creating 3D models of IoT devices

365. **When integrating Ptolemy II and LabVIEW, what is a key factor to ensure successful communication between systems?**

    a. Consistent data formats and communication protocols

    b. Matching hardware specifications

    c. Synchronizing graphical user interfaces

    d. Standardizing code libraries

366. **Which LabVIEW feature can facilitate real-time data logging from a Ptolemy II simulation?**

    a. DataSocket

    b. Shared variables

    c. Network streams

    d. File I/O functions

367. **How might LabVIEW's real-time module be used in conjunction with Ptolemy II?**

    a. To handle real-time data processing and control tasks based on Ptolemy II simulations

    b. To directly embed Ptolemy II models into LabVIEW

    c. To create graphical user interfaces for Ptolemy II models

    d. To simulate data acquisition hardware

368. **What is the advantage of using a custom middleware solution for Ptolemy II and LabVIEW integration?**

    a. It allows for tailored data handling and communication between systems

    b. It provides pre-built integration tools

    c. It simplifies user interface design

    d. It directly controls hardware components

369. **Which of the following is a typical use case for integrating Ptolemy II and LabVIEW in an IoT application?**

    a. Developing and simulating complex control systems in Ptolemy II, then implementing real-time control and data visualization in LabVIEW

    b. Replacing LabVIEW's hardware with Ptolemy II's virtual models

    c. Creating web-based user interfaces for Ptolemy II models

    d. Managing database transactions and user authentication data visualization in LabVIEW

370. **What is the purpose of parameterized models in Ptolemy II?**

    a. To create user-defined control elements

    b. To allow models to be adjusted with different parameters for various scenarios

    c. To design graphical user interfaces

    d. To interface with external hardware

371. In Ptolemy II, how can multi-domain modeling be described?

    a. Modeling different hardware components

    b. Integrating multiple domains like continuous time, discrete event, and dataflow within a single model

    c. Creating multiple graphical user interfaces

    d. Handling different types of data storage

372. What does Ptolemy II's hierarchical modeling feature enable?

    a. Designing a complex system by breaking it down into simpler sub-models

    b. Creating detailed data visualization

    c. Managing real-time data streams

    d. Implementing user interface elements

373. Which of the following is a primary function of Ptolemy II's Modeling and Simulation environment?

    a. Direct hardware control

    b. Visualizing and analyzing complex systems and their behaviors

    c. Managing user authentication

    d. Creating network protocols

374. How does Ptolemy II support interoperability between different models?

    a. By using common data formats and interfaces for model integration

    b. By directly embedding external code

    c. By creating custom graphical components

    d. By providing hardware abstraction layers

375. In LabVIEW, what does the VI Server allow you to do?

    a. Manage real-time data acquisition

    b. Access and control VIs programmatically, including remote access

    c. Create user interface components

    d. Simulate hardware components

376. What is the function of LabVIEW's data acquisition (DAQ) system in IoT?

    a. To perform network communication

    b. To handle data from sensors and other measurement devices

    c. To design graphical user interfaces

    d. To create data storage solutions

377. **Which of the following LabVIEW features supports real-time processing of data?**

    a. Real-Time Module

    b. Simulation Module

    c. Vision Development Module

    d. Data Acquisition Module

378. **What does LabVIEW's project explorer allow users to manage?**

    a. Network communication

    b. Multiple VIs and associated files within a project

    c. Data acquisition hardware

    d. Graphical user interfaces

Join our Discord space

Join our Discord workspace for latest updates, offers, tech happenings around the world, new releases, and sessions with the authors:

https://discord.bpbonline.com

Answers

Q.No.	Answers	Q.No.	Answers	Q.No.	Answers	Q.No.	Answers	Q.No.	Answers
1	d	37	c	73	c	109	a	145	b
2	b	38	c	74	b	110	c	146	b
3	b	39	b	75	c	111	c	147	b
4	c	40	c	76	b	112	a	148	a
5	b	41	c	77	b	113	a	149	b
6	b	42	b	78	c	114	a	150	a
7	c	43	c	79	b	115	c	151	a
8	c	44	c	80	b	116	b	152	d
9	b	45	b	81	c	117	c	153	a
10	c	46	c	82	b	118	c	154	c
11	b	47	c	83	d	119	b	155	a
12	b	48	b	84	c	120	a	156	d
13	c	49	c	85	c	121	c	157	b
14	c	50	c	86	b	122	b	158	a
15	b	51	c	87	c	123	b	159	a
16	c	52	b	88	b	124	c	160	a
17	b	53	b	89	b	125	a	161	a
18	b	54	c	90	c	126	a	162	b
19	c	55	b	91	b	127	d	163	a
20	c	56	b	92	d	128	a	164	a
21	b	57	c	93	c	129	a	165	c
22	c	58	b	94	b	130	c	166	d
23	c	59	a	95	b	131	b	167	a
24	b	60	c	96	c	132	b	168	a
25	c	61	b	97	c	133	b	169	c
26	c	62	b	98	b	134	a	170	a
27	b	63	c	99	c	135	b	171	b
28	c	64	c	100	b	136	a	172	a
29	c	65	b	101	b	137	b	173	a
30	b	66	c	102	b	138	b	174	a
31	c	67	b	103	c	139	d	175	a
32	b	68	b	104	b	140	a	176	a
33	b	69	c	105	c	141	b	177	a
34	c	70	b	106	a	142	a	178	a
35	b	71	b	107	a	143	a	179	a
36	b	72	c	108	c	144	a	180	a

Q.No.	Answers	Q.No.	Answers	Q.No.	Answers	Q.No.	Answers	Q.No.	Answers
181	a	221	c	261	b	301	b	341	a
182	b	222	b	262	b	302	c	342	a
183	a	223	c	263	b	303	b	343	b
184	d	224	b	264	c	304	c	344	b
185	a	225	a	265	a	305	b	345	a
186	a	226	c	266	b	306	c	346	c
187	b	227	c	267	b	307	a	347	a
188	a	228	c	268	b	308	b	348	d
189	a	229	c	269	a	309	a	349	c
190	a	230	b	270	b	310	b	350	b
191	a	231	b	271	b	311	a	351	b
192	a	232	a	272	b	312	c	352	a
193	a	233	a	273	c	313	c	353	b
194	a	234	b	274	d	314	b	354	b
195	a	235	b	275	b	315	c	355	b
196	a	236	a	276	c	316	a	356	a
197	a	237	c	277	b	317	d	357	b
198	a	238	b	278	a	318	b	358	a
199	b	239	b	279	b	319	b	359	a
200	b	240	b	280	c	320	a	360	a
201	b	241	b	281	b	321	a	361	b
202	b	242	b	282	d	322	c	362	b
203	b	243	b	283	c	323	b	363	a
204	c	244	a	284	a	324	a	364	a
205	b	245	b	285	b	325	b	365	a
206	c	246	b	286	c	326	b	366	a
207	c	247	c	287	a	327	c	367	a
208	b	248	c	288	a	328	a	368	a
209	c	249	b	289	c	329	b	369	a
210	b	250	a	290	b	330	b	370	b
211	b	251	b	291	b	331	a	371	b
212	b	252	b	292	b	332	b	372	a
213	c	253	b	293	a	333	d	373	b
214	c	254	c	294	b	334	b	374	a
215	b	255	b	295	b	335	b	375	b
216	c	256	a	296	b	336	b	376	b
217	b	257	a	297	c	337	c	377	a
218	c	258	c	298	a	338	a	378	b
219	b	259	c	299	a	339	a		
220	c	260	c	300	b	340	b		

CHAPTER 7
IoT Ecosystem

Introduction

The digital transformation of numerous industries is collectively driven by a vast and interconnected matrix of devices, systems, and technologies that comprise the **Internet of Things (IoT)** ecosystem. The IoT ecosystem is fundamentally composed of a diverse array of smart devices that are outfitted with sensors and actuators, and that continuously generate and collect data from the physical world. These devices are connected through a variety of communication protocols, including Wi-Fi, Bluetooth, Zigbee, and cellular networks, which facilitate the seamless transmission of data to centralized or distributed cloud platforms for processing and analysis. The IoT ecosystem also incorporates sophisticated data analytics, artificial intelligence, and machine learning algorithms to convert unstructured data into actionable insights, thereby facilitating real-time decision-making and the automation of processes. The development of smart applications, including industrial automation, healthcare, agriculture, and smart homes and communities, is facilitated by the synergy between hardware, software, and communication networks within this ecosystem. Furthermore, the IoT ecosystem is supported by security frameworks and standards that are intended to safeguard data integrity, privacy, and system resilience in the face of cyber threats. It is on the brink of unlocking new opportunities for innovation, efficiency, and sustainability as IoT continues to develop, rendering it a critical enabler of the digital age.

IoT is a network of networked gadgets, automobiles, appliances, and other items that can gather and exchange data without human interaction. This network needs a diverse ecosystem of technologies, frameworks, and platforms to develop and evolve. Understanding the IoT ecosystem is essential to realizing its disruptive potential. Let us take a look:

- **Devices and hardware**: Devices are the foundation of the IoT ecosystem. These include smart thermostats, fitness trackers, industrial sensors, and smart city infrastructure. Each gadget has sensors or actuators to acquire data or act.

- **Connectivity:** IoT devices need network connectivity to communicate data. Communication technologies, including Wi-Fi, Bluetooth, LoRaWAN, Zigbee, and cellular networks, enable this. Application requirements for range, power consumption, and data transmission speeds determine the connection.

- **Data processing and storage:** Data must be processed after collection. Here comes cloud platforms and data centers. They host and process massive volumes of data. Advanced analytics, machine learning, and AI algorithms can then interpret the data and provide actionable insights.

- **Software and programs**: Users need programs to access and interact with data. Software makes data actionable for end-users, whether it is a smartphone app to manage a smart home device or an enterprise-level program to monitor an industrial IoT system. It simplifies complicated data into usable insights.

- **Security:** IoT devices handle sensitive data, making security a crucial aspect of the ecosystem. User trust and IoT network efficiency depend on secure data transfer, encrypted storage, and threat prevention.

- **Standards and protocols:** IoT ecosystem harmony requires standardization. Organizations are developing global standards and protocols to ensure device and platform compatibility.

- **Analytics and machine learning**: IoT data analysis enables informed decision-making. The ecosystem uses machine learning and AI to anticipate outcomes, automate processes, and customize user experiences.

Multiple choice questions

1. **What does IoT stand for?**
   a. Internet of Techniques
   b. Internet of Telecommunications
   c. Internet of Things
   d. Internet of Time

2. **Which statement best describes the IoT ecosystem?**
   a. A single connected device communicating with the internet.
   b. A network of interconnected devices that can communicate and exchange data.

c. A standalone device that does not require internet connectivity.

d. A group of unrelated devices that do not interact with each other.

3. **What is the primary purpose of IoT devices in the ecosystem?**

a. Entertainment

b. Collecting data and enabling automated actions

c. Aesthetics

d. None of the above

4. **Which of the following is not an example of an IoT device?**

a. Smart thermostat

b. Refrigerator with internet connectivity

c. Traditional wristwatch

d. Smart doorbell

5. **What does a sensor do in an IoT ecosystem?**

a. Provides power to devices

b. Connects devices to the internet

c. Collects data from the environment

d. Displays information on screens

6. **Which technology enables IoT devices to communicate wirelessly over short distances?**

a. Wi-Fi

b. Bluetooth

c. Ethernet

d. USB

7. **What role do actuators play in an IoT ecosystem?**

a. They sense environmental data.

b. They store data for later use.

c. They process data.

d. They perform actions based on received data.

8. **Which of the following is an example of a consumer IoT application?**

   a. Industrial automation

   b. Smart agriculture

   c. Wearable fitness tracker

   d. Smart city infrastructure

9. **What is the purpose of IoT gateways in an ecosystem?**

   a. To control devices locally

   b. To provide internet access to devices

   c. To secure devices from external threats

   d. To store data generated by devices

10. **Which layer of the IoT architecture deals with data processing and analysis?**

    a. Perception layer

    b. Network layer

    c. Application layer

    d. Database layer

11. **Which communication protocol is commonly used for IoT devices due to its low power consumption?**

    a. Bluetooth

    b. Wi-Fi

    c. Zigbee

    d. Ethernet

12. **What is the main advantage of edge computing in an IoT ecosystem?**

    a. Centralized data processing

    b. Reduced latency

    c. Higher bandwidth

    d. Greater device mobility

13. **Which of the following is not an example of a smart city application in the IoT ecosystem?**

    a. Personal fitness tracker

    b. Smart refrigerator

    c. Traffic management system

    d. Home automation system

14. **In the IoT ecosystem, what is the purpose of the cloud platform?**
    a. It provides power to IoT devices.
    b. It connects IoT devices through wires.
    c. It stores and processes data from IoT devices.
    d. It physically locates IoT devices.

15. **What does the term interoperability mean in the context of the IoT ecosystem?**
    a. The ability of devices to be standalone without any connectivity.
    b. The capability of devices to communicate and work together seamlessly.
    c. The requirement for devices to function only with specific brands.
    d. The need for devices to communicate using different communication protocols.

16. **Which of the following is a key challenge in the IoT ecosystem?**
    a. Lack of data security concerns
    b. Unlimited power supply for devices
    c. Standardization of communication protocols
    d. Reduced complexity in device interactions

17. **What is the main goal of data analytics in the IoT ecosystem?**
    a. To slow down data processing for accuracy.
    b. To analyze data for the sake of analysis.
    c. To generate unnecessary reports.
    d. To extract meaningful insights from collected data.

18. **Which layer of the IoT architecture involves the collection of data from the physical world?**
    a. Perception layer
    b. Network layer
    c. Application layer
    d. Presentation layer

19. **Which technology enables the identification and tracking of objects using radio waves?**
    a. GPS
    b. Bluetooth
    c. RFID
    d. NFC

20. **Which of the following is a security concern in the IoT ecosystem?**

    a. Devices always having physical connections.

    b. Devices sharing data too quickly.

    c. Devices being too expensive to replace.

    d. Devices are vulnerable to hacking and data breaches.

21. **Which layer of the IoT architecture is responsible for connecting IoT devices to the internet?**

    a. Perception layer

    b. Network layer

    c. Application layer

    d. Database layer

22. **What term describes the ability of IoT devices to communicate and interact without human intervention?**

    a. Human-machine interface

    b. Device autonomy

    c. Machine-to-machine communication

    d. Device synchronization

23. **How does the IoT ecosystem contribute to efficient resource utilization?**

    a. By increasing resource consumption

    b. By enabling better waste management

    c. By relying solely on non-renewable resources

    d. By decreasing resource optimization

24. **What role do APIs play in the IoT ecosystem?**

    a. They are physical connectors for IoT devices.

    b. They allow IoT devices to communicate with each other.

    c. They only work with specific IoT devices.

    d. They are used to power IoT devices.

25. **Which of the following is not a potential benefit of implementing an IoT ecosystem?**

    a. Improved efficiency and productivity

    b. Enhanced user privacy concerns

    c. Real-time monitoring and control

    d. Better decision-making based on data insights

26. **What role does fog computing play in the IoT ecosystem?**

    a. It generates fake data to confuse hackers.

    b. It enhances security by isolating IoT devices from the network.

    c. It acts as an intermediary layer between IoT devices and the cloud.

    d. It solely focuses on optimizing device energy consumption.

27. **Which technology allows IoT devices to communicate over long distances using cellular networks?**

    a. Wi-Fi

    b. Bluetooth

    c. LTE-M/NB-IoT

    d. Zigbee

28. **What is the role of blockchain technology in the IoT ecosystem?**

    a. It enhances device aesthetics.

    b. It ensures data security and tamper-proof records.

    c. It connects IoT devices to the cloud.

    d. It replaces the need for IoT gateways.

29. **What is the significance of edge devices in the IoT ecosystem?**

    a. They are only decorative elements in IoT environments.

    b. They process data locally, reducing latency and bandwidth usage.

    c. They have no role in IoT data processing.

    d. They solely rely on cloud processing for all tasks.

30. **Which layer of the IoT architecture involves the presentation and visualization of data?**

    a. Perception layer

    b. Network layer

    c. Application layer

    d. Presentation layer

31. **What is the purpose of IoT data analytics in the ecosystem?**

    a. To increase data collection frequency

    b. To interpret data patterns and derive insights

    c. To store data indefinitely

    d. To replace the need for data collection

32. **What is the term for the unique identifier assigned to each IoT device for network communication?**

   a. IP address

   b. MAC address

   c. Serial number

   d. Barcode

33. **How does the IoT ecosystem contribute to environmental sustainability?**

   a. By promoting excessive resource consumption

   b. By encouraging waste generation

   c. By optimizing energy usage and reducing carbon footprint

   d. By disregarding ecological concerns

34. **What is the primary goal of IoT security measures in the ecosystem?**

   a. To make IoT devices more aesthetically pleasing

   b. To eliminate all data collection from IoT devices

   c. To ensure the confidentiality, integrity, and availability of data

   d. To remove the need for device authentication

35. **Which protocol is commonly used for communication between IoT devices and the cloud?**

   a. Message Queuing Telemetry Transport (MQTT)

   b. Simple Mail Transfer Protocol (SMTP)

   c. Secure Shell Protocol (SSH)

   d. File Transfer Protocol (FTP)

36. **How do IoT devices contribute to data-driven decision-making in the ecosystem?**

   a. By limiting the amount of data collected

   b. By making decisions autonomously without human intervention

   c. By collecting and analyzing data for insights and actionable information

   d. By ignoring data insights and relying solely on intuition

37. **What is the role of machine learning in the IoT ecosystem?**

   a. It only focuses on enhancing device aesthetics.

   b. It analyzes data and adapts IoT devices' behavior based on patterns.

   c. It reduces the need for data analysis in IoT applications.

   d. It eliminates the need for network connectivity.

38. **How does the IoT ecosystem contribute to the concept of smart homes?**

    a. By making homes less secure and more vulnerable to attacks

    b. By automating home processes and enhancing energy efficiency

    c. By increasing electricity consumption in homes

    d. By disconnecting home devices from the internet

39. **What is the primary purpose of IoT device management in the ecosystem?**

    a. To make devices more expensive

    b. To ensure devices are not connected to the internet

    c. To monitor, control, and update IoT devices remotely

    d. To eliminate the need for device maintenance

40. **How does the IoT ecosystem contribute to enhancing healthcare services?**

    a. By making healthcare services less accessible

    b. By enabling remote patient monitoring and personalized treatment

    c. By promoting misinformation about health

    d. By reducing the role of doctors and healthcare professionals

41. **Which layer of the IoT architecture deals with data storage and management?**

    a. Perception layer

    b. Network layer

    c. Application layer

    d. Database layer

42. **What is the role of AI in the IoT ecosystem?**

    a. It is solely used for device aesthetics.

    b. It enhances data security and privacy.

    c. It enables devices to communicate only with each other.

    d. It analyzes data patterns and provides predictive insights.

43. **How does the IoT ecosystem contribute to improving agricultural practices?**

    a. By promoting excessive use of water and fertilizers

    b. By automating irrigation and monitoring crop health

    c. By reducing the need for data collection in farming

    d. By limiting access to essential farming data

44. **What is the term for the seamless communication between IoT devices and the services they provide?**

    a. User interface

    b. API

    c. Device communication interface

    d. Service integration protocol

45. **How does the IoT ecosystem contribute to enhancing industrial processes?**

    a. By increasing inefficiencies and downtime

    b. By reducing the need for process automation

    c. By enabling predictive maintenance and real-time monitoring

    d. By solely relying on manual labor for operations

46. **What is the role of predictive analytics in the IoT ecosystem?**

    a. It predicts the number of IoT devices in the future.

    b. It anticipates future security threats.

    c. It foresees potential issues based on data trends.

    d. It forecasts weather patterns.

47. **How does the IoT ecosystem contribute to improving transportation systems?**

    a. By increasing traffic congestion and accidents

    b. By promoting fuel wastage

    c. By enabling real-time traffic monitoring and navigation

    d. By eliminating the need for public transportation

48. **What is the term used when IoT devices are given unique IP addresses and can access the internet?**

    a. Device autonomy

    b. Device aesthetics

    c. Device connectivity

    d. Device integration

49. **How does the IoT ecosystem contribute to enhancing energy efficiency in smart buildings?**

    a. By increasing energy consumption

    b. By optimizing lighting, HVAC systems, and appliances

   c. By promoting unnecessary resource usage

   d. By eliminating the need for energy management

50. **Which of the following is a challenge in the IoT ecosystem related to data privacy?**

   a. Too much data being collected

   b. Inability to store data

   c. Unauthorized access to sensitive information

   d. Data being too accurate

51. **What is the purpose of a digital twin in the IoT ecosystem?**

   a. To create a virtual replica of physical objects

   b. To replace physical objects with digital counterparts

   c. To create simulated data for testing scenarios

   d. To increase the complexity of IoT networks

52. **How does the IoT ecosystem contribute to improving supply chain management?**

   a. By increasing inefficiencies in logistics

   b. By promoting inaccurate inventory tracking

   c. By enabling real-time tracking and monitoring of goods

   d. By reducing the need for data sharing between suppliers

53. **What is the role of location-based services in the IoT ecosystem?**

   a. To track users' personal information

   b. To deliver context-aware content

   c. To promote unnecessary data collection

   d. To improve device aesthetics

54. **How does the IoT ecosystem contribute to enhancing environmental monitoring?**

   a. By promoting increased pollution

   b. By enabling real-time monitoring of air and water quality

   c. By ignoring climate change concerns

   d. By limiting access to environmental data

55. **Which layer in the IoT architecture handles the processing and analysis of data collected from IoT devices?**

    a. Perception layer

    b. Network layer

    c. Application layer

    d. Database layer

56. **What is the term for a network of physical devices, vehicles, buildings, and other objects embedded with sensors, software, and connectivity to enable data exchange?**

    a. Internet of Things (IoT)

    b. Internet of Computers (IoC)

    c. Internet of Networks (IoN)

    d. Internet of Communication (IoC)

57. **How does the IoT ecosystem contribute to improving disaster management?**

    a. By increasing the impact of disasters

    b. By promoting ineffective response strategies

    c. By enabling real-time monitoring and early warnings

    d. By solely relying on traditional disaster management methods

58. **What is the role of fog nodes in edge computing within the IoT ecosystem?**

    a. To generate fog to cool down devices

    b. To process data only in the cloud

    c. To act as intermediaries between edge devices and the cloud

    d. To solely perform data storage tasks

59. **How does the IoT ecosystem contribute to improving waste management?**

    a. By increasing littering and waste generation

    b. By enabling real-time monitoring of waste levels and collection

    c. By discouraging recycling efforts

    d. By ignoring waste disposal concerns

60. **Which layer of the IoT architecture is responsible for the physical sensing of the environment?**

    a. Perception layer

    b. Network layer

    c. Application layer

    d. Presentation layer

61. **What is the term for the integration of IoT devices and systems into existing physical environments?**

    a. Digital intrusion

    b. IoT assimilation

    c. IoT integration

    d. Device adaptation

62. **How does the IoT ecosystem contribute to enhancing water management?**

    a. By increasing water wastage

    b. By promoting water pollution

    c. By enabling real-time monitoring of water consumption and quality

    d. By eliminating the need for water conservation efforts

63. **What is the role of big data analytics in the IoT ecosystem?**

    a. It generates big data for IoT devices.

    b. It processes data exclusively on edge devices.

    c. It analyzes massive amounts of data for insights.

    d. It limits data collection in IoT applications.

64. **How does the IoT ecosystem contribute to enhancing retail operations?**

    a. By increasing stock shortages and customer dissatisfaction

    b. By enabling real-time inventory management and personalized shopping experiences

    c. By discouraging online shopping

    d. By reducing the need for customer data collection

65. **What is the term for devices or sensors that operate in an autonomous manner, without human intervention, to perform specific tasks?**

    a. Connected devices

    b. Autonomous devices

    c. Robotic devices

    d. Automated devices

66. **How does the IoT ecosystem contribute to improving public safety and security?**

    a. By promoting unsafe environments

    b. By enabling real-time surveillance and emergency response

    c. By increasing crime rates

    d. By limiting access to emergency services

67. **What is the role of cloud computing in the IoT ecosystem?**

    a. It solely focuses on device aesthetics.

    b. It provides local data processing on edge devices.

    c. It stores and processes data from IoT devices remotely.

    d. It eliminates the need for device communication.

68. **How does the IoT ecosystem contribute to enhancing waste recycling?**

    a. By promoting improper waste disposal

    b. By enabling real-time monitoring of recycling bins

    c. By discouraging sustainable practices

    d. By increasing landfill usage

69. **What is the role of microcontrollers in IoT devices?**

    a. They enhance device aesthetics.

    b. They connect devices to the internet.

    c. They solely focus on energy consumption.

    d. They control device operations and data processing.

70. **How does the IoT ecosystem contribute to enhancing air quality monitoring?**

    a. By increasing air pollution

    b. By enabling real-time monitoring of pollutants and air quality indexes

    c. By promoting activities harmful to air quality

    d. By reducing the importance of clean air

71. **What is the purpose of mesh networking in the IoT ecosystem?**

    a. To enable self-healing multi-hop

    b. To connect devices in a linear fashion

    c. To create complex device hierarchies

    d. To enable devices to communicate directly with each other

72. **How does the IoT ecosystem contribute to enhancing agriculture precision?**

    a. By promoting excessive use of pesticides and fertilizers

    b. By enabling data-driven decision-making in farming practices

    c. By eliminating the need for weather forecasts

    d. By ignoring soil health concerns

73. **What is the term for the process of transferring data from one device to another without human intervention?**

    a. Device synchronization

    b. Data communication

    c. Machine communication

    d. Machine-to-machine communication

74. **How does the IoT ecosystem contribute to improving wildlife conservation efforts?**

    a. By increasing threats to endangered species

    b. By enabling real-time monitoring and tracking of wildlife

    c. By encouraging habitat destruction

    d. By promoting illegal wildlife trade

75. **What is the role of 5G technology in the IoT ecosystem?**

    a. It only focuses on improving device aesthetics.

    b. It enhances data security on IoT devices.

    c. It enables faster and more reliable wireless communication.

    d. It eliminates the need for data processing.

76. **How does the IoT ecosystem contribute to enhancing disaster recovery and response?**

    a. By making disasters more destructive

    b. By enabling real-time communication and coordination during disasters

    c. By increasing response time and inefficiency

    d. By disregarding disaster management efforts

77. **What is the role of predictive maintenance in the industrial IoT ecosystem?**

    a. It predicts when IoT devices need to be replaced.

    b. It anticipates maintenance requirements based on data analysis.

    c. It eliminates the need for device maintenance altogether.

    d. It focuses solely on aesthetic maintenance.

78. **How does the IoT ecosystem contribute to enhancing smart energy management?**

    a. By increasing energy wastage

    b. By enabling real-time monitoring and optimization of energy usage

    c. By ignoring energy conservation efforts

    d. By reducing the importance of renewable energy sources

79. **What is the term for the process of integrating digital information with the physical world using sensors and other devices?**

    a. Data transformation

    b. Digital integration

    c. Digital transformation

    d. Digital transformation

80. **How does the IoT ecosystem contribute to enhancing urban planning?**

    a. By increasing urban sprawl and traffic congestion

    b. By enabling real-time monitoring of infrastructure and public services

    c. By discouraging sustainable development

    d. By limiting access to urban amenities

81. **What is the primary function of an IoT device?**

    a. Data processing

    b. Data storage

    c. Data collection and communication

    d. Data deletion

82. **Which of the following is an example of an IoT device?**

    a. Smart thermostat

    b. Desktop computer

    c. DVD player

    d. Analog radio

83. **What protocol is commonly used by IoT devices for wireless communication?**

    a. HTTP

    b. FTP

    c. MQTT

    d. SMTP

84. **Which sensor type is often used in IoT devices for environmental monitoring?**

    a. Temperature sensor

    b. Motion sensor

    c. Proximity sensor

    d. Light sensor

85. **What is the primary function of wearables in the IoT ecosystem?**

    a. Playing music and videos

    b. Monitoring and transmitting real-time health and activity data

    c. Replacing smartphones

    d. Enhancing social media engagement

86. **What is a common security concern in IoT systems?**

    a. Battery life

    b. Device compatibility

    c. Data breaches

    d. User interface design

87. **Which technology can be used to ensure data integrity in IoT devices?**

    a. VPN

    b. Firewalls

    c. Blockchain

    d. Load balancers

88. **What is the purpose of encryption in IoT security?**

    a. To increase data speed

    b. To enhance user experience

    c. To protect data confidentiality

    d. To reduce power consumption

89. **Which of the following is a secure communication protocol used in IoT?**

    a. HTTP

    b. TLS/DTLS

    c. FTP

    d. Telnet

90. **What is the role of an intrusion detection system (IDS) in IoT?**

    a. To detect power failures

    b. To monitor and analyze traffic for signs of attacks

    c. To backup data

    d. To manage device updates

91. **Which network topology is commonly used in IoT?**

    a. Star topology

    b. Ring topology

    c. Mesh topology

    d. Bus topology

92. **What does LPWAN stand for in IoT networking?**

    a. Low Power Wireless Area Network

    b. Local Private Wireless Area Network

    c. Long Protocol Wide Area Network

    d. Low Power Wide Area Network

93. **Which wireless technology is known for its low power consumption suitable for IoT?**

    a. Wi-Fi

    b. Bluetooth

    c. Zigbee

    d. LTE

94. **What is the primary benefit of using IPv6 in IoT networks?**

    a. Faster data transmission

    b. Larger address space

    c. Enhanced security

    d. Lower latency

95. **Which type of network is often used to connect IoT devices within a limited area?**

    a. PAN

    b. WAN

    c. MAN

    d. GAN

96. **Which of the following is an example of an IoT-enabled wearable device?**

    a. Smartwatch

    b. Smart refrigerator

    c. Wireless router

    d. Bluetooth speaker

97. **How does an IoT gateway enhance security?**

    a. By reducing power consumption

    b. By filtering out malicious data

    c. By increasing data speed

    d. By storing large amounts of data

98. **What is edge computing in the context of IoT?**

    a. Processing data at a central cloud

    b. Processing data at the edge of the network

    c. Storing data on local servers

    d. Sending data directly to the user

99. **Which protocol is often used by IoT gateways for device communication?**

    a. SMTP

    b. FTP

    c. MQTT

    d. IMAP

100. **What is a benefit of using fog computing with IoT gateways?**

    a. Increased latency

    b. Reduced bandwidth usage

    c. Enhanced data encryption

    d. Simplified network management

101. **What is the role of the cloud in IoT ecosystems?**

    a. Data storage and analysis

    b. Device management

    c. User interface management

    d. Power supply

102. **Which of the following is a popular cloud service for IoT?**

     a. Azure IoT Hub

     b. MySQL

     c. Apache Kafka

     d. Redis

103. **What is the main advantage of using cloud computing in IoT?**

     a. Increased hardware costs

     b. Improved data accessibility and scalability

     c. Reduced security

     d. Complex setup

104. **Which type of data is typically stored in IoT cloud applications?**

     a. Static data

     b. Time-series data

     c. Video data only

     d. Text documents

105. **What does the term analytics refer to in IoT cloud applications?**

     a. Data storage techniques

     b. Processing and analyzing data to generate insights

     c. Device management

     d. Network configuration

106. **What is a smart device in the context of IoT?**

     a. A device that can operate without power

     b. A device that can connect and communicate over the internet

     c. A device that only stores data

     d. A device that does not require updates

107. **Which component in an IoT device is responsible for sensing physical conditions?**

     a. Microcontroller

     b. Sensor

     c. Actuator

     d. Transceiver

108. **What is the function of a transceiver in an IoT device?**

    a. To store data

    b. To sense environmental data

    c. To transmit and receive data

    d. To process data

109. **Which energy source is commonly used for powering IoT devices?**

    a. Solar power

    b. Fossil fuels

    c. Nuclear power

    d. Wind power

110. **What does low-power mean in the context of IoT devices?**

    a. Devices that operate with minimal electricity

    b. Devices that do not use any power

    c. Devices that require frequent charging

    d. Devices with high power consumption

111. **What is a common method to secure data transmission in IoT?**

    a. Using plain text communication

    b. Encrypting data

    c. Disabling data transmission

    d. Using analog signals

112. **What is two-factor authentication (2FA) in IoT security?**

    a. A method of encrypting data

    b. A user authentication process involving two different verification methods

    c. A way to store data

    d. A device management protocol

113. **Which of the following is a major challenge in IoT security?**

    a. Large storage capacity

    b. Device interoperability

    c. Limited processing power for security protocols

    d. High power consumption

114. **What is the purpose of a firewall in IoT networks?**
    a. To physically protect devices
    b. To control incoming and outgoing network traffic
    c. To increase data speed
    d. To manage user interfaces

115. **Which symmetric encryption method is commonly used in securing IoT devices?**
    a. Advanced Encryption Standard (AES)
    b. RSA
    c. Data Encryption Standard (DES)
    d. MD5

116. **What is a Zero Trust security model?**
    a. A model where no devices are trusted and verification is continuously required
    b. A model that trusts all devices by default
    c. A model with no security requirements
    d. A model that does not use encryption

117. **What is a common technique for mitigating IoT device vulnerabilities?**
    a. Regular software updates
    b. Deactivating device communication
    c. Using outdated protocols
    d. Limiting device functionality

118. **Which of the following is a technique to secure IoT networks?**
    a. VPN
    b. Open access
    c. Disable all communications
    d. Use only local storage

119. **What is device hardening in IoT security?**
    a. Adding physical barriers to devices
    b. Configuring devices to minimize security vulnerabilities
    c. Increasing the device's power supply
    d. Reducing device functionality

120. **What does QoS stand for in IoT networks?**
    a. Quality of Service
    b. Quantity of Storage
    c. Quality of Security
    d. Quantity of Signals

121. **Which protocol is often used for low-power IoT networks?**
    a. TCP/IP
    b. HTTP
    c. CoAP
    d. IMAP

122. **What is the function of a network router in an IoT setup?**
    a. To connect multiple devices and manage data traffic
    b. To provide power to devices
    c. To sense environmental conditions
    d. To store data

123. **What does network latency refer to?**
    a. The speed at which data is processed by devices
    b. The time delay in data transmission across the network
    c. The amount of data stored in the network
    d. The frequency of network updates

124. **Which technology is used to connect IoT devices over long distances with low power consumption?**
    a. Bluetooth
    b. Zigbee
    c. Long Range (LoRa)
    d. Wi-Fi

125. **What role does an IoT gateway play in data processing?**
    a. It performs initial data processing before sending it to the cloud
    b. It only stores data
    c. It sends data directly to users
    d. It performs data encryption

126. **Which of the following is a key feature of IoT gateways?**

    a. Support for multiple communication protocols

    b. Data deletion capabilities

    c. High power consumption

    d. Lack of security features

127. **What is a protocol converter in the context of IoT gateways?**

    a. A device that converts data to different formats for compatibility

    b. A device that stores data

    c. A device that only senses data

    d. A device that provides power to IoT devices

128. **What is the benefit of using edge analytics in IoT gateways?**

    a. Increased data transmission time

    b. Reduced need for cloud resources

    c. Increased power consumption

    d. Decreased data accuracy

129. **Which feature of IoT gateways helps in managing large numbers of devices?**

    a. Device management interfaces

    b. Low power consumption

    c. Data storage capabilities

    d. Limited communication range

130. **What is scalability in the context of IoT cloud applications?**

    a. The ability to increase or decrease resources based on demand

    b. The speed at which data is processed

    c. The physical size of cloud servers

    d. The frequency of software updates

131. **Which cloud computing model provides the highest level of management and control?**

    a. Software as a service (SaaS)

    b. Platform as a service (PaaS)

    c. Infrastructure as a service (IaaS)

    d. Function as a service (FaaS)

132. **What does schema-on-read refer to in cloud applications?**

    a. A centralized repository for storing large amounts of unstructured data

    b. A specific type of database

    c. A temporary data storage solution

    d. A method for data encryption

133. **Which cloud-based service is used for real-time data processing in IoT?**

    a. Data warehousing

    b. Batch processing

    c. Stream processing

    d. Data backup

134. **What does serverless computing mean in the context of IoT cloud applications?**

    a. Computing without physical servers

    b. A model where users do not manage the server infrastructure

    c. A computing model with reduced security

    d. A model that requires extensive hardware setup

135. **Which of the following is an important consideration for designing IoT devices?**

    a. Power efficiency

    b. Size of the device only

    c. Device weight

    d. Aesthetic design

136. **What type of IoT device uses voice recognition technology?**

    a. Smart speaker

    b. Smart refrigerator

    c. Smart thermostat

    d. Smart lock

137. **Which component of an IoT device is responsible for executing control commands?**

    a. Sensor

    b. Actuator

    c. Transceiver

    d. Microcontroller

138. **What is interoperability in the context of IoT devices?**

   a. The ability of devices to work together and communicate effectively

   b. The capacity of a device to operate independently

   c. The power consumption of devices

   d. The storage capacity of devices

139. **Which of the following is a common interface for IoT devices?**

   a. VGI

   b. HDMI

   c. Ethernet

   d. Bluetooth

140. **What is a common secure authentication method for authenticating IoT devices?**

   a. Using passwords only

   b. Using digital certificates

   c. Using manual verification

   d. Using physical tokens only

141. **What does vulnerability assessment involve in IoT security?**

   a. Identifying and evaluating security weaknesses in IoT systems

   b. Increasing device functionality

   c. Enhancing device aesthetics

   d. Reducing data storage needs

142. **Which approach helps in mitigating denial of service (DoS) attacks on IoT devices?**

   a. Rate limiting and traffic filtering

   b. Disabling all network connections

   c. Increasing power supply

   d. Using unencrypted protocols

143. **What is a security patch?**

   a. An update designed to fix security vulnerabilities

   b. A physical cover for a device

   c. A method to increase device speed

   d. A tool for data backup

144. **Which protocol helps in managing secure connections between IoT devices and cloud services?**

    a. TLS

    b. POP3

    c. IMAP

    d. MQTT-TLS

145. **What is a mesh network in IoT?**

    a. A network topology where each node connects directly to several other nodes

    b. A network that only uses wireless connections

    c. A network with a central hub

    d. A network that does not support multiple devices

146. **What is the primary use of a base station in IoT networks?**

    a. To connect and manage communication between IoT devices and the network

    b. To store data locally

    c. To power IoT devices

    d. To provide backup storage

147. **Which of the following protocols is used for high-bandwidth IoT applications?**

    a. 6LoWPAN

    b. LTE

    c. Zigbee

    d. LoRa

148. **What is network slicing in the context of IoT?**

    a. Creating virtual networks on the same physical network infrastructure

    b. Reducing network speed

    c. Increasing physical network size

    d. Disabling network connections

149. **What does bandwidth refer to in IoT networks?**

    a. The amount of data that can be transmitted over a network in a given time

    b. The physical size of network cables

    c. The power consumption of network devices

    d. The length of network cables

150. What is a data aggregator in an IoT gateway?

    a. A component that collects and consolidates data from multiple sources

    b. A device that performs data encryption

    c. A device that only stores data

    d. A component that powers devices

151. Which feature of IoT gateways helps with interoperability?

    a. Support for multiple communication protocols

    b. High power consumption

    c. Limited storage capacity

    d. Lack of security features

152. What is protocol bridging in the context of IoT gateways?

    a. The capability to translate between different communication protocols

    b. The process of increasing network speed

    c. The method of powering multiple devices

    d. The technique of data encryption

153. How do IoT gateways typically handle data before sending it to the cloud?

    a. By filtering, aggregating, and preprocessing the data

    b. By directly forwarding raw data without processing

    c. By storing it on local disks

    d. By encrypting data only

154. What is the advantage of using cloud gateways in IoT systems?

    a. They allow for seamless integration with cloud services

    b. They only provide local data storage

    c. They do not support remote device management

    d. They increase device power consumption

155. Which service model in cloud computing offers tools for developing and managing IoT applications?

    a. Platform as a service (PaaS)

    b. Software as a service (SaaS)

    c. Infrastructure as a service (IaaS)

    d. Function as a service (FaaS)

156. What is data sovereignty in the context of cloud applications?

    a. The concept that data is subject to the laws and regulations of the country where it is stored

    b. The ability to access data from anywhere

    c. The process of encrypting data

    d. The method of storing data on local devices

157. Which cloud service model allows users to deploy their own applications and manage them?

    a. Infrastructure as a service (IaaS)

    b. Software as a service (SaaS)

    c. Platform as a service (PaaS)

    d. Function as a service (FaaS)

158. What does multi-tenancy mean in cloud computing?

    a. Multiple users or organizations share the same cloud infrastructure while keeping their data separate

    b. Multiple servers for a single application

    c. Multiple data storage methods

    d. Multiple physical locations for cloud data centers

159. Which cloud computing feature is essential for handling large-scale IoT data?

    a. Elastic scalability

    b. Fixed storage capacity

    c. Local-only processing

    d. Single-user access

160. Which technology is used for short-range wireless communication in IoT devices?

    a. Wi-Fi

    b. Zigbee

    c. LoRa

    d. 4G LTE

161. What does device firmware refer to?

    a. The software that controls the hardware of an IoT device

    b. The physical components of a device

    c. The power supply system of a device

    d. The device's outer casing

162. **What is device provisioning in IoT?**

    a. The process of configuring and setting up a device for use in a network

    b. The process of powering a device

    c. The process of physical assembly of a device

    d. The process of installing device software

163. **Which type of IoT device is commonly used in smart home applications?**

    a. Smart light bulbs

    b. Analog watches

    c. Old-style thermostats

    d. Non-networked refrigerators

164. **What is the purpose of a microcontroller in an IoT device?**

    a. To manage and execute control processes within the device

    b. To power the device

    c. To store data

    d. To provide network connectivity

165. **What is public key infrastructure (PKI) used for in IoT security?**

    a. To manage digital certificates and encryption keys

    b. To store device data

    c. To increase device speed

    d. To enhance physical security

166. **Which security measure helps protect IoT devices from physical tampering?**

    a. Physical enclosures and tamper-evident seals

    b. Data encryption

    c. Network firewalls

    d. Regular software updates

167. **What is identity and access management (IAM) in IoT security?**

    a. The system for managing user access and permissions to IoT devices and data

    b. The process of storing device information

    c. The method for device data encryption

    d. The technique for device energy management

168. **What does endpoint security refer to in IoT?**
    a. The protection of individual devices that connect to a network
    b. The security of the network infrastructure
    c. The security of cloud applications
    d. The security of data storage solutions

169. **What is security by design in the context of IoT?**
    a. The practice of incorporating security features into the design phase of IoT devices
    b. The process of post-deployment security updates
    c. The use of external security solutions only
    d. The focus on physical device design without considering security

170. **Which IoT network technology supports very low data rates and long-range communication?**
    a. LoRaWAN
    b. Bluetooth
    c. Zigbee
    d. Wi-Fi

171. **What does network congestion refer to?**
    a. The situation where network traffic exceeds the capacity, leading to delays and packet loss
    b. The high speed of data transfer
    c. The number of connected devices
    d. The physical size of the network infrastructure

172. **What is network redundancy in IoT networks?**
    a. Implementing backup communication paths to ensure network reliability
    b. Using only a single network path
    c. Reducing the number of network devices
    d. Increasing network latency

173. **Which technology provides high-speed internet access for IoT devices?**
    a. 5G
    b. Zigbee
    c. Bluetooth
    d. LoRa

174. What is dynamic spectrum allocation in IoT networks?

a. The method of adjusting the use of frequency bands to optimize network performance

b. The process of increasing network latency

c. The physical allocation of network devices

d. The static assignment of network channels

175. What is device management in the context of IoT gateways?

a. The process of configuring, monitoring, and maintaining IoT devices

b. The physical placement of devices

c. The method of data encryption

d. The design of device enclosures

176. Which feature of IoT gateways supports remote management?

a. Cloud-based management interfaces

b. Local-only access

c. Manual device configuration

d. Physical security measures

177. What is the purpose of data buffering in IoT gateways?

a. To temporarily store data before it is processed or transmitted

b. To increase the device's power consumption

c. To directly forward data without processing

d. To perform encryption on data

178. What is firmware over-the-air (FOTA) in IoT gateways?

a. The capability to update the device's firmware remotely

b. A method for physical device upgrades

c. A tool for data backup

d. A technique for device authentication

179. Which of the following is a common method for securing IoT gateway communications?

a. VPN

b. Open network protocols

c. Unencrypted data transmission

d. Physical isolation from networks

180. **Which cloud service model allows developers to deploy code without managing servers?**

    a. Function as a service (FaaS)

    b. Platform as a service (PaaS)

    c. Infrastructure as a service (IaaS)

    d. Software as a service (SaaS)

181. **What is data encryption at rest?**

    a. Encrypting data when it is stored on disk

    b. Encrypting data during transmission

    c. Encrypting data in memory

    d. Encrypting data only during processing

182. **Which service model provides a full suite of managed applications in the cloud?**

    a. Software as a service (SaaS)

    b. Platform as a service (PaaS)

    c. Infrastructure as a service (IaaS)

    d. Function as a service (FaaS)

183. **What does elasticity mean in cloud computing?**

    a. The ability to scale resources up or down based on demand

    b. The physical size of cloud data centers

    c. The speed of data transfer

    d. The amount of data stored

184. **Which technology is commonly used to ensure high availability in cloud applications?**

    a. Load balancing

    b. Single server deployment

    c. Local-only storage

    d. Manual failover processes

185. **How do IoT-enabled wearables transmit data?**

    a. Through USB cables

    b. Using wireless communication technologies like Bluetooth, Wi-Fi, or LTE

    c. By manual data entry

    d. Using infrared signals

186. **Which of the following is a key benefit of using wearables in healthcare?**

    a. Enhanced gaming experience

    b. Real-time health monitoring and alerts

    c. Improved battery life for mobile devices

    d. Increased internet speed

187. **Which IoT device is specifically designed for tracking location?**

    a. GPS tracker

    b. Smart thermostat

    c. Smart light bulb

    d. Smart lock

188. **What does low-power wide-area network (LPWAN) refer to?**

    a. A network designed for low power consumption and long-range communication

    b. A high-speed local area network

    c. A network with high data throughput

    d. A network with frequent data updates

189. **What is the main advantage of using smart sensors in IoT devices?**

    a. The ability to process and analyze data locally

    b. The physical durability of the sensors

    c. The lack of need for data communication

    d. The low cost of production

190. **What is 2FA used for in IoT security?**

    a. To provide an additional layer of security for user access

    b. To store device data securely

    c. To encrypt data in transit

    d. To monitor device performance

191. **Which type of security attack involves overwhelming a network with traffic?**

    a. Denial of service (DoS) attack

    b. Phishing attack

    c. Man-in-the-middle attack

    d. SQL injection

192. **What is intrusion detection in the context of IoT security?**

    a. The process of monitoring network traffic for suspicious activities

    b. The process of encrypting data

    c. The method of data backup

    d. The technique of physical device protection

193. **Which protocol provides secure communication over the internet for IoT devices?**

    a. HyperText Transfer Protocol Secure (HTTPS)

    b. File Transfer Protocol (FTP)

    c. Telnet

    d. HyperText Transfer Protocol (HTTP)

194. **What is device authentication in IoT security?**

    a. The process of verifying the identity of a device before granting access

    b. The process of encrypting data stored on a device

    c. The method of physical security for devices

    d. The technique of managing user access

195. **Which technology is used for short-range communication between IoT devices?**

    a. BLE

    b. LoRa

    c. 4G LTE

    d. Zigbee home automation

196. **What does IP addressing refer to in IoT networks?**

    a. The method of assigning unique addresses to devices for network communication

    b. The technique of encrypting data

    c. The process of managing device power

    d. The method of storing device data

197. **Which of the following is a common challenge in IoT network management?**

    a. Ensuring efficient data routing and low latency

    b. Increasing device physical size

    c. Reducing the number of network devices

    d. Minimizing network communication

198. **What does bandwidth management involve in IoT networks?**

    a. Controlling the amount of data transmitted over the network to avoid congestion

    b. Increasing device power usage

    c. Decreasing network speed

    d. Reducing the number of connected devices

199. **Which network protocol is suitable for IoT applications requiring real-time data?**

    a. Message Queuing Telemetry Transport (MQTT)

    b. File Transfer Protocol (FTP)

    c. Simple Mail Transfer Protocol (SMTP)

    d. Simple Network Management Protocol (SNMP)

200. **What is data preprocessing in the context of IoT gateways?**

    a. The process of preparing data for further analysis or transmission

    b. The method of storing data locally

    c. The process of increasing device power

    d. The technique of data encryption

201. **Which feature of IoT gateways supports protocol compatibility?**

    a. Protocol translation

    b. High power consumption

    c. Limited storage capacity

    d. Physical security features

202. **What does local data processing mean for IoT gateways?**

    a. Processing data on the gateway itself before sending it to the cloud

    b. Storing data only on local disks

    c. Encrypting data during transmission

    d. Managing network traffic

203. **What is network traffic management in IoT gateways?**

    a. The process of directing and controlling data flow within the network

    b. The method of data storage

    c. The technique of device authentication

    d. The process of device configuration

204. Which of the following is a benefit of using IoT gateways?

    a. Improved network efficiency and device management

    b. Increased data redundancy

    c. Reduced device functionality

    d. Decreased security measures

205. What is auto-scaling in cloud applications?

    a. The automatic adjustment of computing resources based on demand

    b. The manual increase of server capacity

    c. The physical scaling of data centers

    d. The reduction of data storage

206. Which of the following best describes serverless computing?

    a. A cloud computing model where developers deploy code without managing servers

    b. A method of using physical servers for computing tasks

    c. A technique for increasing server size

    d. A process of managing server hardware

207. What is data replication in cloud environments?

    a. The process of creating copies of data to ensure availability and reliability

    b. The method of compressing data

    c. The technique of encrypting data

    d. The process of deleting old data

208. Which cloud feature allows users to pay only for the resources they use?

    a. Pay-as-you-go pricing

    b. Fixed monthly fees

    c. Subscription-based pricing

    d. Lifetime licensing

209. What does disaster recovery involve in cloud computing?

    a. The strategies and processes to restore services and data after a disaster

    b. The method of physical server replacement

    c. The process of manual data backup

    d. The technique of improving server performance

Answers

Q.No.	Answers	Q.No.	Answers	Q.No.	Answers	Q.No.	Answers	Q.No.	Answers
1	c	31	b	61	c	91	c	121	c
2	b	32	b	62	c	92	c	122	a
3	b	33	c	63	c	93	c	123	b
4	c	34	c	64	b	94	b	124	c
5	c	35	a	65	b	95	a	125	a
6	b	36	c	66	b	96	a	126	a
7	d	37	b	67	c	97	b	127	a
8	c	38	b	68	b	98	b	128	b
9	a	39	c	69	d	99	c	129	a
10	c	40	b	70	b	100	b	130	a
11	a	41	d	71	d	101	a	131	c
12	b	42	d	72	b	102	a	132	a
13	a	43	b	73	d	103	b	133	c
14	c	44	b	74	b	104	b	134	b
15	b	45	c	75	c	105	b	135	a
16	c	46	a	76	b	106	b	136	a
17	d	47	c	77	b	107	b	137	b
18	a	48	c	78	b	108	c	138	a
19	c	49	b	79	d	109	a	139	d
20	d	50	c	80	b	110	a	140	b
21	b	51	a	81	c	111	b	141	a
22	c	52	c	82	a	112	b	142	a
23	b	53	b	83	c	113	c	143	a
24	b	54	b	84	a	114	b	144	a
25	b	55	c	85	b	115	a	145	a
26	c	56	a	86	c	116	a	146	a
27	c	57	c	87	c	117	a	147	b
28	b	58	c	88	c	118	a	148	a
29	b	59	b	89	b	119	b	149	a
30	d	60	a	90	b	120	a	150	a

Q.No.	Answers	Q.No.	Answers	Q.No.	Answers
151	a	171	a	191	a
152	a	172	a	192	a
153	a	173	a	193	a
154	a	174	a	194	a
155	a	175	a	195	a
156	a	176	a	196	a
157	c	177	a	197	a
158	a	178	a	198	a
159	a	179	a	199	a
160	b	180	a	200	a
161	a	181	a	201	a
162	a	182	a	202	a
163	a	183	a	203	a
164	a	184	a	204	a
165	a	185	b	205	a
166	a	186	b	206	a
167	a	187	a	207	a
168	a	188	a	208	a
169	a	189	a	209	a
170	a	190	a		

Join our Discord space

Join our Discord workspace for latest updates, offers, tech happenings around the world, new releases, and sessions with the authors:

https://discord.bpbonline.com

CHAPTER 8
IoT Platforms

Introduction

The IoT has rapidly grown into a network of billions of connected devices, generating vast amounts of data and enabling new levels of automation and intelligence across industries. Central to this ecosystem are IoT platforms, which serve as the backbone for managing device connectivity, data collection, processing, and analysis. These platforms provide the necessary tools and infrastructure to streamline the development, deployment, and management of IoT solutions, making it easier to harness the full potential of IoT technology in various applications. The IoT has revolutionized technology by linking billions of devices. IoT systems underpin this complex network. The intermediary layer between device data gathering and application data use is these platforms. Understanding IoT platforms and their importance is key to maximizing the paradigm's potential. IoT platforms enable developers to efficiently connect, manage, and extract data from devices. They simplify IoT infrastructure development and deployment by providing tools and capabilities.

The following are the key features:

- Users may register, categorize, monitor, and remotely manage devices on IoT systems. This covers firmware upgrades, diagnostics, and troubleshooting.

- Data processing and analysis. Platforms process data in real time to provide actionable insights. Finding abnormalities, forecasting device failures, and improving processes are examples.

- To guarantee devices can transmit and receive data smoothly, IoT systems enable many communication protocols. This might include Wi-Fi, LTE, MQTT, and CoAP connectivity.

- IoT commonly interacts with other corporate systems. Therefore, platforms provide integration tools and APIs. This allows data to flow across systems, improving data-driven decision-making.

- Connecting several devices poses hazards; thus, security is crucial. Security features on platforms include encrypted communications, device authentication, and permission.

IoT platform types

Despite the word IoT platform seeming solitary, it refers to several functionalities. Connection/M2M platforms: Prioritize secure device connection:

- **Application enablement platforms (AEPs)**: Help build and deploy IoT apps fast. Advanced analytics platforms: Highlight data analytics, machine learning, and AI.

- **Device management platforms**: Manage device lifespans. Several major businesses dominate the market. Examples include IBM Watson IoT, Microsoft Azure IoT Suite, Google Cloud IoT, **Amazon Web Services (AWS)** IoT Core, Cisco, PTC, and SAP.

Each platform caters to different demands and industries with its own characteristics.

Multiple choice questions

1. **What is the primary purpose of an IoT platform?**
   a. Data visualization
   b. Data encryption
   c. Device management and data analysis
   d. Device manufacturing

2. **Which of the following is not a common IoT platform provider?**
   a. Google Cloud IoT
   b. Microsoft Azure IoT
   c. AWS IoT
   d. IoT Foundation

3. **Which IoT platform component is responsible for collecting data from IoT devices?**
   a. IoT cloud
   b. IoT analytics engine

c. IoT gateway

d. Device registry

4. What does MQTT stand for in the context of IoT communication protocols?

a. Message Queuing Telemetry Transport

b. Multi-Query Transaction Transfer

c. Managed Query Transport Technology

d. Mobile Query Telemetry Transmission

5. What is the primary function of IoT protocols like MQTT and CoAP?

a. Data storage

b. Data transmission between devices and the platform

c. Device registration

d. Device manufacturing

6. Which layer of the IoT architecture is responsible for data processing and analysis?

a. Perception layer

b. Network layer

c. Application layer

d. Business layer

7. What is the primary role of IoT gateways in an IoT platform architecture?

a. Data analysis

b. Data storage

c. Data transmission

d. Data encryption

8. Which of the following is not a common challenge in IoT platform development?

a. Scalability

b. Security

c. Low device diversity

d. Interoperability

9. What is the primary benefit of using cloud-based IoT platforms?

a. Reduced scalability

b. Lower latency

c. Limited data storage options

d. Reduced accessibility

10. **What is the role of IoT APIs in an IoT platform?**

   a. To create IoT devices

   b. To enable communication between different software components

   c. To establish device connections

   d. To analyze data

11. **What is the significance of IoT platform interoperability?**

   a. It ensures that IoT devices cannot communicate with each other

   b. It allows IoT devices from different manufacturers to work together

   c. It increases the complexity of IoT systems

   d. It improves data security

12. **In IoT platform development, what does OTA typically refer to?**

   a. Online technical assistance

   b. Over-the-air updates

   c. On-time analytics

   d. Open transport architecture

13. **What is the primary role of IoT device shadowing in IoT platforms?**

   a. To create physical replicas of IoT devices

   b. To manage device configurations and updates

   c. To encrypt data transmissions

   d. To provide physical security for IoT devices

14. **What is the primary purpose of IoT cloud services in an IoT platform architecture?**

   a. Data encryption

   b. Data analysis

   c. Data storage and retrieval

   d. Data transmission and device management

15. **Which of the following is a challenge in IoT platform development related to data privacy?**

   a. Device compatibility

   b. Scalability

   c. Security concerns

   d. Data transmission speed

16. **What is the primary role of an IoT dashboard in an IoT platform?**
    a. Data encryption
    b. Device management
    c. Displaying real-time data and insights
    d. Data analysis

17. **Which IoT platform is known for its focus on industrial applications and the Industrial Internet of Things (IIoT)?**
    a. GE Predix
    b. Google Cloud IoT
    c. AWS IoT Core
    d. IBM Watson IoT

18. **What does the term IoT ecosystem refer to?**
    a. A network of interconnected IoT devices and platforms b
    b. A specific type of IoT sensor
    c. The physical devices connected to the internet
    d. A type of IoT analytics engine

19. **What is the primary function of IoT edge devices in an IoT platform architecture?**
    a. Data storage
    b. Data analysis
    c. Data transmission
    d. Data encryption

20. **Which IoT communication protocol is designed for constrained devices and low bandwidth environments?**
    a. MQTT
    b. CoAP
    c. HTTP
    d. SMTP

21. **What is the primary role of IoT device management in an IoT platform?**
    a. Data analysis
    b. Data encryption
    c. Device configuration, monitoring, and updates
    d. Data storage

22. **Which of the following is a cloud-based IoT platform offered by Amazon Web Services (AWS)?**

    a. IoT Foundation

    b. Google Cloud IoT

    c. AWS IoT Core

    d. Microsoft Azure IoT

23. **In IoT platform architecture, what does data ingestion refer to?**

    a. Data analysis and insights generation

    b. Data storage and retrieval

    c. The process of collecting data from IoT devices

    d. Data transmission between devices

24. **Which IoT platform component manages device registrations and authentication?**

    a. IoT cloud

    b. IoT gateway

    c. Device registry

    d. IoT analytics engine

25. **What is the primary advantage of using fog computing in IoT platforms?**

    a. Enhanced security

    b. Reduced latency

    c. Lower data storage costs

    d. Decreased device compatibility

26. **Which of the following is not a common IoT platform provider?**

    a. Oracle IoT Cloud

    b. Facebook IoT Connect

    c. SAP Leonardo IoT

    d. IBM Watson IoT

27. **What does SAP Leonardo IoT focus on?**

    a. Cloud computing services

    b. IoT solutions

    c. Social media analytics

    d. On-premises ERP systems

28. **What is MQTT for Sensor Networks (MQTT-SN) used for in IoT platforms?**

    a. To create IoT devices

    b. To send messages between IoT devices and the platform

    c. To manage device registrations

    d. To create virtual replicas of IoT devices

29. **Which layer of the IoT architecture deals with physical sensors and actuators?**

    a. Perception layer

    b. Network layer

    c. Application layer

    d. Business layer

30. **What is the primary database technology used by SAP Leonardo IoT?**

    a. SQL Server

    b. SAP HANA

    c. Oracle

    d. PostgreSQL

31. **What is a digital twin in the context of SAP Leonardo IoT?**

    a. A database backup solution

    b. A digital representation of a physical asset

    c. A virtual reality tool

    d. A duplicate of cloud storage

32. **What is the primary advantage of using a hybrid IoT platform that combines both cloud and edge computing?**

    a. Lower latency

    b. Reduced device support

    c. Enhanced device compatibility

    d. Decreased scalability

33. **What does digital twin mean in the context of IoT platforms?**

    a. A virtual replica of an IoT device

    b. An IoT analytics engine

    c. A type of IoT sensor

    d. A cloud-based IoT platform

34. **What is the primary function of IoT orchestration in an IoT platform?**

    a. Device registration

    b. Data storage

    c. Workflow automation and coordination

    d. Device manufacturing

35. **Which of the following is a key feature of IoT platforms related to data analytics?**

    a. Device management

    b. Real-time data processing

    c. Device manufacturing

    d. Data encryption

36. **Which IoT platform component is responsible for data security, including encryption and access control?**

    a. IoT cloud

    b. IoT gateway

    c. Device registry

    d. IoT security module

37. **Which industries can benefit from SAP Leonardo IoT?**

    a. Manufacturing

    b. Retail

    c. Healthcare

    d. All of the above

38. **What is the purpose of SAP Leonardo IoT Edge?**

    a. Centralized data storage

    b. Local data processing and analytics

    c. Real-time cloud synchronization

    d. Blockchain management

39. **What is an IoT platform primarily designed for?**

    a. Data storage

    b. Data analytics

    c. Data transmission

    d. Data encryption

40. Which of the following is a key feature of IoT platforms?

    a. Limited scalability

    b. Incompatibility with multiple devices

    c. Device management and monitoring

    d. Lack of security measures

41. What does the term IoT platform refer to in the context of the Internet of Things?

    a. The physical devices connected to the internet

    b. Software that connects, manages, and analyzes IoT devices and data

    c. A specific type of IoT sensor

    d. IoT protocols used for data transmission

42. Which component of an IoT platform is responsible for collecting data from various devices and sensors?

    a. Edge devices

    b. IoT gateways

    c. Cloud server

    d. IoT analytics engine

43. Which of the following is not a common IoT platform provider?

    a. Microsoft Azure IoT

    b. IBM Watson IoT

    c. AWS IoT

    d. Netflix IoT

44. What is the role of IoT platforms in data analytics?

    a. Storing data for future reference

    b. Generating random data

    c. Analyzing data to extract meaningful insights

    d. Transmitting data to IoT devices

45. Which IoT platform characteristic ensures that devices can seamlessly connect and communicate with the platform?

    a. Interoperability

    b. Complexity

    c. Limited device support

    d. Closed ecosystem

46. **What is the purpose of device management in IoT platforms?**

    a. Encrypting data

    b. Tracking user behavior

    c. Monitoring and controlling IoT devices

    d. Predicting future data trends

47. **Which type of data is not typically processed by IoT platforms?**

    a. Sensor data

    b. User login information

    c. Location data

    d. Weather data

48. **Which of the following is not a common communication protocol used in IoT platforms?**

    a. HTTP

    b. CoAP

    c. SMTP

    d. MQTT

49. **What is the primary function of IoT platform security?**

    a. To make IoT devices communicate faster

    b. To prevent any data transmission

    c. To protect IoT devices and data from unauthorized access and cyber threats

    d. To reduce the number of IoT devices in use

50. **How does SAP Leonardo IoT support predictive maintenance?**

    a. Through manual data collection

    b. By using machine learning to predict equipment failures

    c. By eliminating IoT sensors

    d. By using static data

51. **What does the term edge computing refer to in IoT platforms?**

    a. Computing that occurs on the cloud servers

    b. Computing that takes place on IoT devices themselves or on gateways

    c. A type of IoT communication protocol

    d. Data encryption technique

52. **Which of the following is an example of a cloud-based IoT platform?**

    a. AWS IoT Core

    b. Raspberry Pi

    c. Arduino

    d. Zigbee

53. **What is the primary benefit of using fog computing in IoT platforms?**

    a. Enhanced security

    b. Reduced latency

    c. Lower data storage costs

    d. Decreased device compatibility

54. **Which IoT platform component manages the registration and authentication of devices?**

    a. Device gateway

    b. Device registry

    c. Data analytics engine

    d. IoT cloud

55. **Which of the following is not a challenge in IoT platform development?**

    a. Scalability

    b. Security

    c. Interoperability

    d. Lack of IoT devices

56. **What type of analytics is primarily used in SAP Leonardo IoT?**

    a. Prescriptive analytics

    b. Predictive analytics

    c. Descriptive analytics

    d. None of the above

57. **Which of the following is not a common use case for IoT platforms?**

    a. Smart home automation

    b. Industrial automation and monitoring

    c. Weather forecasting

    d. Healthcare monitoring

58. Which of the following is a feature of SAP Leonardo IoT?

    a. Real-time data visualization

    b. Offline-only processing

    c. Legacy system compatibility without updates

    d. Manual configuration only

59. What is the primary advantage of using MQTT as an IoT communication protocol?

    a. High bandwidth usage

    b. Real-time data transmission

    c. High energy consumption

    d. Limited device support

60. Which IoT platform component is responsible for data storage and retrieval?

    a. IoT gateway

    b. IoT analytics engine

    c. IoT database

    d. IoT API

61. Which of the following is an example of an IoT platform for industrial applications?

    a. Fitbit

    b. GE Predix

    c. Nest

    d. Philips Hue

62. What does AWS IoT Core primarily provide?

    a. Storage services

    b. Database management

    c. Device connectivity and messaging

    d. Content delivery

63. What is the purpose of AWS IoT Device Management?

    a. To manage the AWS infrastructure

    b. To handle device security patches and updates

    c. To manage user permissions and roles

    d. To manage data analytics

64. **Which protocol does AWS IoT Core support for device communication?**

   a. FTP

   b. HTTP

   c. MQTT

   d. SMTP

65. **What is the main purpose of AWS IoT Analytics?**

   a. To analyze and visualize device data

   b. To manage device firmware

   c. To handle user authentication

   d. To manage device connectivity

66. **Which AWS service allows you to create and manage IoT rules for processing incoming device data?**

   a. AWS Lambda

   b. AWS IoT Rules Engine

   c. AWS CloudFormation

   d. AWS CloudTrail

67. **What is AWS IoT Greengrass used for?**

   a. Managing device certificates

   b. Running local computing and machine learning at the edge

   c. Storing IoT data

   d. Creating device management policies

68. **How does AWS IoT Core handle device authentication and authorization?**

   a. By using IAM roles

   b. Through device certificates and policies

   c. By leveraging Lambda functions

   d. Using AWS CloudTrail

69. **Which AWS IoT service enables you to manage device identities and access control?**

   a. AWS IAM

   b. AWS IoT Device Defender

   c. AWS IoT Device Management

   d. AWS Security Hub

70. **Which protocol is not supported by AWS IoT Core?**

    a. MQTT

    b. HTTP

    c. CoAP

    d. WebSocket

71. **What is the role of AWS IoT Device Defender?**

    a. To provide device authentication

    b. To monitor and audit IoT device behavior

    c. To manage device connectivity

    d. To create device firmware

72. **Which service is used to deploy machine learning models to IoT devices?**

    a. Amazon SageMaker

    b. AWS Lambda

    c. AWS IoT Greengrass

    d. Amazon Rekognition

73. **Which AWS IoT service provides a way to manage the lifecycle of IoT devices?**

    a. AWS IoT Device Management

    b. AWS IoT Core

    c. AWS IoT Greengrass

    d. AWS IoT Analytics

74. **What is the purpose of AWS IoT Events?**

    a. To collect device data

    b. To monitor IoT device security

    c. To detect and respond to events from IoT sensors

    d. To manage device connectivity

75. **Which AWS service can be used to visualize and analyze IoT data in real time?**

    a. Amazon QuickSight

    b. AWS Glue

    c. Amazon RDS

    d. AWS Kinesis

76. **What is the purpose of AWS IoT SiteWise?**
    a. To manage IoT devices at scale
    b. To collect and analyze industrial equipment data
    c. To manage device connectivity
    d. To deploy machine learning models

77. **Which AWS IoT service helps in managing and analyzing large volumes of time-series data?**
    a. AWS IoT SiteWise
    b. AWS IoT Analytics
    c. AWS IoT Core
    d. AWS IoT Greengrass

78. **Which AWS service provides integration with Amazon S3 for storing IoT data?**
    a. AWS IoT Core Rules Engine
    b. AWS IoT Analytics
    c. AWS IoT Device Management
    d. AWS IoT Greengrass

79. **What is the main function of AWS IoT Device Shadows?**
    a. To maintain the state of a device
    b. To manage device firmware updates
    c. To handle device connectivity
    d. To visualize device data

80. **Which AWS service allows you to perform machine learning inference on IoT data at the edge?**
    a. AWS Lambda
    b. AWS SageMaker
    c. AWS IoT Greengrass
    d. Amazon Comprehend

81. **What is the purpose of AWS IoT Things Graph?**
    a. To model and deploy IoT applications using visual workflows
    b. To manage device connectivity
    c. To analyze device data
    d. To provide security for IoT devices

82. **Which AWS service provides real-time data streaming for IoT applications?**

    a. AWS Kinesis Data Streams

    b. AWS IoT Core

    c. AWS Lambda

    d. Amazon DynamoDB

83. **What type of certificate is used for secure communication between IoT devices and AWS IoT Core?**

    a. Self-signed certificates

    b. CA-signed certificates

    c. OAuth tokens

    d. JWT tokens

84. **Which AWS service can be used to automatically scale resources for IoT applications based on demand?**

    a. AWS Auto Scaling

    b. AWS Lambda

    c. Amazon CloudWatch

    d. AWS IoT Core

85. **Which service allows you to integrate IoT data with AWS machine learning services?**

    a. AWS IoT Analytics

    b. AWS IoT Greengrass

    c. Amazon SageMaker

    d. AWS Lambda

86. **What is AWS IoT Core's feature for aggregating and analyzing large volumes of device data?**

    a. AWS IoT Analytics

    b. AWS IoT Events

    c. AWS IoT SiteWise

    d. AWS IoT Greengrass

87. **Which AWS IoT service is used for monitoring and managing device security configurations?**

    a. AWS IoT Device Defender

    b. AWS IoT Core

    c. AWS IoT Device Management

    d. AWS IoT Events

88. **What is the role of AWS IoT Core Rules Engine in IoT applications?**

    a. To process and route messages from IoT devices

    b. To manage device connectivity

    c. To deploy machine learning models

    d. To handle device firmware updates

89. **What does AWS IoT SiteWise do with industrial equipment data?**

    a. Stores data in Amazon S3

    b. Analyzes and visualizes data

    c. Manages device connectivity

    d. Deploys machine learning models

90. **What is the purpose of AWS IoT Core's message broker?**

    a. To handle device connectivity

    b. To store device data

    c. To manage the exchange of messages between devices

    d. To perform data analytics

91. **Which AWS IoT service helps in creating and managing digital twins of physical assets?**

    a. AWS IoT SiteWise

    b. AWS IoT Greengrass

    c. AWS IoT Core

    d. AWS IoT Device Management

92. **How does AWS IoT Core ensure message delivery between devices and the cloud?**

    a. By using TCP connections

    b. By using MQTT and HTTP protocols

    c. By employing UDP for fast transmission

    d. By using WebSocket connections

93. **Which AWS service provides the ability to run and manage containers on IoT devices?**

    a. AWS Lambda

    b. AWS ECS

    c. AWS IoT Greengrass

    d. Amazon EKS

94. **What type of policies can be defined in AWS IoT Core for devices?**

    a. Security policies

    b. Connectivity policies

    c. Authorization and access policies

    d. Data processing policies

95. **Which AWS service is used for creating visual dashboards for IoT data?**

    a. Amazon QuickSight

    b. AWS IoT Core

    c. AWS CloudWatch

    d. AWS IoT Analytics

96. **What role does AWS IoT Core play in edge computing?**

    a. Provides local data processing

    b. Manages device connectivity

    c. Enables cloud-based data processing

    d. Facilitates communication between cloud and edge devices

97. **Which AWS service helps to manage and deploy updates to IoT devices at scale?**

    a. AWS IoT Device Management

    b. AWS IoT Core

    c. AWS IoT SiteWise

    d. AWS IoT Greengrass

98. **SAP Leonardo IoT helps businesses:**

    a. Reduce operational costs

    b. Increase productivity

    c. Automate processes

    d. All of the above

99. **Which AWS IoT service provides insights into device connectivity and performance?**

   a. AWS IoT Core

   b. AWS IoT Device Defender

   c. AWS IoT SiteWise

   d. AWS IoT Analytics

100. **What is the primary use case for AWS IoT Events?**

   a. Real-time analytics of IoT data

   b. Monitoring and responding to events from IoT devices

   c. Managing device firmware updates

   d. Handling device connectivity issues

101. **Which AWS IoT service is used for creating custom rules for processing IoT data?**

   a. AWS IoT Core Rules Engine

   b. AWS IoT Analytics

   c. AWS IoT Greengrass

   d. AWS IoT Device Management

102. **How does AWS IoT Greengrass enhance edge computing?**

   a. By running containerized applications

   b. By providing local data storage

   c. By executing Lambda functions locally

   d. By managing device connectivity

103. **What is the purpose of AWS IoT Device Shadows?**

   a. To manage device firmware

   b. To store and retrieve device state information

   c. To visualize device data

   d. To handle device connectivity

104. **What is the purpose of AWS IoT Device Defender's audit feature?**

   a. To monitor device performance

   b. To perform security audits on IoT device configurations

   c. To manage device connectivity

   d. To analyze device data

105. **What is the primary service in Azure for managing IoT devices and data?**
    a. Azure Blob Storage
    b. Azure IoT Hub
    c. Azure Functions
    d. Azure SQL Database

106. **Which Azure service provides real-time analytics for IoT data streams?**
    a. Azure Data Factory
    b. Azure Stream Analytics
    c. Azure Cognitive Services
    d. Azure SQL Data Warehouse

107. **What protocol does Azure IoT Hub support for device communication?**
    a. HTTP
    b. MQTT
    c. FTP
    d. SMTP

108. **What role does machine learning play in SAP Leonardo IoT?**
    a. Data storage management
    b. Analyzing data patterns for intelligent insights
    c. Replacing human workforce
    d. Simplifying IoT device setup

109. **What is the purpose of Azure IoT Central?**
    a. To provide a fully managed IoT application platform
    b. To handle device firmware updates
    c. To manage Azure virtual machines
    d. To store IoT data

110. **What is Azure IoT Edge used for?**
    a. Running containerized applications and services at the edge
    b. Storing IoT data in the cloud
    c. Managing device connectivity
    d. Creating virtual machines

111. **Which service helps to analyze and visualize IoT data stored in Azure?**

    a. Azure Data Lake Storage

    b. Azure Synapse Analytics

    c. Azure Power BI

    d. Azure Machine Learning

112. **What is the purpose of Azure Time Series Insights?**

    a. To manage IoT device connectivity

    b. To provide a scalable analytics platform for time-series data

    c. To run machine learning models on IoT data

    d. To handle real-time streaming data

113. **How does SAP Leonardo IoT handle large volumes of data?**

    a. By ignoring redundant data

    b. By leveraging SAP HANA for in-memory processing

    c. By restricting data collection

    d. By using flat-file storage

114. **Which Azure service allows for device-to-cloud and cloud-to-device messaging?**

    a. Azure IoT Hub

    b. Azure Event Grid

    c. Azure Logic Apps

    d. Azure Service Bus

115. **What is Azure Digital Twins used for?**

    a. To create digital replicas of physical environments

    b. To handle IoT device connectivity

    c. To store IoT data

    d. To manage device updates

116. **Which Azure service provides a platform for building IoT applications with minimal coding?**

    a. Azure IoT Central

    b. Azure DevOps

    c. Azure Logic Apps

    d. Azure Functions

117. **What feature of Azure IoT Hub ensures secure communication between IoT devices and the cloud?**

    a. Device Identity Management

    b. Device Provisioning Service

    c. Device Authentication and Authorization

    d. Device Shadowing

118. **Which Azure service helps in managing and analyzing IoT data from industrial equipment?**

    a. Azure IoT Hub

    b. Azure IoT Central

    c. Azure IoT Edge

    d. Azure Time Series Insights

119. **Which protocol is not supported by Azure IoT Hub for device communication?**

    a. MQTT

    b. HTTP

    c. AMQP

    d. CoAP

120. **What is the purpose of Azure IoT Hub's message routing?**

    a. To send and receive messages between devices and the cloud

    b. To process and route messages based on specific conditions

    c. To store messages in Azure Blob Storage

    d. To handle device firmware updates

121. **Which Azure service provides automated device provisioning and configuration?**

    a. Azure IoT Hub

    b. Azure IoT Central

    c. Azure Device Provisioning Service

    d. Azure IoT Edge

122. **What is the role of Azure IoT Edge runtime?**

    a. To provide cloud-based analytics for IoT data

    b. To execute containerized applications on edge devices

    c. To manage device connectivity

    d. To handle device security

123. **Which Azure service provides a framework for building and deploying IoT applications with pre-built templates?**
    a. Azure IoT Central
    b. Azure DevOps
    c. Azure Resource Manager
    d. Azure Functions

124. **What feature does Azure IoT Hub provide for ensuring device security?**
    a. Device certificates
    b. Role-based access control
    c. Multi-factor authentication
    d. Virtual private network

125. **Which service provides the ability to execute business logic in response to IoT data events?**
    a. Azure Functions
    b. Azure Logic Apps
    c. Azure Service Bus
    d. Azure Event Grid

126. **What is Azure IoT Central's main advantage for IoT solutions?**
    a. Provides a custom IoT platform
    b. Offers a fully managed, scalable IoT SaaS solution
    c. Manages edge device provisioning
    d. Handles IoT device firmware updates

127. **What does Azure IoT Hub's Device Provisioning Service do?**
    a. Manages IoT device updates
    b. Automates the process of provisioning devices to IoT Hub
    c. Analyzes IoT device data
    d. Manages device connectivity

128. **Which Azure service provides a comprehensive view of IoT device health and security status?**
    a. Azure Security Center
    b. Azure IoT Central
    c. Azure IoT Hub
    d. Azure Monitor

129. **What does Azure IoT Edge offer for processing data locally?**

    a. Cloud-based analytics

    b. Local data processing and containerized workloads

    c. Device connectivity management

    d. Real-time data streaming

130. **Which Azure service allows you to create scalable, serverless applications for IoT data processing?**

    a. Azure Functions

    b. Azure App Service

    c. Azure Kubernetes Service

    d. Azure Logic Apps

131. **What is Azure IoT Hub's role in edge computing?**

    a. To manage device provisioning

    b. To provide device-to-cloud and cloud-to-device messaging

    c. To run containerized applications locally on edge devices

    d. To perform data analytics in the cloud

132. **What feature of Azure IoT Hub ensures the secure handling of messages between devices and the cloud?**

    a. Device management

    b. Message routing

    c. Device authentication and encryption

    d. Device provisioning

133. **Which service is designed to help with the integration of IoT data with other Azure services?**

    a. Azure Event Grid

    b. Azure Logic Apps

    c. Azure Service Bus

    d. Azure Data Factory

134. **What does Azure IoT Central provide out of the box?**

    a. IoT device management

    b. Custom IoT solution development

    c. Pre-built dashboards and analytics

    d. Edge computing support

135. **What is the role of Azure Digital Twins in IoT?**

    a. To provide a cloud-based data storage solution

    b. To create digital representations of physical assets

    c. To manage IoT device configurations

    d. To analyze IoT data in real-time

136. **Which service allows you to execute business logic in response to events from IoT devices?**

    a. Azure Logic Apps

    b. Azure Functions

    c. Azure Service Bus

    d. Azure Event Grid

137. **What does Azure IoT Edge enable in terms of processing?**

    a. Local data processing with containers

    b. Cloud-based data processing

    c. Device management and updates

    d. Data visualization and analytics

138. **Which Azure service provides a scalable platform for building IoT applications?**

    a. Azure IoT Central

    b. Azure DevOps

    c. Azure Machine Learning

    d. Azure Logic Apps

139. **What does Azure IoT Hub's message routing feature allow you to do?**

    a. Store and manage device data

    b. Route messages to different endpoints based on message content

    c. Handle device firmware updates

    d. Monitor device health

140. **Which Azure service is used for time-series data storage and analytics?**

    a. Azure SQL Database

    b. Azure Time Series Insights

    c. Azure Cosmos DB

    d. Azure Blob Storage

141. What role does Azure IoT Hub play in device management?

    a. Provides analytics and visualization tools

    b. Manages device provisioning and communication

    c. Handles local data processing

    d. Manages user authentication

142. Which service allows for seamless integration of IoT data with machine learning models?

    a. Azure Machine Learning

    b. Azure IoT Central

    c. Azure Data Factory

    d. Azure Functions

143. What is the key benefit of integrating SAP Leonardo IoT with SAP S/4HANA?

    a. Improved financial reporting

    b. Enhanced end-to-end business processes

    c. Reduced need for cloud services

    d. Replacement of ERP systems

144. Which Azure service helps to create and manage custom IoT solutions with minimal coding?

    a. Azure IoT Central

    b. Azure IoT Hub

    c. Azure Logic Apps

    d. Azure Digital Twins

145. What is Azure IoT Hub's Device Provisioning Service used for?

    a. Device monitoring

    b. Automating device provisioning and configuration

    c. Handling device communication

    d. Analyzing device data

146. Which Azure service provides a managed platform for deploying containerized applications on IoT devices?

    a. Azure Kubernetes Service

    b. Azure IoT Edge

c. Azure App Service

d. Azure Functions

147. What is the main advantage of using Azure IoT Central for IoT solutions?

a. Provides a high degree of customization for IoT solutions

b. Offers a pre-built, fully managed IoT SaaS solution with ease of use

c. Handles device-to-cloud and cloud-to-device messaging

d. Manages IoT device security and compliance

148. Which Google Cloud service is primarily used for managing IoT devices and their data?

a. Google Cloud Storage

b. Google Cloud IoT Core

c. Google Cloud Pub/Sub

d. Google Cloud Functions

149. What protocol does Google Cloud IoT Core use for device communication?

a. HTTP

b. MQTT

c. CoAP

d. WebSocket

150. Which service allows you to store and analyze time-series data from IoT devices on Google Cloud?

a. Google Cloud Bigtable

b. Google Cloud Storage

c. Google Cloud Spanner

d. Google BigQuery

151. What is the purpose of Google Cloud Pub/Sub in the context of IoT?

a. To store IoT data

b. To manage device provisioning

c. To provide messaging between devices and services

d. To analyze IoT data

152. **Which Google Cloud service provides serverless compute for IoT applications?**

    a. Google Cloud Functions

    b. Google App Engine

    c. Google Compute Engine

    d. Google Kubernetes Engine

153. **Which service is used to securely connect and manage IoT devices in Google Cloud?**

    a. Google Cloud IoT Core

    b. Google Cloud VPN

    c. Google Cloud Identity

    d. Google Cloud Endpoints

154. **What does Google Cloud IoT Core use for secure device authentication?**

    a. OAuth 2.0

    b. API Keys

    c. X.509 Certificates

    d. JWT Tokens

155. **Which Google Cloud service allows you to analyze and visualize IoT data in real-time?**

    a. Google Cloud Dataflow

    b. Google Data Studio

    c. Google Cloud Pub/Sub

    d. Google BigQuery

156. **What is the primary use of Google Cloud Functions in an IoT architecture?**

    a. To manage device firmware updates

    b. To run serverless code in response to IoT events

    c. To store IoT data

    d. To handle device provisioning

157. **Which service provides managed messaging and integration with IoT devices in Google Cloud?**

    a. Google Cloud Pub/Sub

    b. Google Cloud Storage

    c. Google Cloud SQL

    d. Google Cloud Spanner

158. **What is the purpose of Google Cloud IoT Core's Device Manager?**

   a. To handle device data analytics

   b. To manage and organize IoT devices

   c. To provide device authentication

   d. To route device messages

159. **Which Google Cloud service is used for processing and transforming streaming data from IoT devices?**

   a. Google Cloud Dataflow

   b. Google Cloud Pub/Sub

   c. Google Cloud Storage

   d. Google BigQuery

160. **What is the role of Google Cloud IoT Core's Pub/Sub topic?**

   a. To store IoT device logs

   b. To receive and route device data

   c. To manage device configurations

   d. To visualize IoT data

161. **What is the purpose of Google Cloud IoT Core's telemetry data feature?**

   a. To send and receive messages from IoT devices

   b. To store device data

   c. To process data in real-time

   d. To monitor device performance

162. **Which Google Cloud service helps in building real-time dashboards for IoT applications?**

   a. Google Data Studio

   b. Google Cloud Functions

   c. Google BigQuery

   d. Google Cloud Storage

163. **Which service allows for serverless data processing and integration with IoT data streams?**

   a. Google Cloud Dataflow

   b. Google Cloud Pub/Sub

   c. Google Cloud Functions

   d. Google Cloud Spanner

164. **Which Google Cloud service provides analytics for large-scale data from IoT devices?**
    a. Google BigQuery
    b. Google Cloud SQL
    c. Google Cloud Storage
    d. Google Cloud Dataproc

165. **What does Google Cloud IoT Core's registry feature do?**
    a. Manages device configurations
    b. Stores device data
    c. Organizes and manages IoT devices
    d. Handles device firmware updates

166. **Which service is used to create scalable and reliable messaging between IoT devices and cloud applications?**
    a. Google Cloud Pub/Sub
    b. Google Cloud Functions
    c. Google Cloud Spanner
    d. Google Cloud Storage

167. **Which service is used for real-time processing of streaming data from IoT devices?**
    a. Google Cloud Dataflow
    b. Google Cloud Pub/Sub
    c. Google BigQuery
    d. Google Cloud Storage

168. **Which Google Cloud service is used to run containerized applications at scale, including those for IoT?**
    a. Google Kubernetes Engine
    b. Google Cloud Functions
    c. Google Compute Engine
    d. Google App Engine

169. **What is Google Cloud IoT Core's Device Manager used for?**
    a. Managing device connectivity
    b. Storing device data
    c. Organizing and managing IoT devices
    d. Handling real-time data processing

170. **Which service provides managed, scalable storage for time-series data from IoT devices?**
   a. Google Cloud Bigtable
   b. Google Cloud SQL
   c. Google Cloud Datastore
   d. Google Cloud Spanner

171. **Which service enables running event-driven serverless code in response to IoT events?**
   a. Google Cloud Functions
   b. Google App Engine
   c. Google Cloud Run
   d. Google Kubernetes Engine

172. **What is the purpose of Google Cloud IoT Core's X.509 certificates?**
   a. To provide device authentication
   b. To encrypt IoT data
   c. To manage device provisioning
   d. To store device configurations

173. **Which Google Cloud service is designed for large-scale, real-time data analytics?**
   a. Google BigQuery
   b. Google Cloud SQL
   c. Google Cloud Spanner
   d. Google Cloud Dataflow

174. **What role does Google Cloud Pub/Sub play in IoT applications?**
   a. Provides secure device connections
   b. Manages real-time messaging between devices and services
   c. Handles data storage
   d. Runs serverless code

175. **Which Google Cloud service is used to process and transform data streams from IoT devices?**
   a. Google Cloud Dataflow
   b. Google Cloud Bigtable
   c. Google Cloud SQL
   d. Google BigQuery

176. **Which service enables the integration of IoT data with machine learning models?**

    a. Google Cloud AI Platform

    b. Google Cloud Pub/Sub

    c. Google Cloud Storage

    d. Google Cloud Functions

177. **Which protocol is commonly used by IoT devices in SAP Leonardo IoT?**

    a. HTTP

    b. MQTT

    c. FTP

    d. SMTP

178. **Which Google Cloud service provides a fully managed database for time-series data?**

    a. Google Cloud Bigtable

    b. Google Cloud SQL

    c. Google Cloud Datastore

    d. Google Cloud Spanner

179. **What does Google Cloud IoT Core's device provisioning service facilitate?**

    a. Secure device communication

    b. Device management and configuration

    c. Real-time data analytics

    d. Data encryption

180. **Which Google Cloud service is used for building and deploying serverless applications for IoT?**

    a. Google Cloud Functions

    b. Google Cloud Run

    c. Google App Engine

    d. Google Kubernetes Engine

181. **SAP Leonardo IoT enables real-time decision-making by:**

    a. Storing data for future use

    b. Providing historical reports only

    c. Utilizing real-time sensor data and analytics

    d. Relying solely on manual inputs

182. **Which service provides a framework for real-time event processing and transformation in GCP?**

    a. Google Cloud Dataflow

    b. Google Cloud Spanner

    c. Google Cloud SQL

    d. Google BigQuery

183. **What is the role of blockchain in SAP Leonardo IoT?**

    a. Data encryption

    b. Tracking and verifying transactions in IoT ecosystems

    c. Replacing traditional storage methods

    d. Eliminating the need for cloud services

184. **Which service provides a scalable platform for querying and analyzing IoT data?**

    a. Google BigQuery

    b. Google Cloud SQL

    c. Google Cloud Storage

    d. Google Cloud Datastore

185. **How does SAP Leonardo IoT improve supply chain operations?**

    a. By predicting demand and preventing stock-outs

    b. By eliminating warehouse management systems

    c. By relying on manual inventory checks

    d. By using paper-based reports

186. **Which Google Cloud service enables the deployment of containerized applications for IoT?**

    a. Google Kubernetes Engine

    b. Google Cloud Functions

    c. Google Compute Engine

    d. Google App Engine

187. **What role does Google Cloud Functions play in an IoT architecture?**

    a. Provides real-time data analytics

    b. Manages device provisioning

    c. Executes serverless code in response to IoT events

    d. Stores IoT data

188. **Which service provides secure and scalable messaging between IoT devices and applications?**

    a. Google Cloud Pub/Sub

    b. Google Cloud Storage

    c. Google Cloud SQL

    d. Google BigQuery

189. **What is the benefit of IoT-enabled predictive analytics in SAP Leonardo?**

    a. Eliminates the need for machine learning

    b. Identifies potential failures before they occur

    c. Reduces the need for IoT devices

    d. Replaces cloud-based systems

190. **Which of the following is not a feature of SAP Leonardo IoT?**

    a. IoT data integration

    b. Manual data entry only

    c. Predictive maintenance

    d. Real-time analytics

191. **What is the primary purpose of the Artik Cloud IoT platform?**

    a. Data storage

    b. Device management and connectivity

    c. Data visualization

    d. Cloud hosting

192. **Which protocol is commonly used by Artik Cloud for communication between devices and the cloud?**

    a. HTTP

    b. MQTT

    c. CoAP

    d. WebSocket

193. **What feature of Artik Cloud allows you to securely manage device credentials?**

    a. Device management

    b. Device authentication

    c. API management

    d. Data encryption

194. **Which service within Artik Cloud helps in aggregating and analyzing data from multiple IoT devices?**

    a. Artik Cloud Data Management

    b. Artik Cloud Analytics

    c. Artik Cloud Data Pipeline

    d. Artik Cloud Dashboard

195. **What does Artik Cloud's Event System provide?**

    a. Real-time data processing

    b. Event-driven notifications and triggers

    c. Data storage

    d. Device updates

196. **Which feature of Artik Cloud enables real-time data visualization?**

    a. Artik Cloud Dashboard

    b. Artik Cloud Analytics

    c. Artik Cloud Storage

    d. Artik Cloud API

197. **What does Artik Cloud's Rules Engine allow you to create?**

    a. Data storage policies

    b. Custom business logic for handling IoT data

    c. Device provisioning workflows

    d. API integrations

198. **Which service is used to manage and control IoT devices in the Artik Cloud platform?**

    a. Artik Cloud Device Manager

    b. Artik Cloud Data Management

    c. Artik Cloud API

    d. Artik Cloud Connectivity

199. **What kind of data does Artik Cloud primarily handle?**

    a. Time-series data

    b. Relational data

    c. Document-based data

    d. Graph-based data

200. How does Artik Cloud ensure data security during transmission?

    a. Using HTTP

    b. Using OAuth 2.0

    c. Using HTTPS and TLS

    d. Using API keys

201. Which protocol is used by Artik Cloud for device-to-cloud communication?

    a. CoAP

    b. AMQP

    c. MQTT

    d. XMPP

202. What is the role of Artik Cloud's Data Pipeline feature?

    a. To process and analyze data

    b. To visualize data

    c. To handle data integration and transformation

    d. To store data

203. Which tool in Artik Cloud helps you manage device firmware updates?

    a. Artik Cloud Device Manager

    b. Artik Cloud Firmware Manager

    c. Artik Cloud Rules Engine

    d. Artik Cloud API

204. How does Artik Cloud support device provisioning?

    a. Through device manager

    b. Through API integration

    c. Through device shadowing

    d. Through event triggers

205. What is Artik Cloud's Device Shadow feature used for?

    a. To manage device connectivity

    b. To store and manage the state of devices

    c. To handle device firmware updates

    d. To visualize device data

206. **Which service provides scalability for Artik Cloud's data handling?**

    a. Artik Cloud Data Management

    b. Artik Cloud Storage

    c. Artik Cloud API

    d. Artik Cloud Analytics

207. **What feature allows Artik Cloud to integrate with other cloud services?**

    a. Artik Cloud API

    b. Artik Cloud Dashboard

    c. Artik Cloud Rules Engine

    d. Artik Cloud Data Pipeline

208. **How does Artik Cloud handle data from different IoT devices?**

    a. Through data aggregation

    b. Through data encryption

    c. Through device authentication

    d. Through device management

209. **Which Artik Cloud service provides real-time alerts based on specific data conditions?**

    a. Artik Cloud Alerts

    b. Artik Cloud Rules Engine

    c. Artik Cloud Dashboard

    d. Artik Cloud Data Pipeline

210. **What type of data can you visualize with Artik Cloud's Dashboard?**

    a. Historical data

    b. Real-time data

    c. Processed data

    d. Both historical and real-time data

211. **Which Artik Cloud feature helps in managing and scaling IoT device networks?**

    a. Artik Cloud Device Manager

    b. Artik Cloud Analytics

    c. Artik Cloud API

    d. Artik Cloud Data Pipeline

212. **What does Artik Cloud's Event System enable?**

    a. Secure data transmission

    b. Real-time event-driven processing

    c. Device firmware updates

    d. Data storage

213. **How does Artik Cloud ensure secure access to its APIs?**

    a. Using IP whitelisting

    b. Using OAuth 2.0 authentication

    c. Using HTTP Basic Authentication

    d. Using API keys

214. **Which service provides automated rules for processing and handling IoT data in Artik Cloud?**

    a. Artik Cloud Rules Engine

    b. Artik Cloud Data Management

    c. Artik Cloud Dashboard

    d. Artik Cloud Alerts

215. **What is the role of Artik Cloud's Data Management feature?**

    a. To process data in real-time

    b. To store and manage data securely

    c. To visualize data trends

    d. To handle device provisioning

216. **Which tool in Artik Cloud allows for the creation of custom data pipelines?**

    a. Artik Cloud API

    b. Artik Cloud Data Pipeline

    c. Artik Cloud Dashboard

    d. Artik Cloud Rules Engine

217. **What kind of data analytics does Artik Cloud Analytics provide?**

    a. Historical data analysis

    b. Real-time data analysis

    c. Predictive analytics

    d. Both real-time and historical data analysis

218. **Which service helps in monitoring and managing device health in Artik Cloud?**

    a. Artik Cloud Device Manager

    b. Artik Cloud Analytics

    c. Artik Cloud Data Management

    d. Artik Cloud Alerts

219. **What does Artik Cloud's Device Management feature primarily focus on?**

    a. Device provisioning and authentication

    b. Data analytics and visualization

    c. Data storage and security

    d. Event-driven notifications

220. **How does Artik Cloud support integration with third-party services?**

    a. Through API integration

    b. Through Data Pipelines

    c. Through Device Shadows

    d. Through Rules Engine

221. **Which feature allows Artik Cloud to handle multiple IoT device types and protocols?**

    a. Artik Cloud Device Manager

    b. Artik Cloud Data Pipeline

    c. Artik Cloud API

    d. Artik Cloud Analytics

222. **What does Artik Cloud's Dashboard feature provide in terms of data presentation?**

    a. Historical data reports

    b. Real-time data visualization and trends

    c. Data encryption status

    d. Device firmware status

223. **Which service is used to create custom alerts based on IoT data conditions in Artik Cloud?**

    a. Artik Cloud Alerts

    b. Artik Cloud Rules Engine

    c. Artik Cloud Data Pipeline

    d. Artik Cloud API

224. How does Artik Cloud handle device state management?

    a. Through Device Shadows

    b. Through Device Management

    c. Through Data Pipelines

    d. Through Data Storage

225. Which tool in Artik Cloud helps with the real-time processing of IoT data streams?

    a. Artik Cloud Data Pipeline

    b. Artik Cloud Analytics

    c. Artik Cloud Dashboard

    d. Artik Cloud API

226. What is the purpose of Artik Cloud's Rules Engine?

    a. To manage device provisioning

    b. To define and execute custom data processing rules

    c. To visualize device data

    d. To store device data

227. Which service in Artik Cloud helps manage IoT data security?

    a. Artik Cloud Data Management

    b. Artik Cloud Device Manager

    c. Artik Cloud API

    d. Artik Cloud Analytics

228. What type of data does Artik Cloud's Device Manager primarily handle?

    a. Device state and configuration data

    b. Historical data

    c. Real-time data

    d. Processed data

229. Which service provides real-time and historical data insights in Artik Cloud?

    a. Artik Cloud Analytics

    b. Artik Cloud Dashboard

    c. Artik Cloud Data Pipeline

    d. Artik Cloud Device Manager

230. **How does Artik Cloud ensure the scalability of data handling?**

    a. Through Data Pipelines

    b. Through Device Management

    c. Through Data Storage

    d. Through Analytics

231. **What is Artik Cloud's primary method for handling large volumes of IoT data?**

    a. Data aggregation

    b. Data visualization

    c. Data encryption

    d. Data pipelines

232. **Which tool in Artik Cloud supports real-time event processing and automation?**

    a. Artik Cloud Rules Engine

    b. Artik Cloud Data Pipeline

    c. Artik Cloud Analytics

    d. Artik Cloud API

233. **What does Artik Cloud's Device Authentication feature ensure?**

    a. Secure data transmission

    b. Secure device identity and access

    c. Device state management

    d. Data visualization

234. **Which Artik Cloud feature allows for the creation and management of data-driven events?**

    a. Artik Cloud Event System

    b. Artik Cloud Rules Engine

    c. Artik Cloud Dashboard

    d. Artik Cloud API

235. **What does Artik Cloud's Data Management feature focus on?**

    a. Managing device configurations

    b. Handling data storage and security

    c. Processing real-time data

    d. Creating data pipelines

236. **Which service provides real-time alerts and notifications based on device data conditions?**

    a. Artik Cloud Rules Engine

    b. Artik Cloud Data Pipeline

    c. Artik Cloud Device Manager

    d. Artik Cloud Dashboard

237. **How does Artik Cloud support multi-device and multi-protocol environments?**

    a. Through Device Manager

    b. Through Data Pipeline

    c. Through Analytics

    d. Through API Integration

238. **What role does Artik Cloud's API play in an IoT solution?**

    a. Provides real-time data visualization

    b. Enables integration with third-party services and applications

    c. Manages device firmware updates

    d. Handles data encryption

239. **Which feature helps in scaling IoT solutions and managing large amounts of data in Artik Cloud?**

    a. Artik Cloud Storage

    b. Artik Cloud Data Pipeline

    c. Artik Cloud Analytics

    d. Artik Cloud Device Manager

240. **What is the primary benefit of Artik Cloud's Device Shadows?**

    a. Managing and controlling device connectivity

    b. Storing and managing device state information

    c. Analyzing historical data

    d. Visualizing real-time data

241. **What is the primary function of the IBM Watson IoT platform?**

    a. Data analytics

    b. Device management

    c. Cloud storage

    d. Application development

242. **Which protocol is commonly used by IBM Watson IoT for device communication?**

   a. HTTP

   b. MQTT

   c. CoAP

   d. AMQP

243. **What feature of IBM Watson IoT helps in integrating IoT data with artificial intelligence?**

   a. Watson Assistant

   b. Watson Discovery

   c. Watson Machine Learning

   d. Watson Visual Recognition

244. **Which IBM Watson IoT service is used for analyzing time-series data from IoT devices?**

   a. IBM Watson Analytics

   b. IBM Cloud Pak for Data

   c. IBM Cloud Data Services

   d. IBM Watson IoT Platform

245. **What does IBM Watson IoT's Device Management feature provide?**

   a. Data storage

   b. Device configuration and monitoring

   c. Data encryption

   d. Real-time analytics

246. **How does IBM Watson IoT ensure secure data transmission?**

   a. Using HTTPS and TLS

   b. Using OAuth 2.0

   c. Using API keys

   d. Using IP whitelisting

247. **Which IBM Watson IoT service helps with the visualization of IoT data?**

   a. IBM Watson Studio

   b. IBM Watson IoT Dashboard

   c. IBM Watson Analytics

   d. IBM Cloud Pak for Data

248. What role does IBM Watson IoT's Rules Engine play?

    a. Manages device firmware updates

    b. Processes and routes IoT data based on custom rules

    c. Handles device provisioning

    d. Provides real-time data storage

249. Which service allows IBM Watson IoT to integrate with external data sources and applications?

    a. IBM Watson API

    b. IBM Watson IoT API

    c. IBM Watson Studio

    d. IBM Watson Discovery

250. What does IBM Watson IoT's Event Processing feature provide?

    a. Real-time data visualization

    b. Real-time event-driven data processing

    c. Historical data analysis

    d. Device management

251. Which IBM Watson IoT service is used for predictive analytics on IoT data?

    a. IBM Watson Machine Learning

    b. IBM Watson Studio

    c. IBM Watson Assistant

    d. IBM Watson Discovery

252. How does IBM Watson IoT support device provisioning?

    a. Through Device Manager

    b. Through API Integration

    c. Through Device Shadows

    d. Through Rules Engine

253. What feature does IBM Watson IoT's Device Shadows provide?

    a. Device state management

    b. Data encryption

    c. Real-time data analytics

    d. Device firmware updates

254. **Which tool in IBM Watson IoT helps manage large-scale data streams from devices?**

    a. IBM Watson IoT Platform

    b. IBM Cloud Pak for Data

    c. IBM Watson Analytics

    d. IBM Watson Studio

255. **What role does IBM Watson IoT's API Gateway play?**

    a. Provides real-time data analytics

    b. Manages API requests and integrates with external systems

    c. Handles device provisioning

    d. Manages data storage

256. **Which IBM Watson IoT service helps with machine learning model deployment?**

    a. IBM Watson Machine Learning

    b. IBM Watson Assistant

    c. IBM Watson Studio

    d. IBM Watson Discovery

257. **What is the primary benefit of IBM Watson IoT's Asset Management feature?**

    a. Device configuration

    b. Data visualization

    c. Real-time asset tracking and management

    d. Predictive maintenance

258. **Which IBM Watson IoT service provides a unified view of device data and analytics?**

    a. IBM Watson IoT Dashboard

    b. IBM Watson Analytics

    c. IBM Watson Studio

    d. IBM Cloud Pak for Data

259. **What does IBM Watson IoT's Rules Engine help to automate?**

    a. Device updates

    b. Data storage

    c. Event-driven actions based on specific conditions

    d. Data encryption

260. **Which service in IBM Watson IoT is designed for real-time event monitoring and response?**

   a. IBM Watson IoT Event Processing

   b. IBM Watson Analytics

   c. IBM Watson Machine Learning

   d. IBM Watson Studio

261. **What type of data does IBM Watson IoT's Data Storage service handle?**

   a. Real-time data

   b. Historical data

   c. Processed data

   d. Both real-time and historical data

262. **Which IBM Watson IoT feature is used for integrating IoT data with business applications?**

   a. IBM Watson IoT API

   b. IBM Watson IoT Dashboard

   c. IBM Watson Analytics

   d. IBM Watson Studio

263. **How does IBM Watson IoT support real-time data analysis?**

   a. Through Data Pipelines

   b. Through Watson Analytics

   c. Through Watson Studio

   d. Through Event Processing

264. **Which feature in IBM Watson IoT allows for seamless integration with external data sources?**

   a. IBM Watson IoT API

   b. IBM Watson Analytics

   c. IBM Watson Studio

   d. IBM Watson Machine Learning

265. **What is IBM Watson IoT's Device Management primarily used for?**

   a. Device state management

   b. Device provisioning and monitoring

   c. Data encryption

   d. Real-time analytics

266. **Which service provides tools for building and deploying AI models within the IBM Watson IoT platform?**

   a. IBM Watson Studio

   b. IBM Watson Machine Learning

   c. IBM Watson Assistant

   d. IBM Watson Discovery

267. **What role does IBM Watson IoT's Asset Management feature play?**

   a. Manages device firmware updates

   b. Provides real-time asset visibility and status

   c. Handles data encryption

   d. Manages data visualization

268. **Which service allows you to create and manage custom rules for IoT data in IBM Watson IoT?**

   a. IBM Watson IoT Rules Engine

   b. IBM Watson Analytics

   c. IBM Watson Studio

   d. IBM Watson API

269. **What does IBM Watson IoT's Device Shadows feature help with?**

   a. Managing device firmware updates

   b. Storing and managing device states

   c. Data visualization

   d. Event processing

270. **How does IBM Watson IoT support predictive maintenance?**

   a. Through real-time data analysis

   b. Through asset management

   c. Through machine learning models

   d. Through device provisioning

271. **Which IBM Watson IoT feature allows for the creation of custom APIs?**

   a. IBM Watson IoT API

   b. IBM Watson Studio

   c. IBM Watson Analytics

   d. IBM Watson Assistant

272. **What is the purpose of IBM Watson IoT's Event Processing feature?**

    a. Real-time event-driven data processing

    b. Data storage

    c. Device management

    d. Data encryption

273. **Which IBM Watson IoT service is best suited for handling large-scale IoT data streams?**

    a. IBM Watson IoT Platform

    b. IBM Watson Analytics

    c. IBM Watson Machine Learning

    d. IBM Watson Studio

274. **What is IBM Watson IoT's primary tool for analyzing and visualizing data from IoT devices?**

    a. IBM Watson IoT Dashboard

    b. IBM Watson Analytics

    c. IBM Watson Studio

    d. IBM Cloud Pak for Data

275. **Which IBM Watson IoT feature helps manage device connectivity and authentication?**

    a. IBM Watson IoT Device Management

    b. IBM Watson IoT API

    c. IBM Watson Studio

    d. IBM Watson Analytics

276. **How does IBM Watson IoT handle real-time data processing?**

    a. Through Event Processing

    b. Through Data Pipelines

    c. Through Device Shadows

    d. Through Data Encryption

277. **Which IBM Watson IoT service integrates with external machine learning tools and platforms?**

    a. IBM Watson Machine Learning

    b. IBM Watson Studio

c. IBM Watson Analytics

d. IBM Watson Assistant

278. **What does IBM Watson IoT's Data Management feature focus on?**

a. Managing data storage and security

b. Real-time data analytics

c. Device management

d. Data visualization

279. **Which tool helps in monitoring and analyzing data from various IoT devices in IBM Watson IoT?**

a. IBM Watson IoT Dashboard

b. IBM Watson Machine Learning

c. IBM Watson Studio

d. IBM Watson Discovery

280. **What type of data does IBM Watson IoT's Rules Engine process?**

a. Historical data

b. Real-time data

c. Device firmware data

d. Both historical and real-time data

281. **Which IBM Watson IoT feature helps in the management of device firmware updates?**

a. IBM Watson IoT Device Management

b. IBM Watson IoT API

c. IBM Watson Machine Learning

d. IBM Watson Studio

282. **How does IBM Watson IoT facilitate the integration of IoT data with AI-driven insights?**

a. Through IBM Watson Machine Learning

b. Through IBM Watson Studio

c. Through IBM Watson Analytics

d. Through IBM Watson Assistant

283. **What feature of IBM Watson IoT provides a unified view of IoT device data and performance?**

    a. IBM Watson IoT Dashboard

    b. IBM Watson Analytics

    c. IBM Watson Machine Learning

    d. IBM Watson Studio

284. **Which service in IBM Watson IoT provides real-time alerts and notifications based on specific conditions?**

    a. IBM Watson IoT Rules Engine

    b. IBM Watson Analytics

    c. IBM Watson Machine Learning

    d. IBM Watson Studio

285. **How does IBM Watson IoT's Data Pipeline feature assist in managing data?**

    a. By creating custom data pipelines for integration and transformation

    b. By handling device connectivity

    c. By providing real-time analytics

    d. By managing device firmware updates

286. **What role does IBM Watson IoT's API Gateway play?**

    a. Manages API requests and integrations

    b. Provides real-time data analytics

    c. Handles device provisioning

    d. Manages data encryption

287. **Which service helps IBM Watson IoT users to build and deploy custom machine learning models?**

    a. IBM Watson Studio

    b. IBM Watson Machine Learning

    c. IBM Watson Assistant

    d. IBM Watson Discovery

288. **How does IBM Watson IoT manage and process large-scale IoT data?**

    a. Through Data Pipelines

    b. Through Device Management

c. Through Real-time Analytics

d. Through Event Processing

289. **Which feature of IBM Watson IoT supports real-time decision-making based on IoT data?**

a. IBM Watson IoT Rules Engine

b. IBM Watson Analytics

c. IBM Watson Machine Learning

d. IBM Watson Studio

290. **What is the primary use of IBM Watson IoT's Device Shadows?**

a. To manage and update device firmware

b. To store and manage the current state of IoT devices

c. To analyze historical data

d. To provide real-time data visualization

Join our Discord space

Join our Discord workspace for latest updates, offers, tech happenings around the world, new releases, and sessions with the authors:

https://discord.bpbonline.com

Answers

Q.No.	Answers	Q.No.	Answers	Q.No.	Answers	Q.No.	Answers	Q.No.	Answers
1	c	31	b	61	b	91	a	121	c
2	d	32	a	62	c	92	b	122	b
3	c	33	a	63	b	93	c	123	a
4	a	34	c	64	c	94	c	124	a
5	b	35	b	65	a	95	a	125	a
6	c	36	d	66	b	96	d	126	b
7	c	37	d	67	b	97	a	127	b
8	c	38	b	68	b	98	d	128	a
9	b	39	b	69	c	99	b	129	b
10	b	40	c	70	c	100	b	130	a
11	b	41	b	71	b	101	d	131	b
12	b	42	b	72	c	102	c	132	c
13	b	43	d	73	a	103	b	133	b
14	c	44	c	74	c	104	b	134	c
15	c	45	a	75	a	105	b	135	b
16	c	46	c	76	b	106	b	136	b
17	a	47	b	77	a	107	b	137	a
18	a	48	c	78	b	108	b	138	a
19	c	49	c	79	a	109	a	139	b
20	b	50	b	80	c	110	a	140	b
21	c	51	b	81	a	111	c	141	b
22	c	52	a	82	b	112	b	142	a
23	c	53	b	83	b	113	b	143	b
24	c	54	b	84	a	114	a	144	a
25	b	55	d	85	c	115	a	145	b
26	b	56	b	86	a	116	a	146	b
27	b	57	c	87	a	117	c	147	b
28	b	58	a	88	a	118	d	148	b
29	a	59	b	89	b	119	d	149	b
30	b	60	c	90	c	120	b	150	a

Q.No.	Answers	Q.No.	Answers	Q.No.	Answers	Q.No.	Answers	Q.No.	Answers
151	c	181	c	211	a	241	b	271	a
152	a	182	a	212	b	242	b	272	a
153	a	183	b	213	b	243	c	273	a
154	c	184	a	214	a	244	d	274	a
155	b	185	a	215	b	245	b	275	a
156	b	186	a	216	b	246	a	276	a
157	a	187	c	217	d	247	b	277	a
158	b	188	a	218	a	248	b	278	a
159	a	189	b	219	a	249	b	279	a
160	b	190	b	220	a	250	b	280	b
161	a	191	b	221	a	251	a	281	a
162	a	192	b	222	b	252	a	282	a
163	c	193	b	223	b	253	a	283	a
164	a	194	b	224	a	254	a	284	a
165	c	195	b	225	a	255	b	285	a
166	a	196	a	226	b	256	a	286	a
167	a	197	b	227	a	257	c	287	a
168	a	198	a	228	a	258	a	288	a
169	c	199	a	229	a	259	c	289	a
170	a	200	c	230	c	260	a	290	b
171	a	201	c	231	d	261	d		
172	a	202	c	232	a	262	a		
173	a	203	b	233	b	263	d		
174	b	204	a	234	b	264	a		
175	a	205	b	235	b	265	b		
176	a	206	b	236	a	266	a		
177	b	207	a	237	a	267	b		
178	a	208	a	238	b	268	a		
179	b	209	b	239	b	269	b		
180	a	210	d	240	b	270	c		

CHAPTER 9

Interview Questions

Introduction

This chapter's offers a concentrated examination of the primary topics and concepts associated with the **Internet of Things (IoT)** that are frequently highlighted in technical interviews. This chapter endeavors to anticipate the types of inquiries that readers may encounter during interviews for positions associated with the IoT. It covers fundamental concepts, including IoT architecture, communication protocols, and security considerations, as well as more advanced topics, such as edge computing, IoT analytics, and real-world applications. In this field, readers can more effectively assess the expectations of employers, identify areas for further study, and develop the confidence to articulate their knowledge by comprehending the scope and depth of interview questions. This chapter is an invaluable asset for individuals who aspire to excel in IoT-related interviews and advance their careers in this swiftly expanding field.

This chapter aims to provide readers with a comprehensive comprehension of the types of questions they may encounter during interviews for positions related to the IoT. The objective of this chapter is to address a wide range of subjects, such as the fundamental principles of IoT, industry-specific applications, problem-solving scenarios, and specific technical skills. IoT is a rapidly evolving technology that connects devices, sensors, and applications to share data and enable intelligent decision-making. Communication between devices is powered by technologies like Bluetooth, **Wireless Fidelity (Wi-Fi)**, Zigbee, **Long Range Wide Area Network (LoRaWAN)**, and **fifth generation (5G)**, depending on distance, power, and application needs. The IoT architecture consists of layers such as perception, network, data, and application, each responsible for sensing, transmitting, storing, and analyzing information. Key protocols such as **Message Queuing Telemetry Transport (MQTT)**, **Constrained Application Protocol (CoAP)**, and **Representational State Transfer Application Programming Interfaces (RESTful APIs)** ensure seamless integration and efficient communication across diverse platforms. Advanced technologies like AI and ML play a major role in anomaly detection, predictive maintenance, and real-time analytics. Similarly, edge computing and gateways enhance performance by processing data closer to the source, while cloud platforms manage large-scale storage and computation. To connect devices effectively, topologies like star and mesh networking are widely adopted, supporting reliability and scalability. However, IoT also faces challenges such as security, privacy, and interoperability, requiring solutions like encryption, **public key infrastructure (PKI)**, and global standards. Overall, IoT represents a powerful ecosystem that integrates digital intelligence with the physical world, transforming industries, smart cities, and everyday life.

Multiple choice questions

1. **What technology enables communication between IoT devices over short distances?**
   a. Wi-Fi
   b. Cellular
   c. Satellite
   d. Bluetooth

2. **Which layer of the IoT architecture is responsible for data storage and management?**
   a. Perception layer
   b. Network layer
   c. Application layer
   d. Data/Support layer

3. **Which communication protocol is commonly used for IoT devices due to its low power consumption?**
   a. Wi-Fi
   b. Bluetooth
   c. Zigbee
   d. 4G LTE

4. **What is the role of application programming interfaces (APIs) in the IoT ecosystem?**
   a. They provide physical connectors for IoT devices
   b. Enable low-level RF communication

    c. They enable data exchange between different software applications

    d. They generate electricity for IoT devices

5. **Which technology enables IoT devices to communicate over long distances using low-power, wide-area networks?**

    a. Wi-Fi

    b. Bluetooth

    c. LoRaWAN

    d. NFC

6. **What is the term for network communication on the internet?**

    a. MAC address

    b. IP address

    c. GPS coordinate

    d. Wi-Fi address

7. **Which layer in the IoT architecture collects data from various devices and organizes it for further analysis?**

    a. Perception layer

    b. Network layer

    c. Application layer

    d. Data layer

8. **What is the term for the process of collecting, storing, and analyzing large volumes of data generated by IoT devices?**

    a. Data warehousing

    b. Data analytics

    c. Data harvesting

    d. Data farming

9. **What is the term for the network topology where each IoT device is directly connected to a central server or cloud?**

    a. Star topology

    b. Mesh topology

    c. Bus topology

    d. Ring topology

10. **What is the role of machine learning in the IoT ecosystem?**

   a. It increases the aesthetic value of IoT devices

   b. It enhances device durability

   c. It enables anomaly detection, predictions, and classification

   d. It eliminates the need for data analysis

11. **What is the term for a network of interconnected devices that communicate and cooperate with each other to achieve a common goal?**

   a. Collaborative network

   b. Cooperative network

   c. Interconnected network

   d. Collaborative intelligence

12. **What is the role of 5G technology in the IoT ecosystem?**

   a. It only focuses on improving device aesthetics

   b. It enhances data security on IoT devices

   c. It enables faster and more reliable wireless communication

   d. It eliminates the need for data processing

13. **What is the purpose of mesh networking in the IoT ecosystem?**

   a. To simplify device interactions

   b. To connect devices in a linear fashion

   c. To create complex device hierarchies

   d. To enable devices to communicate directly with each other

14. **What is the role of predictive maintenance in the industrial IoT ecosystem?**

   a. It predicts when IoT devices need to be replaced.

   b. uses data analysis to forecast when maintenance is required

   c. It eliminates the need for device maintenance altogether.

   d. It focuses solely on aesthetic maintenance.

15. **What is the term for the process of integrating digital information with the physical world using sensors and other devices?**

   a. Data transformation

   b. Digital integration

   c. Digitalization

   d. Digital transformation

16. **How does machine learning benefit the IoT ecosystem?**
    a. By improving the visual design of IoT devices
    b. By extending hardware lifespan
    c. By allowing devices to analyze data and make intelligent decisions
    d. By removing the need for sensors in devices

17. **What is the term for a network of interconnected devices that communicate and cooperate with each other to achieve a common goal?**
    a. Collaborative network
    b. Cooperative network
    c. Interconnected network
    d. Collaborative intelligence

18. **What is the role of 5G technology in the IoT ecosystem?**
    a. It only focuses on improving device aesthetics
    b. It enhances data security on IoT devices
    c. It enables faster and more reliable wireless communication
    d. It eliminates the need for data processing

19. **What is the purpose of mesh networking in the IoT ecosystem?**
    a. To simplify device interactions
    b. To connect devices in a linear fashion
    c. To create complex device hierarchies
    d. To enable devices to communicate directly with each other

20. **How does predictive maintenance enhance efficiency in the industrial IoT environment?**
    a. By identifying the exact time to replace IoT devices
    b. By analyzing data to forecast and schedule maintenance needs
    c. By removing the requirement for any maintenance
    d. By concentrating only on the appearance of devices

21. **What is the term for the process of integrating digital information with the physical world using sensors and other devices?**
    a. Data transformation
    b. Digital integration
    c. Digitalization
    d. Digital transformation

22. **How does machine learning improve the functionality of IoT systems?**

    a. By making IoT devices look more appealing

    b. By making devices physically last longer

    c. By allowing devices to analyze data and make intelligent predictions

    d. By completely replacing the need for data analysis

23. **What is the term for a system where smart devices communicate and work together to accomplish shared objectives?**

    a. Collaborative network

    b. Cooperative network

    c. Interconnected network

    d. Collaborative intelligence

24. **What is the role of 5G technology in the IoT ecosystem?**

    a. It only focuses on improving device aesthetics

    b. It enhances data security on IoT devices

    c. It enables faster and more reliable wireless communication

    d. It eliminates the need for data processing

25. **What is the purpose of mesh networking in the IoT ecosystem?**

    a. To simplify device interactions

    b. To connect devices in a linear fashion

    c. To create complex device hierarchies

    d. To enable devices to communicate directly with each other

26. **Which benefit does predictive maintenance provide in industrial IoT systems?**

    a. It alerts users only after the equipment fails

    b. It schedules maintenance randomly to avoid downtime

    c. It reduces unplanned downtime by forecasting equipment issues

    d. It only monitors external wear and tear

27. **What is the term for the process of integrating digital information with the physical world using sensors and other devices?**

    a. Data transformation

    b. Digital integration

c. Digitalization

d. Digital transformation

28. **Which technology forms the foundation of the IoT ecosystem by connecting devices to the internet?**

a. Bluetooth

b. Internet protocol (IP)

c. NFC

d. Infrared

29. **Which phrase best describes a system where everyday objects are connected and communicated via the internet?**

a. Internet of Technology

b. Internet of Telecommunication

c. Internet of Thoughts

d. Internet of Things

30. **Which component of the IoT ecosystem is responsible for processing and analyzing the collected data?**

a. Sensors

b. Actuators

c. Gateway

d. Cloud

31. **What is the purpose of actuators in the IoT ecosystem?**

a. To sense environmental conditions

b. To process data

c. To perform actions based on received instructions

d. To establish network connections

32. **Which communication protocol is commonly used in IoT devices to connect over short distances with low power consumption in consumer wearables?**

a. Bluetooth

b. Wi-Fi

c. Ethernet

d. 3G/4G

33. **What is the primary function of the perception layer in the IoT architecture?**

    a. Data storage

    b. Data analysis

    c. Data communication

    d. Data sensing

34. **How does the IoT ecosystem enhance agricultural practices?**

    a. By increasing water wastage

    b. By enabling real-time monitoring of soil moisture and crop health

    c. By promoting excessive pesticide use

    d. By eliminating the need for crop management

35. **Which technology enables devices to exchange data with each other without human intervention?**

    a. Artificial intelligence

    b. Machine learning

    c. Machine-to-machine (M2M)

    d. Cloud computing

36. **What is the term for the interconnection of multiple IoT devices to form a network?**

    a. Data integration

    b. Device aggregation

    c. Device-to-device networking

    d. Device connectivity

37. **Which security challenge is associated with the IoT ecosystem?**

    a. Data scarcity

    b. Data privacy

    c. Data duplication

    d. Data processing

38. **What is the role of edge computing in the IoT ecosystem?**

    a. It enhances device aesthetics

    b. It focuses solely on data storage

    c. It enables data processing closer to the data source

    d. It eliminates the need for cloud computing

39. **Which layer of the IoT architecture is responsible for processing and analyzing data received from devices?**

    a. Perception layer

    b. Network layer

    c. Application layer

    d. Data layer

40. **Which technology enables devices to communicate using electromagnetic waves over long distances?**

    a. Wi-Fi

    b. Bluetooth

    c. LoRa

    d. Zigbee

41. **What is the role of data analytics in the IoT ecosystem?**

    a. It solely focuses on data storage

    b. It enables real-time data transmission

    c. It helps extract valuable insights from collected data

    d. It eliminates the need for data collection

42. **Which communication protocol is commonly used in IoT devices for long-range wireless communication?**

    a. Wi-Fi

    b. Bluetooth

    c. NB-IoT

    d. NFC

43. **What is the primary role of a gateway in the IoT ecosystem?**

    a. Data sensing

    b. Data analysis

    c. Data storage

    d. Data communication

44. **Which layer of the IoT architecture is responsible for connecting devices and managing data flow?**

    a. Perception layer

    b. Network layer

    c. Application layer

    d. Data layer

45. **What is the term for a network topology where devices are interconnected in a mesh-like structure?**

    a. Star topology

    b. Mesh topology

    c. Bus topology

    d. Ring topology

46. **What is the term for the unique identifier assigned to each IoT device for identification and communication purposes?**

    a. MAC address

    b. IP address

    c. GPS coordinate

    d. Wi-Fi address

47. **Which layer of the IoT architecture is responsible for aggregating data from multiple devices and preparing it for analysis?**

    a. Perception layer

    b. Network layer

    c. Application layer

    d. Data layer

48. **What is the term for the process of collecting, storing, and analyzing large volumes of data generated by IoT devices?**

    a. Data warehousing

    b. Big data analytics

    c. Data harvesting

    d. Data farming

49. **What is the term for the network topology where each IoT device is directly connected to a central server or cloud?**

    a. Star topology

    b. Mesh topology

    c. Bus topology

    d. Ring topology

50. **What is the role of machine learning in the IoT ecosystem?**

    a. It increases the aesthetic value of IoT devices

    b. It enhances device durability

    c. It enables devices to learn and make predictions based on data

    d. It eliminates the need for data analysis

51. **What is the term for a network of interconnected devices that communicate and cooperate with each other to achieve a common goal?**

    a. Collaborative network

    b. Cooperative network

    c. Interconnected network

    d. Collaborative intelligence

52. **What is the role of 5G technology in the IoT ecosystem?**

    a. It only focuses on improving device aesthetics

    b. It enhances data security on IoT devices

    c. It enables faster and more reliable wireless communication

    d. It eliminates the need for data processing

53. **What is the role of AI-powered analytics in the IoT ecosystem?**

    a. It only focuses on data storage

    b. It enables real-time communication between devices

    c. It helps derive meaningful insights from IoT data

    d. It replaces the need for IoT devices

54. **Which layer of the IoT architecture is responsible for managing communication between devices and providing network connectivity?**

    a. Perception layer

    b. Network layer

    c. Application layer

    d. Processing layer

55. **In IoT, what is the primary function of the perception layer?**

    a. Data processing and analysis

    b. Sensor data collection and interaction with the physical world

    c. Device management and control

    d. Network routing and data forwarding

56. **Which IoT communication protocol is designed for low-power devices and operates over UDP?**

    a. MQTT

    b. CoAP

    c. HTTP

    d. AMQP

57. **What is the key advantage of MQTT over HTTP in IoT applications?**

    a. Higher bandwidth

    b. Better security features

    c. Lower latency and reduced overhead

    d. More complex implementation

58. **Which cryptographic technique is often used in IoT devices to ensure data integrity and authentication?**

    a. Asymmetric encryption

    b. Hash functions

    c. Symmetric encryption

    d. Digital signatures

59. **In an IoT network, what is the primary function of a PKI?**

    a. To provide encryption for data at rest

    b. To manage digital certificates and public-private key pairs

c. To monitor network traffic

d. To ensure the physical security of IoT devices

60. **Which standard defines the framework for IoT device management and interoperability?**

a. ISO/IEC 27001

b. IEEE 802.15.4

c. OneM2M

d. 3GPP

61. **Which protocol is used for device-to-device communication in low-power and low-bandwidth IoT environments?**

a. XMPP

b. Zigbee

c. HTTP/2

d. WebSocket

62. **What is the main challenge in managing data generated by IoT devices in a big data environment?**

a. Data privacy

b. Data storage capacity

c. Data integration and analysis

d. Data transmission speed

63. **Which technology is commonly used to process and analyze streaming data from IoT devices in real-time?**

a. Hadoop

b. Apache Kafka

c. MongoDB

d. MySQL

64. **What is the primary advantage of edge computing in IoT?**

a. Increased cloud storage capacity

b. Reduced data processing latency

c. Enhanced network security

d. Improved device interoperability

65. **Which of the following is not a common use case for edge computing in IoT?**

    a. Real-time analytics

    b. Cloud data backup

    c. Local data processing

    d. Device control and management

66. **Which technology enables IoT devices to communicate over long distances with low power consumption?**

    a. NFC

    b. LoRaWAN

    c. Wi-Fi

    d. Bluetooth

67. **What role does AI play in enhancing IoT systems?**

    a. Managing physical device interfaces

    b. Improving network bandwidth

    c. Analyzing data patterns and making intelligent decisions

    d. Providing basic connectivity

68. **Which of the following is a major challenge for deploying IoT solutions in a smart city environment?**

    a. High bandwidth availability

    b. Scalability of solutions

    c. Availability of standardized hardware

    d. High cost of energy

69. **What is the primary concern related to IoT device interoperability?**

    a. Device power consumption

    b. Communication protocol compatibility

    c. Device physical durability

    d. Device network coverage

70. **Which of the following technologies is used to establish a mesh network for IoT devices?**

    a. LTE

    b. Zigbee

    c. Ethernet

    d. 5G

71. **What is a key benefit of using 5G technology in IoT applications?**

    a. Higher data encryption levels

    b. Improved device battery life

    c. Enhanced data transfer rates and reduced latency

    d. Reduced device size

72. **How can machine learning enhance the performance of IoT systems?**

    a. By improving device hardware capabilities

    b. By automating data analysis and predictive maintenance

    c. By simplifying device installation processes

    d. By increasing network bandwidth

73. **Which protocol is commonly used for remote management and firmware updates of IoT devices?**

    a. SNMP

    b. TR-069

    c. MQTT

    d. CoAP

74. **What is the primary purpose of the device shadow in AWS IoT?**

    a. To handle device authentication

    b. To store and synchronize device state information

    c. To manage device firmware updates

    d. To route messages between devices

75. **Which of the following techniques is used to protect data integrity in IoT communications?**

    a. Encryption with RSA

    b. Hash-based message authentication code (HMAC)

    c. Secure sockets layer (SSL)

    d. Pretty good privacy (PGP)

76. **What is the primary risk associated with inadequate authentication mechanisms in IoT devices?**

    a. Data redundancy

    b. Increased latency

    c. Unauthorized access and control

    d. Higher power consumption

77. **Which approach is commonly used to handle scalability issues in IoT systems?**

    a. Centralized data processing

    b. Edge computing and data aggregation

    c. Increasing the number of communication channels

    d. Enhancing physical device robustness

78. **What is a common technique to ensure data consistency across a large number of IoT devices?**

    a. Data replication

    b. Data sharding

    c. Consensus algorithms

    d. Data warehousing

79. **Which IoT standard provides guidelines for interoperability between IoT devices and platforms?**

    a. Zigbee Alliance

    b. IEEE 802.15.4

    c. ISO/IEC 30141

    d. Open Connectivity Foundation (OCF)

80. **What does the term semantic interoperability refer to in IoT systems?**

    a. The ability of devices to use the same communication protocol

    b. The ability of devices to understand and use the same data formats and meanings

    c. The ability of devices to connect through the same network topology

    d. The ability of devices to authenticate each other

81. **Which framework is commonly used for distributed data processing in large-scale IoT deployments?**

    a. Apache Spark

    b. TensorFlow

    c. Apache Flink

    d. Apache Hive

82. **What is the main benefit of using time-series databases in IoT applications?**

    a. Improved query performance for large datasets

    b. Efficient handling of continuous data streams

    c. Enhanced security features

    d. Simplified data visualization

83. **Which protocol is designed to handle intermittent connectivity in IoT environments?**

    a. HTTP

    b. MQTT

    c. CoAP

    d. XMPP

84. **Which of the following protocols is designed specifically for low-power, wide-area networks in IoT?**

    a. Wi-Fi

    b. Zigbee

    c. LoRaWAN

    d. Bluetooth Low Energy (BLE)

85. **Which API design style is commonly used to enable integration between IoT devices and cloud services?**

    a. RESTful APIs

    b. SOAP APIs

    c. GraphQL APIs

    d. gRPC APIs

86. **What is the main purpose of an IoT gateway in a smart home system?**

    a. To provide internet connectivity

    b. To bridge communication between local IoT devices and the cloud

    c. To store and manage local device data

    d. To perform heavy data processing

87. **What is the purpose of a time-series database in managing IoT data?**

    a. To optimize relational database queries

    b. To efficiently store and retrieve data indexed by time

    c. To provide advanced data analytics capabilities

    d. To manage device firmware versions

88. **Which connectivity technology is well-suited for applications requiring low power consumption and short-range communication?**

    a. Zigbee

    b. LoRaWAN

    c. NB-IoT

    d. 5G

89. **Which of the following technologies is often used in conjunction with IoT for industrial automation?**

    a. Robotics process automation (RPA)

    b. Building management systems (BMS)

    c. Supervisory control and data acquisition (SCADA)

    d. Content delivery networks (CDNs)

90. **Which type of machine learning model is used to predict future values based on historical time-series data from IoT sensors?**

    a. Classification model

    b. Regression model

    c. Clustering model

    d. Reinforcement learning model

91. **Which architectural pattern is commonly used for integrating heterogeneous IoT systems and services?**

    a. Event-driven architecture

    b. Cloud architecture

    c. Layered architecture

    d. Client-server architecture

92. **What is the purpose of an API Gateway in an IoT ecosystem?**

    a. To manage device firmware updates

    b. To provide a single entry point for routing requests and aggregating responses

    c. To store and secure device data

    d. To handle real-time data processing

Conclusion

This chapter is a comprehensive resource for individuals who are preparing for interviews in the swiftly evolving field of the IoT. Readers have encountered a diverse array of multiple-choice questions in this chapter, each of which is intended to assess their comprehension of both fundamental and advanced IoT concepts. IoT connects devices and systems using technologies like Wi-Fi, Bluetooth, Zigbee, LoRaWAN, and 5G to enable smart communication. Protocols such as MQTT and CoAP make data transfer efficient, while AI and ML improve predictive decision-making. With the help of edge computing, cloud platforms, and secure methods like PKI, IoT provides reliable and scalable solutions. Despite challenges like privacy and interoperability, IoT continues to transform industries, healthcare, agriculture, transportation, and smart cities.

Join our Discord space

Join our Discord workspace for latest updates, offers, tech happenings around the world, new releases, and sessions with the authors:

https://discord.bpbonline.com

Answers

Q.No.	Answers	Q.No.	Answers	Q.No.	Answers	Q.No.	Answers	Q.No.	Answers
1	d	21	d	41	c	61	b	81	a
2	d	22	c	42	c	62	c	82	b
3	c	23	d	43	d	63	b	83	b
4	c	24	c	44	b	64	b	84	c
5	c	25	d	45	b	65	b	85	a
6	a	26	b	46	b	66	b	86	b
7	b	27	d	47	b	67	c	87	b
8	b	28	b	48	b	68	b	88	a
9	a	29	a	49	a	69	b	89	c
10	c	30	d	50	c	70	b	90	b
11	d	31	c	51	d	71	c	91	a
12	c	32	a	52	c	72	b	92	b
13	d	33	d	53	c	73	b		
14	b	34	b	54	b	74	b		
15	d	35	c	55	b	75	b		
16	c	36	c	56	c	76	c		
17	d	37	b	57	c	77	b		
18	c	38	c	58	d	78	c		
19	d	39	d	59	b	79	d		
20	b	40	b	60	c	80	b		

Join our Discord space

Join our Discord workspace for latest updates, offers, tech happenings around the world, new releases, and sessions with the authors:

https://discord.bpbonline.com